D0393115

OTHER BOOKS BY THE AUTHORS

By Linda and Richard Eyre

The Nature of Nurturing (2003)
The Happy Family: Restoring the Eleven Essential Elements
Lifebalance
Teaching Your Children Values
3 Steps to a Strong Family
Teaching Your Children Responsibility
How to Talk to Your Child About Sex
Teaching Your Children Sensitivity
Teaching Your Children Joy
*Children's Stories to Teach Joy**
*Alexander's Amazing Adventures: Values for Children***

By Linda Eyre

I Didn't Plan to Be a Witch
A Joyful Mother of Children
The Little Book of Big Ideas About Mothers

By Richard Eyre

Life Before Life
The Discovery of Joy
Spiritual Serendipity
Stewardship of the Heart
The Awakening (a novel)
What Manner of Man
Don't Just Do Something, Sit There
The Wrappings and the Gifts
Simplified Husbandship/Simplified Fathership
Free to Be Free
The Secret of the Sabbath

* Children's book
**Audiotape set

Empty-Nest Parenting

Adjusting Your Stewardship As Your Children Leave Home

Richard and Linda Eyre

WITH SAREN EYRE LOOSLI

BOOKCRAFT

All rights reserved. No part of this book may be reproduced in any form or by any means without permission in writing from the publisher, Deseret Book Company, P. O. Box 30178, Salt Lake City, Utah 84130. This work is not an official publication of The Church of Jesus Christ of Latter-day Saints. The views expressed herein are the responsibility of the authors and do not necessarily represent the position of the Church or of Deseret Book Company.

Bookcraft is a registered trademark of Deseret Book Company.

Visit us at www.deseretbook.com

Library of Congress Cataloging-in-Publication Data

Eyre, Richard M.
    Empty nest parenting / Richard Eyre, Linda Eyre.
      p.   cm.
    Includes bibliographical references and index.
    ISBN 1-57008-731-8 (pbk.)
    1. Parent and adult child.   2. Empty nesters—Family relationships.   3. Parenting   4. Parenting—Religious aspects—Church of Jesus Christ of Latter-day Saints.   I. Eyre, Linda.   II. Title.
HQ755.86 .E95 2002
306.874—dc21   2001007699

Printed in the United States of America   72076-6855
Publishers Printing, Salt Lake City, UT

10   9   8   7   6   5   4   3   2

The most important work
you will ever do . . . is never done.

Foreword

by Stephen R. Covey

I was delivering a seminar to "WPO," the World Presidents Organization. We were at a seaside resort location and some of the attendees—each the president or CEO of his or her corporation—had actually "parked their yachts" at the marina outside the hall where we were meeting. There were individuals in their fifties and sixties who seemed to have everything—wealth, position, power, and the freedom to live where and how they pleased.

As we talked, the focus turned to family, and the mood turned somber. With some probing on my part, a few individuals had the courage and candor to admit the loneliness they felt at this stage of their lives, with their children grown and gone from home. "I thought the goal was independence," one CEO said, "for my children and for me. I sent them to the best schools and they're 'launched' now—doing fine. We talk on the phone every couple of weeks, but we live completely separate lives, and there is this emptiness." Others chimed in, agreeing that the luxurious, independent lifestyle they'd worked so hard and long to achieve was often sad and lonely because it lacked frequent family involvement and interaction.

Whether it's a yacht or a camper or just your general lifestyle, if you are moving in directions that separate you more and more from your children—directions that make you more independent from each other rather than more interdependent with each other—you are probably headed toward that same kind of emptiness. And your children could be losing the ultimate security of belonging to a family that never dissolves.

Not only will this book help you get through the difficult transitions of children moving on, but it will also help you build a beautiful ongoing family culture in your three-generation family—and that is where real happiness lies.

Contents

Chapter 10:

Phase 2: Career—

Chapter 11:

Phase 3: Marriage—

Introduction

If your idea of success is to "finish" with the kids so you can go live in Sun City and spend the next thirty years playing golf, this may not be the book for you.

We're going to make the case that even when your children are grown and gone, *parent* is still the most influential and important role in your life. And although there are plenty of light moments and humor in parental relationships with adult children, this stewardship that we call *empty-nest parenting* is a pretty serious thing. Before you start reading you should know that:

- This is not a book written for people who are content to have "average" families.
- This is not a book written for people who just want a few easy little ideas for staying in touch or setting up trust funds for grandkids.
- This is not a book written for people who think that enduring families or great adult family relationships just happen by luck or by chance.

We're going to try to persuade you (or support you if you already believe) that families and family relationships need constant maintenance. This is a book about:

- Choosing who you want to be for the rest of your life—and centering that choice on family.
- Making family bonds grow stronger rather than weaker as years pass and generations grow up.
- Becoming true patriarchs and matriarchs and leading and supporting your family forever.
- Creating a mutually beneficial and increasingly interdependent relationship with your children as you share your lives, your knowledge, and your love.

Eternal Family Leadership

The reason aging people get "discarded" in America is that they don't take their rightful positions as the continuing heads of their grown families. They suffer for this, and so do their children and grandchildren. We tend to blame the plight of the elderly on "Western society." "In Asia," we say, "parents and grandparents are revered and respected by their adult children." But in fact, we parents of grown children have no one to blame but ourselves. If our goal is to put in our time and do our parental duty until our kids turn eighteen and move out so that we can get on with our own lives and devote ourselves exclusively to our own enjoyment and our own ambitions, then we deserve it when our children fail to listen to us or respect us or look up to us—and when they begin to see us as a burden that they may have to take care of.

Somewhere along the line, here in America, we have come to the common narrow notion that *family* means parents and the young children who live with them, and that once the kids move on to their own families, parents should let them "have their independence" by getting out of the picture. Thus we give up and walk away from the role we ought to play for the rest of our lives—the role that will help our children most and that will preserve our own dignity, respect, and happiness—the ongoing role of parent, advisor, grandparent, and family head. We also give up priceless opportunities to learn from our children, share their lives, and enjoy their friendship.

Empty-nest parenting doesn't mean we don't enjoy the greater freedom and flexibility that come with an empty nest, but it does mean that we continue to be involved and active as the heads of our families and that we develop new and mutually beneficial ways of interacting with our kids.

So, if you thought this book was about disengaging as a parent, don't buy it. It is about engaging, about staying involved, and about loving it!

Saren: Let me insert a word here. I agree that parents should stay involved. but some empty-nest parents go too far, clinging to their children and to the role they played while their kids were young, trying to maintain control or have influence over every little thing in their adult children's lives. Some parents have a very hard time moving into a parenting role that respects their kids' independence while continuing to give support.

Who Should Read This Book—and When?

We are writing to any parent who wants to stay meaningfully involved in a way that *works* for the parents *and* the kids. If none of your kids have left home yet, it's a great time to read this book. You can learn what to expect, become emotionally prepared, and lay out a strategy before the fact. If all of your kids have left and you're now a bona fide empty-nester, it's a great time to read this book. You can reassess and readjust your relationship with your grown children. And if one or more children have left your nest and one or more are still in it, it's a great time to read this book. You can improve your relationship with those who are gone and prepare thoroughly for the time when the next one leaves.

While we hope most of this book would "work" for any empty-nest parent (ENP), it is particularly relevant to Latter-day Saint parents. We say it so often. We even post it on our refrigerators: "Families Are Forever." One clear implication, and one we don't think about often enough or hard enough, is that "Parenting Is Forever."

As a church and as a culture, we have platitudes for that, too. We say, "'Father' and 'Mother' are the only callings from which we will never be released." We know that family relationships can continue beyond this life. Our whole concept of heaven is based on it. We even know that the Church itself is temporary while the family is eternal. We *start* our journey as parents here on this earth, but we end it . . . never.

Yet some of our other favorite concepts, some of our best quotations, if we're not careful, can suggest to us subconsciously that parenting happens only in our homes and that the stewardship ends or diminishes when kids grow up and leave. We say, "No other success can compensate for failure in the home" and "the most important work you will ever do will be within the walls of your own home." But we really know, don't we, that when President McKay and President Lee said "home" they didn't mean "house," they meant *family*, and they meant it for the long term.

Kids moving out is just a change of venue—a road game instead of a home game. They're still ours, our salvation is still linked, our stewardship is still intact.

As LDS parents, we have the insight and the tools to design the second half of our lives according to eternal priorities. It will take faith (which Joseph Smith defined as "working by mental effort rather than physical force"), but we can do it. We can become parents for the ages—literally.

Structure and Sequence

Although we empty-nesters have many needs and feelings in common, each situation is different, and our hope is that you'll use what we've written to stimulate your thoughts and prompt the ideas that will work best in your own unique set of circumstances. Some of our ideas and experiences will have little relevance to you. Others will seem "right on." Still others won't quite fit you personally but will prompt ideas of your own. Make notes and underline and circle what fits. Write your own ideas, "Aha's," and commitments in the margins. Then, when you get to the last page, this will be your book instead of ours. You'll also notice that, in the table of contents, we have included a lot of detail about each chapter of the book so that you'll be able to use it almost like an index to find the issues that are of greatest concern in your family.

In part 1 we share more of our perspective as LDS parents and try to express our convictions about how important and rewarding empty-nest parenting can be. We want you to share in our enthusiasm for this part of life and to understand and appreciate the opportunity we all have to continue shaping our children's lives and sharing both their joys and their challenges. In part 2, we've collected thoughts and ideas from several ENPs (empty-nest parents) whose kids have left—and from dozens of LTNs (leaving-the-nesters)—kids who have recently left home. These thoughts will reassure you that you're not the first who has gone through this stage. They will also give you a chance to "survey" other families, particularly the Eyres, to see how they have coped with some of the same situations and concerns that you are now facing (or will soon face). The thoughts from Saren, her siblings, and other kids who have left their nests may help you understand what your own children are going through (or will go through), and the thoughts from us and other parents will give you ideas and starting points for handling things in your own family.

This book's appendix is the risky part for us. We decided to get personal enough to share the whole process we've gone through in moving from a full nest to an empty one. The reason we made it an appendix is that we think the book is complete without it, and we would not expect or want you to follow exactly the same formula. Indeed, our approach may seem way too involved and complicated— after all, we have nine children! But "case studies" really are the best teacher, and we hope that reading about the process we went through will prompt and catalyze your ideas for your own unique approach to empty-nest parenting.

One way to look at it is that the book goes from the general to the specific. In part 1 we're trying to present the overall concept of empty-nest parenting—and some principles and ideas we think apply pretty much to everyone. In part 2 we address dozens of common questions, some of which you will find more useful than others. Finally, in the appendix, we get down to examples and specific strategies that may save you some time in developing your own approaches to empty-nest parenting.

A Brief Introduction to Our Own Family (as Contributors to This Book)

One final introductory item: Since, over the rest of this book, our families—yours and ours—are going to get pretty close (you'll know ours through what you read, and we'll try to know and anticipate yours through what we write), some introductions are in order. Here's our lineup of kids who have "grown and flown" (and whom you'll be hearing from in the questions-and-answers section of part 2).

Saren: Thirty-something—just barely. Wellesley and Harvard graduate; served a mission to Bulgaria in between; married to Jared Loosli with an unbelievably gorgeous baby boy named Ashton and a new baby on the way; curriculum and education consultant; living and working in San Jose. (Jared, by the way, was a missionary in Italy and is a Silicon Valley engineer and MIT graduate with an exceptionally calm and unflappable demeanor—the perfect complement and partner to Saren—an answer to prayer [hers and ours]!) Saren is our co-author in this book, and you'll be hearing from her throughout.

Shawni: Almost thirty-something. Boston University and Brigham Young University; served a mission to Romania; married to David Pothier and mother of two incomparably beautiful children, Max and Ellie; an artist and designer living in the Washington suburb of McLean, Virginia. (Dave, the first to join our family by the in-law route, is a creative and capable mortgage banker and BYU graduate who served a mission in Taiwan and whom we love as much as our "born" sons.)

Joshua: Late mid-twenties. Brigham Young University graduate in construction management; served a mission in London; waiting a little longer than we'd wish for the right woman; working in Washington, D.C., in the construction and computer industries. We owe him so much for the constant example he's set as the oldest son.

Saydria (Saydi): Early mid-twenties. Wellesley graduate now pursuing a master's degree from Columbia and loving the single life in New York City. Served her mission in Spain. Has a Mother Teresa side that leads her to social work and to humanitarian trips to India, Bolivia, and Kenya.

Jonah: Earlier mid-twenties. He and his new wife, Aja, are both studying anthropology at Harvard, expecting their first child, and living, as coincidence would have it, in the student-housing apartment right next door to the first place we (Linda and Richard) lived as students after our marriage. Served a mission in England. (We love Aja not only for her brilliance and strong opinions but also for making Jonah a vastly happier young man!)

Talmadge: Early twenties. Six-foot-nine-inch basketball scholarship student at Weber State University—living on campus but close enough to come home part time; trying to balance very heavy doses of academics, church involvement, athletics, and dating. Served a mission in Brazil.

Noah: Nearly twenty. Currently on his mission in Santiago, Chile. Our second high-school honorable-mention All-American basketball player who hopes to come home and play with (or maybe against) his brother. Student-body president in high school and a leader with sensitive empathy for everyone.

Frankly, our advice and ideas would lack both credibility and completeness without response and reaction from those with whom we've tried to apply them. Saren, by virtue of her seniority as well as some special interests and abilities, has become our chief partner and collaborator in this book and has frequently polled and debriefed her siblings so that their perspectives can also be included. While regular in-the-nest parenting is something parents themselves principally decide on and work at, empty-nest parenting should be more like an *agreement*, where the parents and kids decide together how to handle various issues of support, communication, and relationships. This is how we've tried to do it, and this is how we've written it.

Years ago, if we'd seen a list of children like the one above from some other family, we'd have said, "Well, there you go. They've finished their parenting." Oh, how little we knew. Each of these "departed seven," as you'll see from their comments in this book, is *in the process* of leaving home, a process that is gradual, multistaged, and ongoing. The physical leaving (for them) and the physical letting go for us, is just the beginning. There is an emotional leaving and letting go that takes much longer, and a social, mental, and spiritual leaving and letting go that is not (and should not) ever be over.

Getting it right—this leaving and letting go—is the challenge all empty-nest parents face.

Saren: I just have to jump in here and comment on my dad's introductions (and this comment may serve notice for how candid I intend to be in this book). I just think it is so interesting how parents seem to have to slant things a little, and how they seem to stay with their early preconceptions of their kids.

The things Dad included in these brief descriptions of us were so typical they made me laugh while making me a bit exasperated. To him, Shawni's always been the artist of the family. She does enjoy dabbling in art, but she's really into interior design as far as fixing up her own house, so it was funny to see my dad describe her as "an artist and designer." She's always wished Dad would think of her as more of an intellectual and a writer. Josh quit his job recently and is trying to move from the construction industry to computers, somewhat against my dad's advice. So Dad keeps his options open and writes that Josh is "in the construction and computer industries." Is it too much for him to admit he has a son who's not working full-time right now? Josh is happy about his situation, but maybe it embarrasses my dad. Saydi is studying social work. It was funny to see that Dad just wrote that she is "pursuing a master's degree at Columbia." I think he's subliminally uncomfortable with admitting that she's not pursuing something more lucrative at Columbia. He said Jonah and his wife Aja are going to Harvard, when actually Aja's at Harvard and Jo's working temp jobs to support them while she finishes, although he is taking a couple of Harvard extension courses. He'll graduate from Utah State sometime, but finishing his degree isn't his highest priority right now. I guess Dad thinks it's more impressive to say they both go to Harvard. Anyway, you get the picture. It mostly makes me laugh. He's very proud of his children, but we all wish he'd be a little more proud of the things we're proud of. I know he likes to brag about us, and we don't mind being feathers in his hat—but I think it'd be better if he'd be proud of realities, not fictions!

Well, after that response, perhaps we should say a little more. First of all, Saren's right. Like most parents, we do have a tendency to brag too much about our children, to exaggerate a bit here and there, and to make their accomplishments a little too much a part of our egos. And we do (especially Richard) sometimes think of our children and their gifts and talents too much as we originally perceived them or as we want them to be rather than as they now are. We should all challenge ourselves to continually get to know our children all over again as they evolve, change, and develop new interests and aptitudes.

Responding to Saren's response also gives us the chance for an update. As we finish this manuscript, we've had quite a summer, with Shawni and Dave having their third child (a daughter) in June, Saren and Jared their second (a son) in July, and Jonah and Aja their first (a daughter) in August. Life goes on!

PART I

Empty-Nest
Perspectives and Priorities

Reemphasizing what we already know—

that family relationships are the highest priority,

now and forever. Then acting on that knowledge.

Chapter 1

The Simple Things That Matter

Let us begin with an interesting counterpoint to the wealthy, empty, wrong-priority CEOs mentioned by Stephen Covey in his foreword.

In the poverty-stricken central mountains of Mexico, in a village called Tamaula, we met the Laguna family. Juana (age seventy-four) and Jesus (age seventy-eight) were the matriarch and patriarch of the village. Over the course of a week we got to know them well. In fact, we came to love them.

As young parents, Juana and Jesus "homesteaded" a remote, mountainous area high above the city of Guanawato. It took hours to get there by foot or by burro, but they built a small adobe house and scratched out a living. Eventually they had ten children, six boys and four girls, and welcomed a few other relatives who wanted to join them in their new village.

Their crops, mostly corn and peppers, along with milk and cheese from their goats, kept them alive, but they had no money to buy building materials to replace their tiny, mud-block adobe huts or to get a small grinder to grind cornmeal for tortillas. Finally, the oldest son, Pedro, decided on the dangerous course of making his way north to the Rio Grande and swimming across in hopes of finding work and sending a little money back to his family. Following his precedent, the other boys, Francisco, Pablo, Rudolpho, Martin, and Jesus Jr., took their turns as "wetbacks" in their early twenties—spending two or three years in the U.S., sending back what money they could to the village. Jesus Laguna Jr. told us of his experience across the border.

All he had ever wanted, he said, was enough money to buy the little bit of lumber, nails, and fixtures that he could put together with homemade bricks to build a house for his little family. There was no way to get money in the village, and if he moved to a Mexican city he would have to be away from his family for much longer to save enough. He walked and hitchhiked his way four hundred miles north to the Rio Grande and swam across in a particularly dangerous stretch, filled with whirlpools where many had drowned. But on the other side he was rounded up by border patrol dogs and helicopters and was sent back. He tried a second time and was picked up by "coyotes" (essentially slave traders who pick up wetbacks and drive them to a farm or factory that pays them for delivering low-cost Mexican laborers). But the coyotes turned out to be bounty hunters who delivered him, instead, to the border patrol, who sent him back again. On the third try he found "real" coyotes who drove him to a chicken soup factory in Georgia. But the trip took three days, in the back of a hot van with other wetbacks and with no food or water. By the time he got there, he had lost nearly twenty pounds and was almost dead.

But Jesus Jr., like his five brothers before him, worked for two years in the chicken soup factory, dutifully sending back small amounts until there was enough to buy building materials for a house. As he talked, there were tears, and Jesus Jr. began to remind me of Vietnam veterans I've spoken to who have to summon all their courage to even think about, let alone talk about, what they have been through.

Anyway, as we got to know the Laguna family, we felt a rare peace and happiness in each family member. Juana and Jesus Sr. have eight of their ten children living there in the village with them (two daughters moved away but come home twice a year, on Mother's Day and

Christmas). They have sixty grandchildren, and one of the highlights of our visit was to watch their delight as they interacted and played with those grandchildren. Their children's families now each have "proper" brick houses, and the family has a one-cylinder grinder to make cornmeal as well as metal plows for their donkeys to pull.

But the Laguna family's happiness has nothing to do with the modest material advances they have made. It has everything to do with their commitment and togetherness as a family. They care for each other. They work together. On Sundays they go to church together. They have family meetings and work things out together. Juana and Jesus call all sixty grandkids by name and seem to have a personal relationship with each one. Their children respect them, seek their advice, and take care of them. They are the matriarch and patriarch of a large, intact, extended family. They will never be lonely or empty. They will always have struggles and challenges, but they'll face them together with their family and grow even closer in the process.

On the first day we went into the village, we pitied Juana and Jesus in their rude, primitive existence. Seven days later, as we left, we envied them, and we respected them for the priorities they had kept and the relationships they had built.

One Thing That's Guaranteed

Whatever you think about the Laguna family and whatever you think about the CEOs in Stephen Covey's foreword, one thing is guaranteed: Covey's CEOs will feel lonely and emotionally empty during much of the twenty or thirty years they have left to live. Juana and Jesus never will. If the Lagunas could see the yachts and lifestyles of the CEOs, they would probably feel some jealousy, but if they looked long enough they would also feel some pity. If the CEOs could see the family unity and security of the Lagunas, they would certainly feel some jealousy, some longing, some regret.

At the end of life, all that matters is our relationships. What we need to understand is that relationships are what matter *before* the end of our lives too. Twenty or thirty or forty years before the end of our lives, our children leave our homes. If our relationships leave with them, we are guaranteed a legacy of loneliness. But if we maintain and build on our relationships with our grown children, we maximize the happiness on both ends.

With that in mind, let's look at some additional perspectives, first from empty-nest parents (ENPs) and then from leaving-the-nesters (LTNs).

Chapter 2

Perspectives from Parent and Child

Somehow, many parents get the idea that when their kids grow up and leave home, they are done with parenting. Well, fellow parent, think again! Parenting isn't finished when kids move away for college or jobs or marriage. The challenges change, but they don't end. In fact, they often get bigger and more complex.

But here's the good news: Just as the worries, problems, and challenges of being a parent don't end when the kids no longer share the same roof, the love, joy, and fulfillment don't end either. And while it's natural for a parent to dread the day when children leave home to be on their own, it's also natural to look forward to the "freedom" you'll have when your kids move on and you have less day-to-day responsibility for them.

If you're an average baby boomer, you will be a parent for nearly sixty years of your life, and only twenty to thirty of those years will be spent parenting your kids while they live with you. You'll spend half to two-thirds of your parental span as an empty-nest parent!

And it doesn't stop there. As Church members, we have so many added insights about the eternally important (and eternally joyful) nature of families. One of the most important of these is that family relationships are the one thing we can take with us from this world into the next. Not only our marriages but also our parenthood can be eternal!

Reminding ourselves of this should be motivation enough to take the time and put forth the effort required to thoroughly think through the empty-nest phase of our lives and to work with our children to create a vision and a plan for the kind of extended family we want to have. We want to build relationships with our children and our grandchildren that will provide them and us with the eternal joy we were sent here to find.

So what kind of an empty-nest parent will you be? How much control and influence should you try to maintain with kids who have grown up and moved on? How much do you want to help them financially? How can you do so without undermining their independence? How much should you influence their decisions about school, jobs, marriage, children? How much do you want to know about their day-to-day needs and problems? How often should you call or write an e-mail? How much do you want to influence where they live and how close they locate to you? How often do you want them to come home? Most important, what do you need from them and what do they need from you?

There are lots of questions—*what* and *how* and *when* and *where* questions. Most parents take a wait-and-see attitude—dealing with issues as they arise and feeling their way along. The thesis of this book is that you're better off with a *plan*—with some well-thought-out goals about what kind of an empty-nest parent you want to be and some specific ideas about how to make it happen!

This book will help you formulate your own objectives and will be a mental grab bag and a thought and idea prompter. There are more methods, techniques, and ideas here than any empty-nest parent will ever use or than any one family could ever want. Every family, every parent, every child, and every situation is different. The key is to examine your own unique family situation, talk with your kids, and set your own goals, and then choose methods and plans that work for *you* to reach *your* unique family aims and objectives.

We're so pleased that we were able to write this book with the real experts on this subject—our own children. Each of them, as you will see, has strong opinions. And in some ways their views may be more valuable to you than ours. Saren, our oldest daughter, has combined her insights with those of her six out-of-the-nest siblings and dozens of other nest-leavers, orchestrating them all into coherent, candid feedback about what it feels like to leave and about what parents can do to make all the transitions work better and build meaningful relationships with their kids.

In the ENP portions of this book, we will share the ideas and approaches that we and other ENPs have come up with over the years, but in the LTN portions—which are always in this typeface—Saren and all the other "departers" will tell you, with firsthand authority, "This is what your children need when they leave home! This is how they feel; this is what they hope you will be to them and give to them." Particularly in part 2, Saren shares these perspectives—the views of the "child" we're still parenting, the son or daughter whose happiness (along with our own) is the goal and the reason for wanting to continue to be the best parents we can.

—Richard and Linda

The Child's Perspective (Telling It Like It Is)

My role in this book is to tell you, bluntly, and with as many examples and stories as possible, what eighteen- to thirty-something kids want and need from their parents. I certainly can't speak for everyone, but I'll do my best to tell you what I can see from my perspective and try to make it as representative as possible of the other "kids" I know.

Throughout college and graduate school, as I worked for several years and lived with roommates, and now as I'm married with one little boy and another one on the way, I've found it fascinating to observe all the different types of relationships that my friends have with their parents and the approaches that their parents have taken as empty-nest parents. I've heard a lot of interesting stories as friends talk about the things their parents and in-laws do that drive them crazy and as they praise the ways their parents help them out. When I add up my experiences with my parents and the experiences that my friends have had, I've learned quite a bit about what works and what doesn't work, from the child's perspective.

I left home twelve years ago, and since then, my parents and I have learned to handle lots of new issues—through trial and error, through talks and fights. I'm the oldest in the family, my parents' guinea pig, so they were really in uncharted waters when I left home. Over the years, we've learned a lot about what we need to "be" to each other as we progress with our lives, and I think my parents have become better and better empty-nest parents as more and more of their kids have left the nest. There were a lot of things my parents did that really helped me make a smooth transition to independent adult-hood and interdependent daughterhood. And there were some things they did that I'm sure we'd all agree didn't help at all.

To help set the stage for the book, let me say a few things on behalf of your children—to you and to my own parents. As your children, we need your love and support and listening ear all the days of our lives. We'll never outgrow our need for your approval for the things we do. But from the moment we leave home and even before, we really want to be treated like adults in a lot of important ways. We need you to respect our opinions. We need to feel that you trust us. We hate it when you think you know the right thing for us when you don't really understand the situation and you say you're listening but you really aren't. We hate it when you try to control our choices by dangling money in front of us or threatening us. A lot of the time, we really do want and need your advice, but we want you to give it without getting all bent out of shape if we don't take it. We want you to love our friends and those we are dating. We want your admiration. We want you to tell us about your problems and seek help from us sometimes. We want you to see us more as peers and friends and less as subordinates. But we still need you to nurture us—to check in with us and make sure we're okay, to worry and call us when we're sick or sad, and to send us the occasional care package. We want you to come visit us and to request our presence in your home quite a bit. We need you. We'll always need you. And we like to know that you need us. But we need to communicate openly so that we can figure out the roles that we need to play in each other's lives as time passes and changes happen.

The big thing, I think, is really understanding what each other is going through—and that requires good communication and good questions. I'm sure it's often hard for parents to accept that their children need them less and less in many ways. Some parents cling too much, and some turn their kids loose too completely and too easily. It bothers me how in most families the whole transition just kind of happens and everyone learns by hit and miss, by trial and error. Sometimes the errors are pretty painful. Sometimes the mistakes or insensitivity of the parent or the child deeply hurt the other, and communication can break down or even pretty much cease for years!

It's so much better to have a basic plan for the transition—to decide in advance about how you'll communicate and how much support will be given—financially and otherwise. Not that every family's plan will be the same, or that every plan will completely work—and adjustments have to be made as time passes. But it's just so important to think about it and to work together to come up with some agreements about your expectations of each other and to keep the channels of communication open.

Using this book as a starting point, I hope you can find the best way to shape your newly configured family of adults and to develop dynamic and meaningful relationships with your kids as you disperse and diversify. After all, no matter how grown up they are, they're still your kids, and there's so much you can do for each other throughout your lives!

—Saren

Chapter 3

What Does Empty-Nest Parenting Mean to You?

T he term *empty-nest parenting* conjures up all kinds of different thoughts and emotions. For as long as we've been working on this book (a long time), we've been bouncing its title off of friends and acquaintances and getting a huge variety of reactions:

"Isn't that an oxymoron—'empty nest' means the kids are raised and you're done!"

"Don't even talk about it. It makes me sad just to think about my kids being gone. It will be the hardest time of my life."

"Sure sounds more peaceful than full-nest parenting!"

"Let me tell you, the parenting problems just get bigger as the kids get older."

"What that means to me is that I'll find gas in the car once in a while—and the radio buttons set to my stations."

"Well, I thought it was empty, but two of them flew back in—to live!"

"I'd be careful of that term. I think once you spin them off, you should let them go. Quit clinging. Let them be on their own."

"Yes. They're gone now. The Ben and Jerry's lasts more than a day. And I found the three sets of retainers they claimed the dog ate."

"Don't kid yourself. They need you more than ever after they leave. Their decisions have bigger consequences, and they continue to need all kinds of help and advice."

"I'd have done anything to keep them home a couple more years."

"I did everything I could to get them to move out sooner."

"The important thing is that they do the right thing when they leave. If they're on missions you'll have a happy empty nest."

"Finances are the big issue. You want to help, but what they really need is a sense of their own independence."

"Well, there's so much to *balance*. How often do you talk on the phone, how often do you see them? How much advice do you give? It's so easy to do too much or to do too little on every question."

"This is what I've waited and worked for. Other than Christmas and a summer reunion, they've got their freedom—and, hey, so do *I!*"

"The hardest part was the first year after he left home—and then the first year after he was married. Those two times nearly tore my heart out!"

"What it means to me is that I can go back to my painting and my music. I can get a life again!"

"Well, the key thing is that you're just turning them back over to Heavenly Father's care. He gave them to you for twenty years and now you're giving them back."

"For me, it's finding that dynamic tension between assistance and independence—because they need both."

"One word—*grandchildren*. That's the part I'm looking forward to!"

"Hi ho, hi ho, it's back to work I go—and I'm looking forward to it!"

"It's like someone peeled off a part of you."

"For moms especially, it's almost unbearable. Your whole priority—all that you've lived and worked for—is suddenly gone."

"I think it's the payoff. After all, the whole goal of parenting is to work yourself out of a job."

"If you've taught them well—if they'll keep the commandments and go to church—they'll be fine."

"Empty nest what?"

"You'd better be ready for it, because it happens so suddenly, and it's gut wrenching."

"I just wish I'd prepared more for it, thought about it more before it happened. I wish I'd had a plan for how we'd handle money needs and other things. We've just tried to figure it out as we go along. We should have had a strategy."

"I say make it a totally empty nest. Leave yourself. Go on a mission or a long trip if you can."

"It's like a career change—only worse!"

"It's like a big promotion—more money, more time—only better!"

"Well, one thing it does is force you to reestablish and re-create your relationship with your spouse."

"Oh, I don't know—I'm not ready to think about that yet."

"The only way our nest will ever be empty is if *we* leave. The kids certainly don't plan to."

How do *you* respond or react to the notion of empty-nest parenting? More important, how do you plan to carry it out?

Before we dive into the nitty-gritty of dangers and dilemmas, of strategies and solutions, let's survey the broader landscape and think for a minute about the *scope* of empty-nest parenting. Most of us feel better when there is a framework, when some parameters have been set wherein everyone is clear on exactly what we're talking about. So before we get into the *hows* of empty-nest parenting (which is the whole point and purpose of this book), let's spend a paragraph or two on the other questions of *who, what, why, when,* and *where*.

Who?

Who are today's new empty-nest parents? Quite simply, they (we) are the largest generation in America's history—the baby boomers. Most parents become empty-nesters within the span that begins ten years before their fiftieth birthday and ends ten years after their fiftieth birthday. Most baby boomers, the post-war generation born between 1946 and 1964, are passing through their empty-nest initiation during the early years of this new millennium. According to *USA Today*, "Every seven seconds, a baby boomer turns 50 . . . about 64 million baby boomers will turn 50 in the next 14 years." (September 20, 2000.)

What's on the minds of these 64 million baby boomers? (Over 80 million if we add those who turned 50 between 1995 and 2000.) Surveys tell us what logic already has—that the two biggest worries of fiftyish Americans are the two generations that "sandwich" them—first, their kids, now in or entering college and leaving home and getting married and needing all kinds of help, and second, their parents, now mostly out of the work force and often burdened with health and finance-related concerns.

These trends and statistics are probably even more exaggerated in the Church, where our families are larger and our parents live longer.

For baby boomers it is truly the best of times and the worst of times. On the positive side, many if not most are at the peak of their professional powers, doing better than they ever have financially and also experiencing the emotional paydays of kids graduating from high school and college, getting married, and presenting them with grandkids. At the same time, on the negative side, the added financial needs and obligations seem to add up faster than the increases in income. It seems that kids turn out to be more demanding financially and emotionally after they leave home than they were when they lived at home, and aging parents extend our purse strings and our heart strings even further.

Often the negatives seem to outweigh the positives, and we just put our heads down and plow ahead, trying to make the extra money to meet the extra needs, trying to be all things to all people whether they're above or below us on the family tree. Perhaps what we need to do is take some brief timeouts and start *thinking* a little harder about what we are and what we aren't, what we can do and what we can't—developing a *strategy* for the roles and relationships of the second half of our lives.

What?

What is the best way to think about and conceptualize empty-nest parenting? First of all, try to view it as a fourth and completing phase or *stage* of your mortal stewardship. First-stage parenting is babies and preschoolers—the incredibly formative time when children acquire 80 percent of their cognitive abilities and need an incredible amount of parenting attention. Second-stage parenting is the elementary school years—sometimes the least turbulent and worrying phase but also the best time to teach children responsibility and values. Third-stage parenting is the adolescent years when children become decision-making young adults.

And then comes fourth-stage parenting—beginning when children first leave home . . . and continuing . . . and continuing . . . and continuing. This is empty-nest parenting, and it can (and should) occupy about half of your adult life here on earth.

This book is *just* about the parenting part of that second half of life. It is not about time management or midlife crisis or "getting a life" or late career burnout or taking care of elderly parents or any of the other issues of this age group *except* as those issues relate to parenting.

Why?

Why acknowledge and prioritize and work at empty-nest parenting? Some of the answers are obvious—they're still your children, your *stewardship*, the biggest part of your heart. Some of the answers are less obvious but equally important—those having to do with the fundamental goal of happiness, which resides in and revolves around family. The fundamental reason for doing your level best at empty-nest parenting is that your efforts there will have more to do with the long-term well-being of your kids, of your family, and of yourself than anything else you can do.

I (Richard) served as the national spokesperson for MasterCard on an ad campaign and a national public opinion poll called "Priceless." The ads showed the prices of various things and connected them to the other things that were "priceless" (basketball tickets: $32.00; hot dogs: $8.50; team pennant: $5.00; time with your son: priceless). My job was to discuss a national poll that, among other things, indicated that on the open-ended question, "What is priceless?" or "What matters most?" more than 80 percent of Americans said "family" or "children." The next highest answer received less than 10 percent. Does family cease to be the priority (or our prime source of happiness) once the kids leave home? No, of course not; nor does it get any easier.

A nuclear family is not just a temporary organization that fulfills the purpose of raising kids to adulthood and then becomes obsolete or redundant. Family, as we all find out sooner or later (through positive or negative experience), is the vehicle for joy and the antidote for loneliness. It is the interdependence between family members that teaches us the most important lessons of life and gives us our best chances for ongoing happiness, and anyone who tries to substitute something other than family to meet his or her long-term emotional needs will eventually feel empty and alone.

When?

Empty-nest parenting is an issue (an opportunity, a challenge) from the day your first child moves out until the day you die. But there are four times, whatever sequence they come in, when new issues and needs arise, and when empty-nest parenting takes on special intensity and importance:

1. When your child first leaves home, often for college.
2. When your child first gets a full-time job.
3. When your child gets married and starts a separate family unit.
4. When your child has a child—and you become a grandparent.

The question of "when" can be answered with a graph:

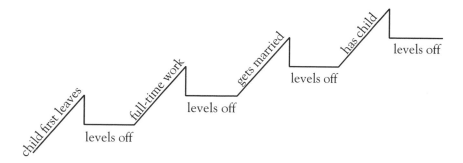

The order and sequence and shape of these four peaks or phases will be different for each child, but the ideal scenario is to be ready for each spike of opportunity (or need) and to talk to your kids ahead of time about each one. Then you will have some objectives in mind and some plans and ideas in place before you need them. If you are already into one or more of the phases, the challenge is to think of and learn and apply some appropriate approaches as soon as possible.

Where?

This may seem like a less relevant question, but the issue of "where?" comes into every phase of empty-nest parenting. Should kids stay close or go far away for college? What are the pros and cons of living close after they're married and start a family? What are the times when it's most important to be with them, and when is it best to leave them on their own?

Another important take on the "where" question is this: "Where is empty-nest parenting a continuation and an extension of in-the-nest-parenting, and where is it something completely different?" Certainly in terms of listening and communicating, of respecting and asking for kids' opinions, of caring and loving unconditionally, parenting is one long continuum, involving the same principles no matter where the kids are. But in other ways, there are distinctive "breaks" and "shifts." Once they are gone, you become more of a consultant than a manager, and the two roles are very different. Your children now make decisions for themselves, and your parenting success will now be based more on your ability to give advice and support than on your ability to discipline.

The "H" Question

If only the one "h" question were as easy to answer as the five "w" questions! *How* is always the tough one, especially in matters of family. We all know we want to trust one another, to continue to grow together, to communicate with and help each other in every possible way. The question is *how* to do each of these things. There is no simple answer, but there are lots of previous experiences we can learn from, lots of good approaches we can adopt, lots of mistakes we can anticipate and avoid rather than fall into, lots of issues we can think ahead on and build strategies for.

Chapter 4

The Emotions of ENP

Just let me (Linda) speak here for a moment on some of the emotions of *mother* ENPs. It's all well and good for Richard to lay out his framework and analysis, but to most women I know, an emptying nest is first and foremost a highly emotional experience.

A dear friend of mine recently gave me a perfect example of what we mothers go through. Picture Bobbi, mother of six (four daughters and two sons) contemplating her life. Her oldest son and daughter moved out, went to college, and got married. The transitions were gradual and felt natural and good. After those two departures, she was delighted at last to have some space for her own art room. She was settling in to enjoy her return to painting when suddenly two more children decided to get married, and she was confronted with the trauma of planning two more weddings within the next five months. Her art room filled with wedding gifts and paraphernalia, and it seemed that every day was crammed with planning events, ordering flowers, finding the perfect dress, finding someone to make the wedding cake or setting up a wedding breakfast—not to mention dealing with the emotional ramifications of losing two more children.

When the dust finally settled, she found herself down to two children and decided that now was the time to redecorate these last two girls' bedrooms with the true designer's flare that she had always dreamed of but had no money to implement while the children were growing up. However, as she announced her plans to the girls, they each dropped an unexpected bomb. One thought she too had found her Prince Charming and had been trying to get up the courage to tell her that yet another marriage was imminent. And the youngest was pondering a move to the sorority house on the nearby university campus.

Back while she was dealing with the everyday hurricane of raising these six children, older more experienced mothers had often said to her, "Just enjoy it while it lasts, because it goes so fast!" "That's easy for you to say," she used to say to herself as she dealt with the constant problems of diapers and fevers and broken arms and teenage car accidents. But now the realization of actually and suddenly having all the children out of the house made those years seem like a moment!

Still reeling from the most recent "exodus" announcements, she channel-surfed onto an Oprah show one afternoon—a show about mothers who had just sent their last child off to college and were trying to deal with their emotions. With a mug of her favorite comfort food—hot chocolate—she sat down to cry with the mothers on the show who were bemoaning the loss of their child-on-board motherhood.

She confided, "Even though they were only talking about losing children to their college careers, not even to marriage, which I had been dealing with, I felt their pain. My tears streamed like a river and I was totally sucked in. By the end of the show, I was a basket case! Why hadn't I finished those rooms sooner, why didn't I appreciate every day they were home more fully, why hadn't I realized what a great time we were having while they were all home?" She began a full-fledged guilt trip.

Suddenly she sat up and began to laugh at herself, mired as she was in misery: "Bobbi, are you crazy? This is the time you have longed for, waited for, and been excited about!" She soaked up the tears and realized that her family *had* spent wonderful times together. They had stocked up more precious memories than she could record, or even remember! She began to giggle about the time her daughter ran through their new brick retaining wall when she was practicing driving. She remembered all the times the kids got lost and all the great vacations they'd had together, as well as the quiet moments helping with homework and panicky moments of breaking the speed limit to get the girls to ballet on time. She remembered all the tears spilled over the piano keys and the kids' friends she and her husband did and didn't like who had eaten at their kitchen bar.

After that kind of reflection, Bobbi told me, "I'm just so grateful that I was able to spend so much time with them when they were young, because now is the time I've looked forward to all my life—a time to spend a little more time on *moi!* In the aftermath of that Oprah show, I dried the last sniffle and realized that this was a rite of passage that I had a right to! I had done my best, and I should now look forward to the next exciting phase of my life!"

The Difficulties of Letting Go

I (still Linda) want to tell you that, with our large number of children, we have had more than our share of farewells and homecomings. In addition to sending kids off to college, new jobs, and marriages, we have also sent all of them off on missions (to Romania, Bulgaria, Spain, England [twice], Brazil, New York City, Chicago, and Chile).

After sending our own children and two semi-adopted children off to college and missions, and after having married five of them off, I thought the process should get easier. Indeed, in some ways it is easier, knowing that the first crop has gone out and come back for short or even extended visits several times and we've all survived. But I must admit that each one is hard.

This year we sent our little Noah (who now stands 6'7") off for his mission to Chile. As a little boy, Noah was the apple of everyone's eye, with his cheeky little grin and engaging personality. Siblings, grandparents, and a constant gaggle of friends thought they had died and gone to heaven when Noah was around. He was a basketball player and student body president of his high school. He could keep us rolling with his *Saturday Night Live* imitations of "Deep Thoughts by Jack Handy," and his sensitivity to the needs of others kept us in awe.

One of the trademarks for his last years of high school and his first year of college was that he only buttoned every other button when he wore a button-down shirt. When he wore a tie he claimed it didn't matter that he only buttoned every other one because you couldn't see the buttons anyway. At first I kept forgetting that he was doing it on purpose and reminded him again and again that some of his buttons were undone. His wry smile reminded me, and I responded, "Oh yeah, I remember." Even tuxedo shirts at the Junior Prom were only half buttoned. Everyone knew that was just Noah.

I must admit it felt like a dagger in my heart when a huge family group saw Noah off at the Missionary Training Center where he began his two years of missionary service. As he entered the door, he pointed to his buttons with a big grin. *All* neatly buttoned, they signified the rite of passage. He was happy and excited to move into another era of his life. But for just that poignant moment, it hurt my heart to say good-bye to my delightful boy, knowing that he was forging on to the new and exciting but scary territory of becoming a man.

Balancing Our Needs with Those of the Children

Even though we have been spinning children off into the world for more than twelve years, we're only now just approaching a truly empty nest as the last two children prepare to "launch." Yet we've also realized that we've sometimes seen the same child come and go several times, and we've learned that dealing with the emotion of empty-nest parenting is an ongoing process no matter how many children you have! Further, as time marches on and they really *are* gone, there are emotional and poignant times when you have to decide just how involved you want to be with the children after they have left the nest.

As a mother, I have quickly learned that, even though I had thought of this era of life as carefree, empty-nest parenting can also become a day-to-day, full-time job if I allow it. There is always a need for phone calls, advice, baby-sitting, and of course, money. When children who have left home are in various kinds of emotional stress, I have to decide when and how much to help. Every other ENP mother I have talked to has had the same experiences and feelings. The following is a list of the "pulls" we feel on our time and energy (from each direction—our own needs and our children's needs).

Our own needs:

- Time to exercise, play tennis, play golf, run or walk, and enjoy nature.
- Time to think and set goals for the future.
- Time to enjoy each other and do things together that we haven't been able to do because of the demands of the children.
- Time to sit down and read all those books we've been stockpiling.
- Time to develop gifts that have lain dormant.
- Time to resume a career or find a job that is meaningful and fulfilling.
- Time to travel without the demands and worries of children at home.
- Time to give service in volunteer work.

The children's continuing needs:

- Letters, e-mail, and "care packages."

- Advice about what classes to take, what to major in, what job to take, how to deal with their own kids, and so on.
- Advice about major decisions on where to live, buying a house, going into debt, and so on.
- Support and help as they deal with a spouse or a child's illness, emotional stress, financial hardships, or difficult circumstances.
- Baby-sitting.
- Requests. ("Please send the robe I left." "Please call someone for me." "Please come visit for a few days.")
- Family reunions and coordination of family events, from weddings to mission farewells.
- Phone calls.
- Money.

As we try to balance these lists, we can quickly see that the balance will be different for different mothers according to our unique needs and preferences. Although there is no right or wrong in many of these decisions, it is important to "begin with the end in mind."

There seem to be two extremes on this spectrum. On one extreme are mothers who feel that they have "done their thing." It is now time for them to fulfill the dreams they have put on hold while the kids were growing up and let the kids take care of themselves. They do not intend to be roped into baby-sitting when they'd rather be working or golfing, and they are essentially saying, "Good-bye, I love you, but you're on your own!" After all, our goal in raising our children is to work our way out of a job, right?

On the other extreme are mothers who have loved parenting their kids so much that they just don't want to give it up. They are so centered on the great times they had in raising their children that they cannot imagine having fun doing anything else. Also, it is so fun to be intimately involved in the lives of their grandchildren while not having the total responsibility of their care. They want to have a hand in guiding their children (the parents of their grandchildren) in matters of discipline, money, and wardrobe. After all, that's what all these years of experience and finally having a little financial stability have been for, right? This time around, they can do a really good job!

Though there are mothers on each end of the spectrum, most of us fall somewhere in between. What we have to ask ourselves in order to find the right balance is: *What do I want for my children and their children at the end of my life?* If I want a truly deep and meaningful relationship with my children and grandchildren, it is going to take some time to develop. Are we willing to make sacrifices to baby-sit when we are desperately needed, even if it's inconvenient, because we realize that each encounter with a grandchild is "money in the bank" for creating a wonderful relationship? For some whose children and grandchildren live too far for baby-sitting to be an issue, giving up part of vacation time or making a long trip to see them may be the sacrifice needed to create a special relationship.

Questions

I've found there are some key questions mothers can ponder to help us establish what we want our emotional relationship with our children and grandchildren to be—and to help guide our decisions as we move into and through the empty-nest years. Thinking about them now might help establish in your mind the relationship you want to have in the end, rather than just working things out as you go and wishing you'd thought some things through more clearly before you got to the end. In order to make things work as you'd like them to in the long run, you have to think through in advance what you want your future relationship to be with your children. Use my following questions as a springboard to help you think of even better ones of your own. At the end of my life:

- How do I want my children to remember me?

- What will each child say about our relationship?
- What will they say they learned from me?
- What specific memories with my grandchildren will be my treasures?
- Did I spend enough time with each grandchild to *really* know him or her?
- Did I pay the price to balance my relationship with my children after they left home? Was I overbearing or aloof?

If you think long and hard about these questions before you get too set in your ways as the children leave home, your chances of being an emotionally stable empty-nester is much greater. If you have a clear idea of what you want in the end, it will make the day-to-day decisions so much easier and the burden of guilt, or wishing you had done better, so much lighter! What it all boils down to is one key question to ask and answer *now*: "What specific things can I do now to ensure the relationship I want to have with my children and grandchildren before I die?"

By the way (Richard speaking now), I think these questions work equally well for ENP fathers. And I think we dads feel most of the same emotions Linda has mentioned. Linda insists that it's harder on moms, but I'd suggest you dads keep on reading this chapter too.

Changing Your Thought Patterns

I (Linda) do believe that mothers have a particularly difficult time with this "letting go" business, so let me tell you about another one of my friends. Dixie, mother of two, who had always been involved in creative projects and is now three years beyond the day when her last child left home, expressed a sort of delight in letting her children go. She had been the PTA president or otherwise deeply involved in the schools and lives of her children while they were home. Her children had been the center of her life, yet when the time came for them to leave, she was so excited about going on to the next phase of her life that she didn't think too much about mourning. With one child married and the other in school, both working and living outside the home, she began to develop her talents for gardening. She also started a small wedding-flower business and nurtured a wonderful flower garden that gave her much pleasure. Though she still loved the contact she had with her children at least once a week, she says that she wouldn't want to go back to full-time mothering for anything. Part of being emotionally stable when your children leave the nest is being ready for the next step. Dixie's advice to the rest of us: Remember your dreams and figure out how you're going to make them come to pass.

Part of the problem is the habits and patterns you have formed that revolve around filling the needs of the children in your care. Your first thoughts in the morning for so many years have probably been like these: "Oops, we're out of milk." "I wonder if Jonathan has a clean shirt." "How am I going to get out of my meeting so that I can take Emily to the orthodontist?" "I think we're out of lunch sacks." "Oh, what I'd give for just one more hour of sleep!" "I wonder what time Andrew finally went to sleep after I finished helping him with his Shakespeare paper."

These habits and thought patterns can continue for as long as we let them. After the children have gone, we can continue our mothering thoughts with, "I wish Angie would listen to my advice about majoring in business management. I'm calling to give her another piece of my mind." "I wonder if baby Katie slept through the night. I'd better call Andrea and see if she took my advice about feeding her cereal just before she went to bed."

There is usually a space of time (between the kids and the grandkids) when we need to break out of habits and appreciate the fact that we don't have to eat any more macaroni and cheese, and we can quit rocking when we're talking to a young mother who is rocking her baby as she talks. You don't have to feel compelled to point out every dump truck and train as you travel along the road, and you can quit checking your watch to figure out who has missed curfew.

Breaking out of these habits and replacing them with new thought patterns may actually make us feel guilty. Waking up with thoughts like, "I think I'll spend my day at the gym" or "I'm just going to hunker down with a good book today and go to lunch with a friend" makes many of us feel uncomfortable. Unusual thoughts like, "What can I do for my husband today?" and "What would I really like to do for myself today?" are new approaches that we sometimes struggle to get comfortable with.

Of course, being totally self-centered or even totally self- and husband-centered is not the answer to becoming a good, emotionally stable empty-nest mother, but allowing yourself more time to take care of yourself and have more fun with your husband is. Just as important is finding new ways to offer service and contribute your skills and talents outside your own immediate family. Finding opportunities for employment or volunteering in a cause you believe in not only fills the cavity that the children made when they left but also provides a great example for them. Balancing your needs for self-fulfillment should always include service that gives you a way to get outside of yourself and concentrate on others' needs.

Especially for Women: What Do You Really Want?

Let me close this little mothers' section with the interesting story of a friend named Dagny. She is the wife of a filmmaker, and they have spent their life in the busy fast lane of Los Angeles. They have raised seven children of their own and a foster child. At one point in their parenting process, Dagny's husband told her that the dream of his life was to own a large range in the wilderness of Oregon where he could retire, enjoy a quiet life, and have time to read and write. She didn't share his need for isolation or open spaces; what she loved was organizing performing groups for youth, particularly teenagers who were her children's ages. She immensely enjoyed being intimately involved with her children and their friends and doing meaningful and exciting things.

Finally though, with just a couple of kids still at home, her husband committed her to trying a life of seclusion and meditation as soon as the last two left the nest. Since she still couldn't imagine that time ever coming, she agreed. When that time *did* come, she followed through on her commitment, and they moved from California to an eighty-acre ranch in Oregon, far from friends, community, shopping, the airport, and any hope for organizing youth singing groups. Before long, she was stretched to the limit with her isolation. She decided that this was definitely *not* her dream! Her husband could see her unhappiness and realized that it wasn't exactly what he had planned either. In addition to doing some writing, he continued making films and traveled often. After six months of reading books and enjoying the scenery, she decided that enough was enough.

The turning point for her came when she realized that in addition to living her husband's dream, she also needed to live her own dreams! By then she had calculated that even though she had turned sixty, with the medical history of her family on both sides, she would probably live a strong, healthy life for at least thirty more years. *Thirty years!* She felt that was an unbearably long time to read and collect stamps! She also realized that just because her children had left the nest, she couldn't just suddenly become somebody else. She decided she had to be who she really was, no matter what the context. As you might have guessed, Dagny sat down and set some goals for her own empty-nest years. She knew that in order to be happy, she had to be actively involved in organizing and helping people as well as having some wonderful quality time with her husband.

Dagny and her husband picked a new dream place nearer to their children in California, and she is now back to organizing performing groups for youth, this time with younger children who are her grandchildren's ages (they have nineteen so far). She is also actively involved in a church job and loves what she is doing. Her husband and children support her wholeheartedly, knowing that she is happy and fulfilling her destiny. Although they regret that she can't be with them every time they'd like to have her, they understand that she has goals and needs. In addition to continuing to support their children's budding families, Dagny and her husband have found a struggling young family near them who they are working with and caring for, feeling that they are making a real difference in their difficulties.

Dagny knows that the life she's chosen for her empty-nest years won't work for everyone. In fact, she has one friend who went back and resumed the full-time career she had enjoyed before having children, and another friend who decided to drop out of "activity" and be a full-time grandmother. Once her children left home, she loved dedicating herself completely to the needs of kids and grandkids. "When I try to get her to come and help me with some of my projects," says Dagny, "she just says how happy she is, not having any pressure to go places and do things." Having no deadlines and having the luxury of time to spend with her children and grandchildren has been her dream, which she is now happily living!

The bottom line: Get in touch with *yourself* and discover what *you* want, what *you* need, and what *you* wish to accomplish in order to fulfill *your* destiny during your remaining time on this earth. Set goals physically, mentally, spiritually, and socially for your empty-nest years—goals that will make it the most productive and fulfilling time of your life!

Chapter 5

Eleven Essential Elements
of Family Relationships

W hile I (Richard) agree with all that Linda has said about making emotional adjustments and defining your own needs, I also know that she agrees with me that as ENPs we need to come to grips *mentally* with this transition and carefully think through what our LTN children are going to need from us and what we are going to need from them. We also need to work hard mentally to understand this one central fact: *We are not "finishing up" as parents—we are transitioning into another, equally important phase of parenting.* So, from a father's standpoint, let me present a more analytical approach.

First, if we take an eternal perspective, we understand that we have just begun a parenting role that lasts forever. We're on page one of a book with infinite pages and chapters. If we think of it in earthly terms, we're about at halftime. In the first half, thirty years give or take, which probably started in our twenties and ends in our fifties or early sixties, our children lived with us in our home. The second half, again thirty years plus or minus, will hopefully take us into our eighties or beyond and be played with our children living outside our home.

Which half is most important? Which half of a basketball game is most important? What a tragedy if our team quit playing, quit trying when the buzzer went off to end the first half!

The fact is that most of the same principles and priorities that applied in the first half continue to be equally important in the second half. To illustrate: We recently published a parenting book titled *The Happy Family: Restoring the Eleven Essential Elements That Make Families Work* (St. Martin's Press, 2001), in which we identified eleven things that our research indicated were present in some form in all succeeding families. We said, "On the first page of *Anna Karenina,* Tolstoy makes a most provocative statement. He says, 'Happy families are all alike; every unhappy family is unhappy in its own way.'"

When we first read that sentence, we disagreed with it on two levels. First, no family is completely happy or completely unhappy, so what was he talking about? Second, no two families, happy or unhappy, are alike anyway.

But maybe Tolstoy didn't mean it the way we first read it. Maybe he simply meant that there are an infinite number of ways to fail as a family, but there is only one way to succeed. Perhaps he was suggesting that there are certain essential elements that are a part of all happy families, certain things that buttress and protect a family from forces that would otherwise tear it apart, and that these elements don't change.

Indeed, all families that last and produce security and happiness for their members do have some fundamental things in common, some elements that may exist in different forms but that are always present:

1. *Commitment* and recommitment (frequently stated as well as demonstrated).

2. A clarity of *purpose*—some kind of formal or informal (written or implied) family mission statement, a conscious parenting approach or strategy.

3. A true *prioritizing* of family and family relationships—personal time management reinvented to reflect family priority.

4. *Communication*—an insistence on it and a constant effort at it.

5. Family *rules*, laws, or standards.

6. Some sort of family *economy*, or a way of dividing family tasks and teaching responsibility and motivation.

7. Fun and lasting family *traditions* that involve humor and service.

8. Some sense of heritage, family history, and *roots*.

9. Efforts to help kids gain or accumulate an *understanding* of other people, of other cultures, and of the larger institutions that have an impact on their lives.

10. Correct *principles* being taught, including faith and belief.

11. A set of clear and recognized *values*, which are even more specific than principles.

The point is that every one of these eleven essential elements is as vital in empty-nest parenting as it is when kids are still at home. To illustrate that, let's ask some self-evident questions about each essential element and see what empty-nest ideas they call to mind.

1. Commitment and Recommitment

Questions: How can you make sure kids who have just left home know that you are still deeply committed to them, to their needs, to their happiness? As they go out to face the world on their own, how much do they need the safety net of our unconditional love and support?

Ideas: Keep telling them! Every letter or e-mail, every phone call, every visit should include a recommitment—a reminder that while so much has changed physically and logistically, nothing has changed emotionally. Always say "I love you" rather than (or in addition to) "Good-bye." Tell them often that while you will respect their independence and try to be wise in what and how much you give them, you will always be there for them and will always be their mom or dad.

Testimony and spiritual commitment ties so closely to family commitment, and a private family testimony meeting on any Sunday when you might be together can strengthen the ties that bind. Similarly, use of the priesthood in the home can deepen both gospel commitment and family commitment. Give father's or grandfather's blessings to those with health needs or those facing important decisions or difficult challenges. Gather as much of your family as you can for blessings and confirmations as well as marriages. Use the great commitment of these ordinances to remind you all of your personal commitments to each other.

2. Clarity of Purpose

Questions: What *is* the purpose of an adult, empty-nest family? Is it important that ENPs and LTNs come together on a purpose and a plan—that they share common goals and have clearly defined expectations of each other? Since most organizations and corporations today have a "mission statement," should families have one too? Can that credo or mission statement embrace the principles you've tried to teach and that you hope your departed children continue to embrace?

Ideas: If we want our families to continue to function and to *exist* after our kids leave home, we'd better have some plans about what they will do and how. Ask each other the basic question, "What *is* our family now, and how should it serve each of us?" Try to get everyone involved in writing a family mission statement. Ask what they think the key principles are that they have learned and incorporate them into the statement. (See the appendix for specifics on a family mission statement.)

3. A True Prioritizing of Family and Family Relationships

Questions: Once our children have left home, are they "out of sight, out of mind"? Are our kids still the most important thing in our lives? Should they be? Do we just need to turn them loose and stop thinking about them so much? Is it time to move on to other priorities? If our kids *do* still come first, how do we show it and live it?

Ideas: Family is always first. The minute we lose that sense, we begin to lose ourselves—our truest identity. They are no less ours when they're gone—our stewardship, our joy, our pride, and our concern. Think about their needs every day. Don't smother them or try to manage them, but always be *aware* of them. When you plan your day (or your week or your month), think of your family first.

There are two simple adjustments you can make in how you make your list of things to do each day that will bring about a more consistent orientation to the priority of kids and family. First, get in the habit of thinking, "What does my family need today?" and writing down the answers that come to you *before* you make your list of "*Things* to do." (After all, *things* are never as important as *people*—especially people who happen to be your children.) Second, draw a vertical line down the middle of your planner page or your list page. Keep the *things* (work, business, and church assignments) on the left. Reserve the right side for family things that may come up. Be willing to "jump the line" and take care of family whenever a need or idea occurs to you.

4. Communication

Questions: How do we stay in close touch while still giving them their independence? What are the key things to communicate about? How should our relationship change now that they're grown and gone? How do we approach them as adults but still as our children? How do we show interest in what they're doing without being too intrusive?

Ideas: This should be a great pleasure and reward of empty-nest parenting—kids whom we can now talk to as adults, as friends, as interesting people who can expand us even as we expand them.

Think of your communication with them as an interest and a joy. Ask questions of genuine interest rather than interrogation. Enjoy them as you would a new friend. Realize that the very technology we often blame for moral and family decline can be assets and powerful keys to our success in empty-nest parenting. E-mail, computer instant messaging, and low rate, long-distance calls can keep communication open and current from any distance. Grab any chance to travel somewhere with an adult child. "Car time" almost always lends itself to an "opening up" type of communication. Encourage your grown children to talk to each other often by phone or through "weekly update" types of e-mail. Consider a brief "online family home evening" once a week from your various locations through an easy-to-set-up computer "chat room."

5. Family Rules and Standards

Questions: Do the rules still apply? How would you or could you or should you enforce them?

Ideas: It's more a question of standards than of rules once children are gone. Now is the time they will make truly independent decisions about their behavior. Encourage them by making full use of the two most important tools you still have: example and confidence. View your own behavior not only in terms of its consequences to you but in terms of its impact on them. Look for every opportunity to show your confidence in them and in their choices. Start a new kind of "rules" that are really more like pledges. ("We're willing to listen, day or night, when someone needs to talk." "We support each other's decisions.")

6. Family Economy

Questions: What expenses should you pay and what should be your children's responsibility? At what stage should they be completely on their own? What are the tradeoffs between gifts and loans?

What approach will maximize their individual initiative and motivation. Do you want them to struggle like you did or to have the advantages you didn't?

Ideas: Talk this out together and come to an *agreement.* Don't figure it out as you go. Kids need to know what to expect and what not to expect. Keep in mind that the goal is independence and self-reliance.

7. Family Traditions

Questions: How many of your family traditions can be continued in some form even though the children are not living at home? What new traditions are starting to form now that they're living elsewhere? Why is it important to hang on to as many traditions as possible? How do you go about establishing new ones (that center around reunions, weekly e-mails, doing similar things on Sunday, and so on)? What difference do your family traditions make to a child once he or she has left home?

Ideas: If traditions are the glue that holds families together, perhaps we need them even more when our kids are living away from us. Write your traditions down or have your children make a list of them to see what they remember. Then calendar these traditions—the holiday ones, the birthday ones, the seasonal ones, the weekly or Sunday ones, the ones that center around the dinner table—whatever they have been, capture them in writing and give a copy to your departed children. Make an effort to keep those traditions alive, even if you have to do them separately or save them up for times when you are together.

8. Family History and Roots

Questions: Why does it matter that kids know something about their grandparents, great-grandparents, and ancestors? Why might this be especially important to children who are now living away from home?

Ideas: We adamantly believe that you don't know who you are until you know where you came from. The older we get, the more we see traits of our parents and grandparents in our children (including a lot of ours—the bad along with the good). Kids can see part of their own dreams, desires, and gifts as they study the lives of those who preceded them on the family tree. Write down any interesting stories you know about any of your ancestors—particularly incidents that illustrate their character or personality—and send these to your live-away children. If you don't already have a pedigree chart, make one. Develop and communicate an interest in the cultures and places where your family has originated. Talk and write about the self-identity we can gain from our roots. Do genealogy together and go to the temple for your own ancestors. Celebrate ancestors' birthdays, complete with cake, birthday song, and stories that have been passed down. Often working together on the roots is the best way to strengthen the branches.

Consider a summer family vacation to the land of your ancestors. Go to the actual places they were born and lived. If your children are not all with you, write descriptive and imaginative accounts of what you learn about your ancestors' origins and circumstances.

9. Understanding of and Healthy Skepticism for Larger Institutions

Questions: If we think of the family as the smallest and most basic institution, where our deepest loyalties should lie, what are the larger institutions that compete for that loyalty and that can undermine the principles and priorities we've learned in our families? Which larger institutions are particular threats to children as they leave home for the first time?

Ideas: Have some adult conversations with your departed (or soon-to-depart) children about the "mixed blessing" of today's large institutions, which on the one hand help us and provide valuable services, but which can also deceive and damage us. (Big financial institutions encourage debt; big merchandising and advertising foster materialism and greed; big media promote violence and recreational sex; big data and information [computer and Internet] can waste time and give access to pornography; big government can overregulate and overtax; and so on.) Help your children become good "critics," with an attitude of healthy skepticism toward the forces in the world—looking for and appreciating the good but also being aware of and cautious about the dangers.

10. Principles

Questions: Do moral and gospel principles become more or less important as children leave? How does Joseph Smith's statement "I teach them correct principles and they govern themselves" apply? How and when should children live less on "borrowed light" and rely more on their own convictions and testimonies?

Ideas: Continue to talk about gospel principles. Hold at least occasional "family home evenings," even if it has to be by conference call or Internet chat room. At family reunions, have each family member prepare and present a talk on a gospel principle that is important to him or her. Have scripture-reading schedules that you all try to follow as a family. Pray specifically for each other and let each other know the things you'd like to have your family pray about for you. Ask missionaries to send home names and details about investigators and members they are working to reactivate so you can pray for them specifically and by name.

11. Values

Questions: In connection with the thoughts just mentioned, how could the values you've tried to teach your children be undermined as they move out on their own? How will they develop their own personal set of values?

How can those values be kept prominent despite countering influences of media and peer group? Away from your home and your influence, won't it be substantially harder for your children to live within those values?

Ideas: Agree together to a list of values and to focus on one of those values each month wherever you are and wherever your children are. Devote one letter or e-mail per month to the "value of the month." Focus on and discuss how values connect to happiness. Make service to others the paramount value of your family and look for chances to serve *together* in various capacities.

Do the eleven essential elements still apply to grown-up, empty-nest families? Of course they do. In fact, the eleven elements can be used as an effective checklist to evaluate and measure how well you are doing with your empty-nest parenting. If you sense slippage on any of the eleven, it may mean that your family is, at least to some small degree, weakening. As if you were mending a fence, prop up and rebuild any of the eleven sections that are sagging a bit. Be *aware* of the condition of each element and make repairs and improvements consistently. In so doing, that fence will stay strong enough to protect your family from outside elements that would undermine and destroy, and it will also hold in a concentration of unity and joy that will make the rest of life worth living!

Four Additional "Essential Elements"

As long as we're talking about essential elements that apply to all families, let's add four more that apply particularly to empty-nest families—four things that have proven, in so many different families, to be helpful in keeping families together emotionally and spiritually, long after they have been separated physically. The four are: 1. *Place* (having a traditional place or location to "gather"), 2. *Family Reunions* (structuring and organizing our gatherings so that they help each family member grow and progress), 3. *Service expeditions* (getting together in adventurous circumstances to serve others), and 4. *"M and FM" and "F and FF"* (dads forming fathers and future fathers clubs with sons and moms forming mothers and future mothers clubs with daughters). Let's look a little deeper at each of the four.

Place (a traditional location to gather)

We're writing this section in a place we call "the Lighthouse," a summer house we built on top of a steep hill overlooking Bear Lake, a natural aqua-blue gem in the mountains on the border of Utah and Idaho. We've been spending family time here for twenty-three summers. More communication, more relaxing, more sharing, and more *fun* seems to happen here in the few days or weeks we spend each year than in all the rest of the time and all the rest of the places put together.

Extended families—families with grown children—especially need a *place* to gather and to communicate. It ought to be a place somewhat removed from the daily routine and rat race—the normal distractions of work and friends and media and commitments. Days seem so much longer at a place like this—there is more time to talk and listen and enjoy each other. There also seems to be more time and more opportunities to discuss problems or choices and to help each other with solutions and decisions.

For some ENPs, this place might just be the family home to which kids return. But the problem there, usually, is that the ENPs have a busy work life and social life revolving around their home, so they are not really "getting away" when the kids visit. A *second* place—somewhere else to go where the dynamics and perspectives change a little—is worth its weight in gold.

And, by the way, it doesn't have to cost very *much* gold. One family we know just uses their old Winnebago. Once they're in it together, they start to talk and have fun on a different level. Another family has a very inexpensive vacation rental that they go to in the off-season. Others just have a good tent and get away to go camping. Friends in Bulgaria and the Ukraine, though they earn vitually nothing by American standards, still have a little "docca"—a tiny country or forest cabin, often that they've built themselves, where they can get away as a family.

In our own case, we started with a one-room-and-loft A-frame at Bear Lake—all we could afford, but a place to start making memories as a family. It has grown and been added onto over the years, and now whenever we want to get together for real talking and real fun, it's here at Bear Lake. This is where so many of our traditions are, and so many of our cherished memories. We're glad we started coming here so early, when our kids were small, but if we hadn't done it before, we'd do it now—for our grown family. Get a *place* to gather and to enoy and re-bond.

Reunions (structuring and organizing our gatherings so they help each family member grow and progress)

Family Reunion. The phrase conjures images of parks or beaches, barbecues, volleyball games, and tug-of-wars. Many of us have those memories from childhood, and the nostalgic feelings they retrieve ought to be reason enough to create the same kind of memories for our children and their children. When LTNs return for reunions, there can be a magical merging of past, present, and future.

To be successful, a family reunion ought to provide generous helpings of three things besides the food:

1. Fun.

2. Opportunities to teach each others the gospel.

3. Progress on the family structure (genealogy, mission statement, finances, and so on).

Fun: When we gather each summer at Bear Lake, water-skiing is the top priority. When the wind is calm and the water becomes a sheet of glass, we drop whatever else we're doing and head for the boat. Reunions also include the annual Eyrealm tennis tournament and the Bear Lake pentathlon (events: sagebrush run, cowpie toss, water rock skip, around-the-deck race, and surf and swim relay), not to mention late-night marathons of "Speed Scrabble" and "Scum" (a hard-to-explain card game).

Gospel Teaching: Each person is assigned in advance a gospel topic to present in one of the "serious sessions" (late-night meetings after kids are in bed).

Family Structure: We'll talk more in the appendix about creating an adult mission statement and a family constitution. We work on these at reunions, along with genealogy, family finances, and other "business."

Service Expeditions (getting together in adventurous circumstances to serve others)

A few years ago, we were invited to join the board of a nonprofit humanitarian group called CHOICE (Center for Humanitarian Outreach Inter Cultural Exchange). The CHOICE philosophy (and there are other similar groups around the country) is that to really serve, people have to give of *themselves* as well as their money. The group accomplishes this by sending out "expeditions" to intensely poor Third- and Fourth-World locations. The expeditions last ten days to two weeks and accomplish some particular project, like building a simple school or health clinic, digging a well, constructing an irrigation project, or setting up micro-enterprise businesses. Expedition members (usually a group of several families) pay their own transportation plus the cost of the materials to accomplish and complete the designated project. An advance team of interns usually gets the materials in place before the expedition arrives.

It wasn't long before we discovered that we could go on one of these expeditions for less money than we'd spend using the same vacation time to go to Disney World, Hawaii, or on a cruise.

We also realized that you don't have to go halfway around the world to derive these benefits from service. A full-family "mini-expedition" to feed the homeless at a shelter provides the same kind of bonding and communication and the same kind of perspective and gratitude.

M&FM or F&FF ("future fathers" and "future mothers" clubs)

Several years ago, when our two oldest daughters had gone away to schol, I (Linda) realized how easy it would be to lose touch with what they were thinking and how they were really feeling. Then, as our first grandchild was about to enter the world, I was worried that my daughters might lose track of how important their role as mothers was as they encoutered the stress and hardships of everyday motherhood. In addition, I felt that our daughters, whether they were mothers yet or not, needed to think about motherhood as a serious career, one that would make not just a little difference but a profound difference in the lives of not only this generation but many yet to come. I realized that unless we organized a time and place to be together so that we could talk about these things that really matter, we might be in danger of being like ships passing in the night, never really sharing our deepest feelings, especially about things that matter most.

From this kernel of thought has sprung the illustrious organization *Mothers and Future Mothers of Eyrealm* (MFME for short). Once a year, usually for three days and two nights, the Eyre women meet at an appointed place and time to exchange ideas, enjoy cultural events, and generally relish being out of our own worlds and in the world of nurturing our love for each other and appreciating each other's ideas. Although motherhood is the underlying theme, it is so exciting for me to learn from these women who have their own perspectives and such good ideas because of their life experiences!

At the first conference, before any of them had children, we talked about motherhood "theoretically." Each conference becomes a little more interesting as our older daughters grapple with the realities of actual mothering. We try to combine communication about motherhood with deep communication about learning and opportunities to share what we've been learning, both about motherhood and the world that surrounds us, since the mother is the primary teacher in the home.

Here are fifteen questions I chose for a recent F & FFE discussion. Hopefully they can serve as a springboard for even better questions you might like to ask your own daughter or daughters:

1. For those who are not yet mothers: What are you looking forward to most about being a mother? What do you think is the hardest part?

2. For those who are now mothers: What surprised you most about being a mother? What *is* the hardest part?

3. How many children would you like to have? (Knowing that you can't always have what you want.)

4. What are the most important things you are learning right now?

5. What is your most memorable experience this year?

6. What do you think you'll be doing five years from now?

7. What should be your criteria when you ask yourself whether or not to have a child?

8. What is the most important thing to know when choosing a marriage partner?

9. What do you dream of doing?

10. What is the most important thing to remember when you are a mother?

11. If you could have lunch with any three people alive, who would they be?

12. What do you love most about what you are doing right now?

13. If you could go anywhere on earth, where would it be?

14. What do you worry about?

15. If you had a magic wand, what is something you would change about yourself?

Later the same day, the girls suggested we go around the circle and tell each person what we each liked best about them and something we wished they would change. It was maybe the most valuable time of all. The things that came out were both gratifying and surprising. Everything was said kindly, but it was a great chance to get some things out on the table that needed to be said. At the end of our time together I gave each daughter a little book where she could put a picture and a short synopsis of our adventures that year. The books became a permanent record of our MFME conference.

Chapter 6

A Word from the LTNs
(and the Basic Purpose of an Empty-Nest Family)

Before we move on to part 2 (where we LTNs really get involved), let me (Saren) jump in as the daughter and make a point or two. I think it is vital, as you think about some of the things my parents have brought up, to involve your kids in that thinking. As your children become adults, they need a new kind of communication where they feel comfortable in bringing up anything that is on their minds.

For some reason, it's really hard to tell your parents that you need certain things or are bothered by certain things they do. When we try, parents can be pretty defensive and annoyed—then things are just unpleasant and pointless. So as long as we have a fairly tolerable relationship and we aren't around each other that much anyway, it's easier to just not say anything.

This book suggests that you, the parent, take the initiative to bring up a full range of subjects—from financial issues to communication ideals to roles you want to play in each others' lives—with your kids. I really appreciate the fact that my parents brought up so many issues and ideas and plans with me before I left home, and that they continue to discuss and adjust the roles they play in my life. Because of these ongoing discussions, I find it fairly easy to bring up my own issues and worries with them. It's my hope that through reading this book and sharing with your kids the thoughts and ideas it inspires, you'll be able to open a door for continually building and strengthening your relationship with them.

Your kids really do want a strong, ongoing relationship with you. To illustrate this, I asked some of my siblings a basic question: "What is the purpose of family once family members don't live together anymore and don't rely on each other for their basic daily needs?" I got some pretty interesting answers:

Saydi: I have found that family relationships are the foundation upon which I have built and continue to build my character. That was easy to see when I was small, living in the same house as my parents and siblings. My parents taught me about life, gave me structure and rules, and provided for me. My siblings were the friends I was around the most, the ones I could be anyone around, be stupid with, say anything to; they would always end up loving me the same. I guess I thought that as we all got older and moved away and started our own lives and families that my family would have less of an impact on me and who I was. Now I see that's not true. Now that I'm older and have been away from home for a while, my family has a different impact on who I am, and perhaps it's a stronger one. Now my family members are my peers, but they have this special place built by unconditional love, so I know they are always honest with me and I know they can give me the most true and real advice because they know me the most, and they know I won't judge them by what they say to me or how they act toward me. My parents and siblings are the ones I go to for advice, for reality checks, for comfort. The purpose of family now is to help me remember who I am and feel good about it, to help me build good character and to love me no matter what I do.

Aja: My thoughts and foundation are still with my family. I don't see my family every day anymore, but I feel them almost all the time. I don't so much think about what they are doing or what's going on at that particular point in time, but I do feel their influence and their love, and I am concerned or joyful for and with them, across all the miles. It seems almost mystical, and maybe it is, but emotionally and spiritually I never really feel like I've left home.

Shawni: The purpose of family once the kids have moved away is to remain as intact and in love as ever, helping each other through different stages of life. I think relationships change and things are different as family members move away and the family is no longer a cohesive unit living in the same house. But I guess the key is figuring out how to keep that cohesive unit in love despite long distances and increasing distractions and chaotic schedules. In some ways I feel even more connected to my family now that I have moved away and been married for a while. As we all grow up, differences in age seem to diminish, and we all kind of relate on a different, more adult level.

I think I'll always be lonely for siblings and parents when I'm not around them a lot. I just love them so much and feel so close to them from all we've been through together that I always feel lonely for them when we're apart. I'm so glad for the phone and the Internet to stay in touch!

Jonah: Now that I'm away from home, family is the memory of all the silly fights and the car rides and all the missing curfews and how you all worked it out and that you are all still together. Family is simple support and knowing that there are people who will always be there to fall back on, whether it's a simple need for love or a desperate need for money. It's important to know that there are always those who will help you in any way they can. Family is not just a place to eat Thanksgiving dinner; rather, it is a place where you know that people really know you. Being out in the student world where kids are trying to fend for themselves, I realize how important it is to know I have a family who cares about me and is willing to fend for me. Physically, parents are with their children 24/7 before the kids move out. Ideally, their influence and support stays with their kids 24/7 if they continue to do their job right.

Chapter 7

Conclusion to Part 1: It's All about Prioritizing

I (Richard) was on an airplane once, seated by a stranger—a psychologist as it happened—who knew a great deal about the Church. (He had several LDS friends and neighbors and had observed them closely.)

"I can't say that I have too many opinions about the doctrine and teachings of your church," he said "but I can tell you this—Joseph Smith and Brigham Young had to be cultural and psychological and sociological *geniuses!*"

"What do you mean by that?" I asked.

"Well," he said, "they somehow anticipated the most common and prevalent developmental problems people would face—even in our day—and put in place systems and programs that would solve them!"

It sounded like he'd thought a lot about this, so I asked him to go on.

"Okay, let's start with kids transitioning into adulthood. Most eighteen- or nineteen-year-olds are too young to make good college, major, and career choices, so they make a lot of false starts and poor choices. You've got your missions at that age. Kids give service, forget themselves, become more mature and sophisticated, see different parts of the world and its cultures, and come home knowing far more about themselves and their aptitudes and their options—ready to make good education and career decisions, not to mention marriage decisions. Your missions are a sociological and personal development masterstroke."

Well, I thought, *I've never looked at it quite that way.* "What else?" I asked.

"The other most difficult developmental phase," he said, "is the empty-nest syndrome and retirement. Most people flounder. They don't feel useful or needed anymore, and there are huge increases in everything from nervous breakdowns to divorce to health problems. But you Mormons have missions for retired couples, and you have that temple and genealogy thing. People not only stay busy but they also perceive that what they are doing is even more important, so their mental and psychological health and their marriage relationships are usually excellent. I just think it's brilliant. Joseph and Brigham were unbelievably farsighted."

I've thought a lot about that discussion. The ideas aren't Joseph's or Brigham's, but they are brilliant. Of course, missions, genealogy, and temple work aren't just for the benefit of those who participate in them, but they are masterstrokes indeed—strokes from the Master.

The whole process and transition of empty-nest parenting is made more positive and more productive for us ENPs and for our LTNs by the inspired programs of God and of his church. Full acceptance and activity in every opportunity we have as members is the most powerful key in unlocking the door to successful empty-nest parenting and a happy and hopefully long second half of life.

Priorities and Commitment

There are lots of books about this transitional time of life—many of them written to and for baby boomers—books with titles like *The Second Half of Life* or *Life After Fifty* or *The Autumn of Life*. Most of the books are about finances or travel or various ways to enjoy our newfound freedom.

But what matters most? And what will ultimately have the most bearing on our happiness? The answer, of course, is our family and our children. So it is ironic that so many of us plan so carefully for every other aspect of our upcoming retirement and our life's second half but think and plan so little for what remains our most important stewardship and the key to our happiness—our families and our ongoing relationships with our children.

There's no single right answer for the issues and challenges of empty-nest parenting. We each have to find our own. But there is one right attitude, and that is to *prioritize* our families, even after they leave, above every other aspect of our lives. After all, we've invested eighteen to twenty years in each child—and we're now nearing the homestretch. This is no time to slack off or slow down. We are now in a position to build the "beautiful family culture of a three-generation family" that Stephen Covey spoke of in the foreword.

It's so interesting to speak (as we often do) to audiences made up of parents of other faiths. While they share the same kind of unconditional love for their children as LDS parents, they often think about commitment and priorities differently than we do. After one speech on the East Coast a person said, in essence, "Before my kids grew up and left, I had to pretty much make every decision with them in mind: the kind of house we lived in, where we went on vacation, what I spent my money on. Pretty much everything had to be oriented to them, and I think I passed that test. Now I'm at a place where I can think about what *I* want."

Not that there's anything so wrong with a little of that kind of thinking, but as Church members with testimonies of eternal families, we are naturally going to be more concerned with preserving and strengthening relationships and with things like family reunions, interfamily advice, mutual assistance, helping with each other's testimonies and lifestyle choices, and so on. For us, there has been no change of priorities, just a change in the address where those priorities live!

Two Related Issues

Preparing Your Children to Leave Home;

Retuning Your Marriage for the Empty-Nest Years

Two Related Issues

This book (all of both of its two parts) is exclusively about *empty-nest parenting*—about being a parent to sons and daughters who have moved out. *But,* there are two related issues that are so relevant and so connected that they can't be ignored. A brief intermission that deals with each of them will, like all good intermissions, enhance our enjoyment of Act II.

The first issue is on the minds of parents who still have one or more children who have *not* yet left home, and who want to do all they can to *prepare* (both the children and themselves) for that day of departure. The second issue is about empty-nest *marriage*—about making the relationship adjustments that married empty-nesters need to make.

Preparing Children to Leave Home—and Preparing Yourself for the Departure

Say you've got an older teenager or two who will be leaving home in the next couple of years. Do you put this book on the shelf and wait until you really need it—or do you start now to think about the transition and to consciously prepare your children for their LTN phase?

Of course it's wisest to anticipate and prepare! The simplest and most effective way to go about this is to sit down with your teenagers and make a list of what they will want to know and be able to do before taking off for college or a mission or whatever. The list can include anything from knowing how to cook a few things to knowing how to budget, how to use a planner, how to be wise in choosing friends, and so on.

We asked our two "still-at-homers"—Eli (seventeen) and Charity Jade (fourteen) what they thought. Actually, we posed four questions to them. Here are some of their answers.

What am I most worried about as I think about leaving home?

Charity Jade: Being the baby of the family, I know that my leaving home will bring many new opportunities for my parents. They will want to travel the world, spend years in tropical locations to golf and lounge away when all of their kids have left. Frankly, this worries me. I want to call home and hear their comforting voices at every worry (without having to track them down). I want to come home to our cozy house for Christmas and Thanksgiving to see the whole family. I know that by the time I have left home, my family will be much larger and more branched off. I am scared that they will all be doing their own thing. I hope they don't forget that I am still hanging on the end.

Because of this worry, I feel that it is very important that parents, while still giving their kids a sense of independence, don't let them go too fast. I know that I will probably be pretty homesick when I first leave home, and I believe that constant support from the parents is very important. I feel that each child deserves to know that there is always a constant person to turn to in times of turmoil. I really believe that parenting should be the same, if not harder, after the children leave home. I will have so many questions when I leave home, and I will need that crutch to lean on.

Because my parents and siblings have taught me both verbally and through example so much about leaving home, I really don't have a long list of worries. This shows me how much preparing your children for life away from home can help them minimize the worries they have about it.

Eli: I have heard from each of my siblings, and it is often said in the world, that you don't truly appreciate something until you no longer have it. I think the thing I am most scared about leaving home is the fact that my parents won't be there, to help me up when I am down, or to remind me about something, or to push me to achieve more.

It is a given that it will be nice to have a little bit more freedom, as far as certain things go. I'll clean my room when I want, come home when I want, and so on. But in pondering this, it isn't all that great. Without my parents I would be nowhere. Seeing as I have never really lived away from home, that has never been a problem. But as I prepare to go to college this fall, I realize how worried I am to be away from the comfort of my parents and family.

There is so much stuff in my life that my parents do for me, often without me even noticing. I worry that, without them, that "stuff" they do won't get done, and thus I will fail.

I am also kind of scared to face the real world, not one sheltered by my own comforts. It is no longer high school where things don't matter all that much. In college, everything I do and learn will somehow affect my life and the path it takes.

What can my family and I do now (while I am still at home) to overcome these worries?

Charity Jade: I think it is important that I develop a strong sense of love and trust with my parents before I leave home. I think they need to let me know they will always be there when I need them. I feel we need to establish that support right now, even before I step foot on my uncharted soil. There should be a promise between us that they will always be around if I need them.

My parents and family can also continue to explain to me what things will be like; they can share their experiences with me. I know that I will be very confident when I leave home because I will know almost exactly what I am getting into and what I am going to experience.

Eli: Let kids practice a little bit of independence. Let them know what the real world is going to be like. Let them know that Mom and Dad aren't always going to be there to pick up after them, to push them along, and to straighten things out when they mess up.

I stress the importance of making sure they know how to handle money. Make them earn it in high school. Don't just give it to them. In the real world, people aren't just going to give you money. In high school, I have had to work for my money; the money that I have spent on clothes and entertainment is money that I have earned. When kids earn their own money, it is then natural for them to take care of it and spend it wisely, whereas if you just give them the money, they won't care what they spend it on, or how fast they spend it.

Don't do everything for your kids; help them out a little or maybe even a lot while they are still at home, but make sure they know you won't always be there to correct their faults and get them out of difficult situations.

Thinking not just about myself, but about kids in general, what are the things that make kids really prepared to be on their own?

Charity Jade: After years of complaining, I have finally come to realize how grateful I am that my parents taught me how to work. Ever since I was eight, I have earned every penny to pay for every item of clothing that I have bought (partly through doing family chores and getting paid to practice the flute). I have also paid for nights out with my friends and other activities. I have sometimes envied my friends with their closets full and their freely giving parents. Now I just feel bad for them. I know that when I am out in the real world, I will be more successful than they. I will know what I am doing. I will handle my money well. I will have more. I appreciate so much that my parents have made me work for my privileges. I am so glad that I know how much money to spend and how much to save and how much to give. This is one of the greatest gifts my parents have given me because I know it is truly preparing me for what's ahead.

I once heard of a mother who decided to clean up after her child and never make her work. She realized that it would take less time if she picked up the toys or did the dishes than it would to tell her daughter to do it and wait for the complaining to stop. Her daughter was pampered with never having to work. Recently, this girl began her freshman year in college. She is miserable. I am so glad that my parents not only made me work for my money and clothes but also taught me how to cook and clean and carry out simple tasks that I will have to do every day of my adult life. I might not be great at it, but this also has made me so much more prepared for "life in the fast lane," and I am so grateful for it.

Parents can also prepare their children for life outside the home by telling them what it will be like and letting them know that they, as parents, will always give a steady stream of support. All children need an idea of what it will be like out there, and it is almost fully the parents' responsibility to prepare them for that. Parents can also start to change roles, from parents that children depend on for the basic needs of life, to parents that children depend on to be friends and sources of support.

Eli: I think the most important thing that prepares kids to be on their own is by hearing experiences. Whether they come from siblings or parents, just knowing what to expect can make worlds of difference. Parents should tell you what they remember about being your age!

The advice of older siblings that have moved away from home is also very important. They know how it works and can tell me what to expect and how to live on my own away from my parents. They can relate stories to me and overall just make the transition easier.

I have seven older siblings that have all gone away to college, and in watching them and hearing their personal experiences, I have better knowledge of what to expect when I leave home.

Even though I don't yet have any experience away from home, I anticipate that what I'll need from my parents during my first year gone will be . . .

Charity Jade: I have said this at least five times before, but I think it is crucial. Before children leave for their first year away, parents need to establish a support system that states they will always be there in hard or great times. I feel that the parents' line should never be busy and that the answer should never be no to a child who wants advice. The support has to be there. Most children as they leave will be homesick and scared at some point. They need people that they can always turn to, that they can rejoice or mourn with. I think this is one thing that I will desperately need my first year away. I have heard the phone ring uncountable times when calls of my older siblings come in. And my parents are always there to talk. I feel that this is one way that they all made it through their first year and beyond, doing so well and being so happy.

Eli: I anticipate that as I move away to college or leave the house, the thing I will need most from my parents is their love and support. I will need to know that they are there for me, to know that they are thinking about me and loving me. I need to know that, if emergency strikes, or just during tough times, I can fall back on them, and they will be there; that I can call them and talk things over when I am having a hard time. This is what I will need from my parents.

Another thing I will need is their advice and ideas. I need to know that I can ask them for advice whenever I feel I need it. It is important, though, that parents give good advice, but if the children don't take it, they can't be offended, and they need to be willing to give advice again the next time it is asked for.

Most of all, I just want to have my parents' support, and I want to know that they will support and love me no matter what decisions I make. The bottom line is that I just need to know that they will be there for me.

Summary

If you still have children living with you in your home, realize that the first step in successful empty-nest parenting is to *prepare* for it. First prepare your family by having some ideas and plans in mind to preserve and maintain the eleven essential elements discussed in the last section of this book. Second, prepare yourself by anticipating the emotions you'll feel and by having some special events or travel in mind to take up the emotional slack when the nest is first empty. (Nothing better than another "honeymoon" where you reinvent your relationship with your spouse and have some leisurely time to think about and discuss your empty-nest parenting strategies.) Third, prepare your children by talking frequently about what it will be like to be gone. Sometimes brief "separations" (a term exchange program or a summer with relations) can be great "previews" of what it will be like to live away and can take a little of the sting out of the real thing.

The Church offers us some pretty amazing opportunities when it comes to both the preparation for and the actual departure of our children. EFY programs and other short-term away-from-home experiences can prepare children emotionally and spiritually. Church universities or institute programs can give them a gospel-centered home away from home. Church-sponsored study-abroad programs can allow short-term "adjusting times." Missions can provide perhaps the best independence and maturity-gaining experience available anywhere. And temple, genealogy, and senior missionary experiences can be the perfect buffer and transitional experience for empty-nest parents.

Most of all, though, the Church and its doctrines of eternal families can give us the profound motivations we need to bridge any gaps, cover any distance, and overcome any challenge in keeping our empty-nest families close and intact.

Retuning Your Marriage

How often have you heard this story: The last child moves out, and within a few months one of the parents moves out too. So, if you are a two-parent family, along with all your efforts at empty-nest parenting, there should be some serious attention paid to *empty-nest partnership*.

Single empty-nest parents have a different set of challenges. If your partner has preceded you to the next phase, you will want to consider what he or she might have thought or felt as you complete on your own the stewardship you started together. If you are divorced or separated, you may still find ways to work together or at least in some kind of tandem agreement on matters relating to your children. If you have remarried or blended families, your relationship with your new spouse will also have a profound influence on your children and on your relationship with them.

If you *are* fortunate enough to still be married to the father or mother of your children, begin with an understanding of the profound importance of that partnership. It is the new and everlasting covenant; it is the relationship that preceded and created and still gives nourishment and security to your relationships with your children. It is the trunk of your family tree, the connection between your roots and branches. It is the ultimate key to your happiness here and hereafter.

The old phrase "The best thing you can do for your kids is to love their mother" (or father) is still true. Nothing gives adult children more security and happiness (not to mention an invaluable example) than seeing that their mom and dad are still in love. Remember that the goal is an eternal family. To be even more direct, the goal is a kingdom—a kingdom within God's kingdom. And the first require-ment for any lasting kingdom is a unified "king" and "queen."

From Orchestra to Duet

Forgive my (Linda's) musical analogy, but let's face it: With kids pulling at our heartstrings for at least two decades, when the children leave home, our marriage is bound to be somewhat, or perhaps even drastically, out of tune. For marriages that have survived, some adjust-ments probably need to be made when our children leave home in order to get our marriage partnership back in full harmony.

For many mother and father "birds," one of the greatest worries living in an empty nest is learning to live together as a couple again after many years of sharing that nest with younger and smaller people and all *their* problems. As we anticipate being on our own, we have empty-nest visions of traveling at will, eating gourmet food, no longer being prisoners to homework, not having to wring our hands when teenagers have missed their curfew, and being able to go to the movies whenever we feel like it. But will we be able to survive each other—just each other—full time? All those years of carpools, juggling sched-ules, and sweating over being late for ballet are gone. Yet somehow, things are not really that much less complicated. There are still career issues and community involvement and church jobs to deal with as well as the inevitable needs of the children even though they are away from home. Life is not easier, but *life is different* in an empty nest. How do we retune our marriage in order to make it into an exciting partnership for the future?

Before we get to the big questions, let's talk about a couple of the little ones that make a big difference. One might be: How does one deal with those annoying habits of a spouse that have sort of gotten swallowed up in the hurricane of life with children? Chances are that those irritating idiosyncrasies will now be exposed and somehow eas-ier to stumble over in that empty nest. For years I have complained sporadically about Richard's habit of flossing his teeth in bed at midnight and been disgruntled by the fact that when he makes the bed, it looks like somebody is still in it. It's easier to dwell on little things like that when there are just the two of us in the house. We have learned that, even though one spouse or the other may be worried about something that may seem to be a silly little thing, the best thing that can go through a spouse's mind when there is a need to change is, *If it's important to you, it's important to me!* (He can be quieter with the floss and neater with the bed. I can be more tolerant on both and keep them in perspective.)

We've also learned that "constructive criticism" is usually destructive. After years of complaining about some of Richard's idiosyncrasies, I have realized that the best way to change behavior is not through criticism but through praise. Praise is a powerful tool, not only to build someone else up but also to help *you* realize how grateful you are for a spouse who is really trying to be the best he can be, even though it may not seem like it at times. Praise focuses your attention on the things you love rather than the things that bother you. Praise is almost like a magic wand to help a spouse feel worthwhile and eager to fulfill expectations. It is a vehicle for choice. It maximizes both spouses' chances to change. Criticism is a judgment, a verdict, and a stifling dead end.

The empty nest is a place (and a time) to consciously change old habits and patterns. Years of dealing with the realities of life produces habits that are sometimes simply modes of survival rather than something that is really helping to enhance your marriage. Even though I tried to be loving and helpful to Richard when all of our children were home, the message that usually came through from day to day was, "I love you but I've got all these kids' needs to attend to today. I can't handle *another* child, so you're just going to have to take care of yourself!" Now mind you, on many days that attitude was absolutely justified, but I think I established a habit of thinking of the kids' needs first. Now that most of them have gone, it has taken a conscious mental shift as well as deliberate physical action to let Richard know that he really is my first priority. This is the person I plan to live with for the rest of my life—and even beyond. Our children will all eventually have their own spouses and their own separate homes and children to care for. The prime relationship for eternity is that of husband and wife.

And that leads us to the fact that a prime relationship deserves prime time! We have decided, now that we are approaching a new phase of life, that we need a new vision statement for our marriage. Since you will be reading in detail about our new family mission statement in the last section of this book, we should just say here that we spent a few days on a business trip talking about what we envisioned for our empty-nest years. We decided to call it "The Mission of Our Marriage." Later we started calling it "Working out our *own* salvation." After several rather long paragraphs containing thoughts that we wanted to include but that we probably weren't going to remember, we decided to simplify our statement to two words: "Love More." These two words are really the heart of our purpose as we progress in our partnership. Developing your own mission for the empty-nest years can give you a sense of purpose and a track to run on.

Learning from Missionaries: "Companionship Testimonies"

Perhaps the biggest ongoing worry of most mission presidents is companionship problems. It was certainly true for me (Richard) in London. Whenever the phone rang, there was a chance that the elder or sister on the line would say, "President, I just can't stand my companion any longer," or "Elder ——— is driving me nuts," or even "Well, President, it finally came to blows. I told you, you should have transferred one of us."

After a year or so in the field, I noticed something. One of the questions I asked in missionary interviews was, "Do you have a private companionship testimony meeting each week as suggested in the white handbook?" *Those who did rarely, if ever, had serious companionship problems.* As I thought about it, and asked about it, I realized that those weekly testimony meetings, besides being an endearing private expression of faith, belief, and love, were also a time to clear the air, to get feelings and frustrations out in an atmosphere that defused them and put them in perspective. After bearing his testimony and telling his companion he loved him, loved the work, loved the investigators, and loved the Lord, it became easier and far less painful or threatening for the missionary to mention something that was bothering him or that could be improved on.

It turned out that this little twenty- or thirty-minute weekly companionship testimony meeting was the single most effective thing we ever found to eliminate companionship complaints, criticisms, and contention.

With the mission in mind, and with the commitment of devoting prime time to our marriage relationship, we decided that we would have a "companionship meeting" of our own every Sunday night.

A few things that make it work best for us:

• Meet in a quiet, private place at the same time every Sunday evening.

• Start with each of you bearing your testimonies—real ones that end "in the name of Jesus Christ." Include things like, "The thing I like most about you is . . ." or "What I admired about what you did this week was . . ."

• Ask what you can do from that week's experience to change for the better.

• Discuss what the challenges of the coming week will be.

• Talk about how to accomplish the things that need to be done during the week and divide responsibilities so that you feel you're working as a team.

• Decide on a time and place for a date that week. Go over the schedule.

Over the years, our favorite part of these partnership meetings is always the private, one-to-one testimony-bearing where we express our feelings about the blessings of our lives. These positive feelings go a long way to get us safely through the week and add greatly to our "emotional bank account," which inevitably has substantial withdrawals from the hassles of the real world during the week.

At our wedding reception thirty-two years ago, we displayed a picture of the two of us gazing off into the sunset. The caption read, "Love does not consist of gazing into each other's eyes but of looking forward together in the same direction." Well, in hindsight, it *is* important to look forward together in the same direction, but it is also important to gaze into each other's eyes!

Different things work for different people, and different things work for men than work for women. I (Linda) smile when I realize that after these thirty-something years, I have discovered that verbally expressing my admiration and appreciation to Richard (along with supplying more frequent back and foot rubs) is the most romantic thing I can do for him. He has discovered that doing the dishes, and seeing what needs to be done around the house and doing it without being asked, goes a long way to aid the romantic atmosphere in my mind. Romance, especially when the children have left home, can be the magnet that draws us back together after many years of fragmentation and distraction.

Even if our marriages weren't perfectly in tune before we started having children, the "orchestration" of the events of our lives as we have lived with children in our homes may have helped create the "duet" that can make life even more rich and vibrant as we begin our empty-nest years. As we retune our marriage and recharge it with love, appreciation, and the excitement of a new era and a new horizon, we hope we'll find that the most beautiful music is yet to come!

The Three Cs

There are plenty of books about rekindling romance after the kids are gone, about learning to be alone together again, about filling the void together that the kids have left. We've read a few of these and think most of the good advice they contain can be summarized into three Cs:

Commitment to each other, and to each other's happiness

Communication with each other, and enjoying being together

Conceptual planning with each other, and working toward common goals

Each of these *becomes* a new challenge and a new opportunity as the kids leave. The requirements and the patterns for each are straightforward but difficult, simple to *say* but downright hard to *do*. But there are two overwhelmingly important reasons for tackling all three with vigor and energy: First, succeeding together at them will bless the lives of your children; second, succeeding together at them will deliver more peace and happiness to you and your spouse than anything else in the world.

So, during this intermission, before the lights start blinking for the next act of empty-nest parenting, let's think hard together about the three crucial elements of empty-nest *partnership*.

1. Renew Your Commitments

We know one couple that actually retook their marriage vows after their last child left their nest. The way they saw it, they were going back to their courtship—back to the one-on-one romantic relationship they had the first time they were married, and they wanted to reformalize that love and personal commitment.

However we do it, we *do* need to recommit to each other as our kids move on and leave us alone together. And when you think about it, it's a pretty exciting thing to fall for each other all over again—you've probably got more money and more freedom than you did the first time, so you may enjoy it even more this time around. Think back to those things you did to win your spouse over in the first place, and do them again—flowers, romantic dates, gifts, and love notes.

Renewed, unconditional commitment is a marvelously powerful and security-giving thing. In the warmth and glow of our spouse's complete commitment, we can relax and truly be ourselves. In our initial courtships, we earned each other's love. In the intervening years of raising children and expanding careers, we have served and helped and loved each other in so many ways. Now, as we move toward some kind of retirement (or at least toward new situations in both our family and our work), we should be capable of even deeper commitment to each other and support for each other.

But that recommitment isn't automatic or assumed. It needs to be *made*. Let us share a written commitment that one husband made to his wife on their thirtieth anniversary as their last child prepared to go away to college:

> My darling: Thirty years ago I pledged to love and be faithful to you in sickness and in health, for time and eternity. In those thirty years we've raised our children and built our careers. We've sacrificed for and supported our children and each other in countless ways. We've disagreed and fought and argued, but we've always made up and gradually come to understand our differences and the way each other thinks. Through all the struggles, we've kept our marriage vows and kept our dream of unity and of growing old together, surrounded by children who still love us and grandchildren who know how much we love them.
>
> On this anniversary and as our youngest child leaves the nest, I feel prompted and prepared to make a simple recommitment to

you—one that carries with it all of the love and all of the faith I have. It is this: Since I believe in the eternity of the soul, that love can outlast death and that relationships can carry over to the next life, I now pledge to love and be faithful to you for eternity. My commitment to you and my love for you is coeternal with my soul and with your soul.

With this eternal commitment comes a new realization—an epiphany I have recently received. It is that there is nothing I would change about you—that with my unconditional love is an unconditional acceptance.

This is not to say that I am under the illusion that you are perfect or that I will not support you in ways that you want to change and progress, but I have realized that there is nothing I would choose to change about you. You are a complex biological and spiritual organism, and I love the *whole* too much to risk changing some *part* of it, which might make the whole something different than what I have come to love. Besides, as the song says, "For every fault you have, I have ten," and "The little faults you do have just make me love you more."

So, my thirtieth anniversary gift to you (and my "second wedding gift" as we start our voyage as empty-nesters) is this: my eternal and unconditional recommitment of love.

What wife wouldn't want to receive that kind of letter—or what husband? We are all warmed and filled by the commitment of our spouse. It is one of the key reasons we get married in the first place. And with a solid *recommitment* from each other, a married couple at this stage of life is ready to face the challenging readjustment of an empty nest.

The goal is not to make our spouses better but to make them happier and to expand the joy we have together. The awesome and sometimes frightening thing about a marriage—especially a long-lasting one—is that we each have more influence on the happiness of our spouse than we do on our own. By now we know how to make each other happy. We simply have to recommit ourselves to doing it!

2. Work at Total, Open Communication

You *think* you've been communicating all these years, but so much of it has been about the kids, and about the life you lived while they were home. When they are gone, it can feel like there's not much left to talk about.

Once again, the whole process is a little like starting over—a little like getting married again. We tell young couples, in our marriage seminar, that there are five things they must talk about openly and constantly, revealing to each other their whole mind and heart. The five things are:

- Finances
- Sex and physical intimacy
- Goals and dreams
- Feelings and beliefs
- Children and parenting

The beginning of the empty-nest phase is a time when all five topics take some shifts and turns, requiring an extra effort at clear communication. Where are the finances now and what kind of budgeting or planning will you do to see that everyone is taken care of? How will your physical intimacy be affected by being alone again—what do you hope for and expect from each other? What goals and plans and hopes do you have for this new season of life? Are you on the same page about how you want your lifestyle to change? How are your testimonies, and what are you both feeling emotionally? Do you each have a different mix of missing and wishing? What continues to need to be discussed about the kids? What kind of empty-nest parents do you want to be?

The bottom line: There is not less to talk about now—there's *more*. This is a new phase, and with it comes lots of issues, lots of opportunities and options, lots of challenges. Step up your communication—open it up—the sooner the better!

One couple we know anticipated their empty-nest phase with some apprehension. They had seen other couples pull apart after their kids were gone, so they had a little plan in place. The first thing they did after the last child left was go away together themselves—two weeks in the Caribbean on a second honeymoon. It was a relaxed, peaceful time to get to know each other again—not as a mother and a father but as sweethearts. They talked a lot about each other's needs and actually avoided talking about their kids. (They'd done plenty of that in the immediate weeks before.) They made new commitments to each other and took the time to really talk about their life as a couple—past and future. They made plans about things they would do together and time they would spend with each other. They talked about their biggest hopes and fears entering this new phase of life. They decided to be patient with each other and to realize and acknowledge that it would take a little time to make this adjustment.

3. Conceptualize and Plan the Rest of Your Life

Out of our renewed commitments and communication should flow some solid conceptual planning about our married life together as empty-nesters. In our own case, even as we've dreaded the day our last one leaves, we've relished and looked forward to having the opportunity to do some things that weren't possible (or at least not practical) while the kids were with us: from simple things like more reading to complex things like travel and humanitarian service on a whole different scale.

It's best not to leave these visions and dreams of what to do with the second half of your lives to chance. Sit down together or take a trip together and plan what you want to do as a couple after the kids are gone. Give yourself some things to look forward to—to balance and counteract the dread you may feel about your children leaving.

Learn to see the empty-nest phase as a natural progression and a great opportunity.

We heard of a couple who went about this in a very organized and systematic way, and while the structure of it might not appeal to all of us, what they were trying to do and what came out of it were very interesting:

• First, they each made a separate, independent list titled "Things I want to do before I die"—places they wanted to visit, adventures they wanted to have, even people they wanted to meet and contributions they hoped to make. They didn't worry much about what was realistic—they each just created a dream list.

• Then they combined their lists—seeing how many matches they had and trying to win each other over into unanimity on their favorites.

• Then they tried to calendar the ones they agreed on—chronologically in terms of *when* they thought they might be able to do them.

• Then they set their completed dream list aside and made a second list—one they called a "hope list"—and it had two columns. On the left they listed the things they still wanted to take care of and feel some responsibility for (their children were at the top, followed by their aging parents and then by things like their health, their small company, their church, their house, and their little summer place). In the right column, they wrote their *hopes* for each thing on the left— the things they wished for each one.

• Finally, they had both lists artistically laid out on parchment by a calligrapher and framed. The lists now hang side by side on the wall of their library.

The husband told us that he had read somewhere that "All happiness starts with hopes and dreams." He said their hope list and their dream list had become a reference point for their plans and goals, and that, since they had created them together, the lists seemed to keep them together mentally and spiritually and lent a certain excitement and anticipation to their life together.

Fifty Empty-Nest
Questions and Answers

Fifty commonly asked questions—and some answers.

Chapter 8

The Most Common Questions of Empty-Nest Parents

A s mentioned earlier, there are four phases of empty-nest parenting when emotions peak and challenges intensify—when the needs of parents and children change dramatically:

Phase 1: When your child first leaves home.

Phase 2: When he or she gets the first full-time job.

Phase 3: When he or she gets married.

Phase 4: When he or she has a child.

Before we get into these phases, let us tell you how we approached the process of writing about them. Writing part 2 was a long and interesting process of asking potential ENPs and LTNs what questions and worries they had (we came up with more than fifty common questions) and then asking seasoned and experienced ENPs and LTNs how they handled those issues and answered these questions.

As you read these questions and answers, you'll see what a variety of perspectives and opinions there are among both ENPs and LTNs. Don't let this variety confuse you. Just zoom in on the ideas that ring true to you. You know yourself, your children, and your situation. You will be drawn to the comments that make sense and work for your own particular conditions.

Part 2 is not so much about final answers or strategies as it is about knowing what the issues are and surveying what a lot of ENPs and LTNs have said about them. Saren has done most of the work in this section, first researching what kind of questions and concerns were most common among ENPs and then getting answers and stories from LTNs that help parents see each issue from the child's point of view. We held some focus groups of parents, too, many of whom were seasoned ENPs, to see "how they did it," but you'll see that most of the section is aimed at giving us a better sense of what our kids have to say about how we can better handle their departure and their needs at various stages of life.

Before we go on, we must say that the answers and ideas we got from our own children have been incredibly insightful! We discovered things that they thought and worried about that we never would have known otherwise. It has opened doors to understanding what they were thinking that we never even knew were there. Also, hearing how other families have dealt with similar situations has been very interesting. In some cases, because we are parents, we could feel the reasons why parents acted as they did, even though the child who was explaining their situation didn't. It made us realize how interesting and complex empty-nest parenting really is. In addition, it was a wake-up call on things that we had neglected to do or even think of as parents of children who have left home.

In retrospect, I (Linda) found myself rationalizing why we did things as we did (for example, we didn't spend much time asking Shawni about her dates because we were too busy helping younger children with their homework and struggling to survive babies who weren't sleeping through the night). Also, it helped me to see that Jonah, our middle child, really could have used more support when he first went away to school. The earlier nest-leavers got lots of attention, but our focus was pulled to other things when it was his turn to leave. Probably the best realization was that even though we did some things backward and upside down, it is never too late to try to set things straight and never too early to try to be a better empty-nest parent.

The questions we asked drew so many interesting responses that we thought you might want a concise list of the questions themselves to ask your own children. (That's one reason we included all of the questions in the table of contents.) Your own children's responses will be even more interesting than the sample answers that follow. Reading others' responses will be sort of like watching a movie. Working out your own and your spouse's responses as well as getting your children's responses will be like being *in* the movie. And any changes you make for the better will certainly be useful in making a movie with a happy ending!

What You've Always Wanted to Know About Children Leaving Home But Haven't Dared Ask (Saren's Introduction to Part 2)

Let me tell you a little about how part 2 of this book came together. First, I worked with my parents to collect the most commonly asked questions from empty-nest parents. Then, through e-mails and focus groups, I addressed these questions to a "panel" of LTNs— people in their twenties and thirties who have stories, examples, and advice to share with parents who want to do a great job with their adult children. I was able to gather insights and experiences along with advice and opinions from a very diverse group of young adults— people who live all over the world, people whose parents are divorced and together, people with close families and more distant relation- ships, people from rich families and poor families, people in and out of the Church, and people in all sorts of schools and careers. You'll see a lot of responses from my siblings—we included a lot of their comments because we want our own family to be a kind of case study for you throughout this book. In addition to material I got through e-mail and focus groups, I included lots of the stories, complaints, and praises that friends have shared with me about their parents over the years. In some cases, real names are used. In others, pseudonyms are used and details are changed slightly. Some stories are written in the first person by those whose experience and opinion is being shared—I got these stories via e-mail and added them to this section pretty much verbatim. Some are written in the third person as I describe the stories and experiences that other people have related to me. But all the stories and examples offered here are true, and the advice is sincere.

As I talked with friends and siblings, I heard so much praise and admiration for parents along with some very constructive criticism. My hope is that this material will point out what works and what doesn't work. You will likely see yourself and your children in many of these stories. You'll surely see some things you'll want to try to do in your family and some things you'll make a point of not doing.

So many times, as friends have shared their frustration with things their parents are doing or not doing, I've asked, "Have you told your parents how you feel about this?" The answer's a fairly predictable no. It's hard to tell our parents how we feel about their parenting techniques. For one thing, we don't want to rock the boat when everything's pretty much okay, we're not together all the time anymore, and the little things that come up don't really affect our daily lives. Also, we don't want to hurt our parents' feelings. We realize how much they love us and want to do right by us—and we don't want them to think that we don't appreciate all they've done for us and continue to do for us. Whatever the reason, a lot of our feelings and opinions about how we could have better relationships with our parents just get swept under the rug. But making our relationships better for us and for you requires that we get things out in the open—even things that aren't urgent and that don't really seem like a big deal at the time.

One great way for you to get things out in the open with your kids and really start talking about taking your relationship to new heights is to read the stuff in this section, then have your kids read it, and then talk about the questions and stories and opinions that resonate most with you and with your kids. Or you may want to start by asking the questions of your kids (use the full list of questions from the table of contents); then you can compare the answers you get with the ones in the book.

A Meeting of ENPs and LTNs

We think the best way to think about part 2 of this book is to imagine yourself sitting in a large room with dozens of other ENPs and about-to-become ENPs talking together about the feelings, challenges, and opportunities that come when kids leave home. There are also lots of LTNs in the room who are willing to talk openly about how it feels to leave the nest—even to give us parents some advice from their point of view. These LTNs are ages eighteen to thirty-five, from all sorts of families, going through all different stages of life.

Into this room full of similar-situations, similar-needs people comes a moderator with a bunch of questions to throw out at all of us. He takes his seat at the front of the auditorium and starts asking things that every ENP wonders about and that most every LTN has an opinion on. He's a good moderator because he draws most of the answers from the kids, knowing that is what the parents need to hear. And he asks for lots of stories, knowing that stories usually help us and stay with us better than plain old advice.

You sit back and listen—jotting down notes on the thoughts that seem relevant to your own family. Now and then you raise your hand and answer a question or share an idea that comes to you. As the meeting goes on, though, you and the other parents say less and less. It's more interesting to listen to what the kids say—to look for insights and clues to what your own children (who have now moved away) might be feeling.

The meeting lasts about a hundred minutes—or one hundred pages—and by the time it's over, you don't feel quite as alone in your worries and concerns, and you feel better understood and better prepared in your own empty-nest parenting.

Chapter 9

Phase 1: Leaving Home For the First Time

Have you "accomplished your mission"
or fallen into an emotional abyss?

Some parents fret and worry about this moment years before it comes; others hardly think about it until it actually happens and they are standing in an emptier house, realizing their baby is gone.

Parents experience a whole gamut of new emotions when children leave home for the first time. We Eyres have felt it ourselves seven different times—felt the deeply intertwined pride and worry that attend a child's striking out on his or her own. We've also sat down in discussion groups with dozens of other parents who have experienced it—and recorded their feelings and observations. We had two purposes in doing so: (1) To help you to know what you'll face, how it will feel, and that you're not the only one facing it or feeling it, and (2) to help you get in mind how you'll respond to your feelings and the issues that arise—and to your children's feelings and issues.

For some families this initial leaving is a celebration and a "mission accomplished" for the parents. For other moms and dads, that first departure for college or an apartment is a trauma and a heartbreak. Whether your children are moving across town or across the country, emotions will run high for a while—many of them bittersweet emotions similar to those felt by your children.

Here are some of the most common questions ENPs have about this first phase—each followed by some ideas and opinions from other parents who may be a lot like you and some answers and advice for LTNs who may be a lot like your children.

In the pages ahead, you'll find the responses of ENPs in regular type and the responses of our children and other LTNs in type that **looks like this**. Each ENP response (other than our own) will be labeled with a first name and last initial, and each LTN response will be labeled with a first name only. We or Saren (or both) will put our own thoughts and summary (labeled "L&R" or "Saren") after the other responses to each question.

One additional note: As we worked in this section, we were involved in lots of lengthy individual conversations and group discussions with our older out-of-the-nest children, and fourteen-year-old Charity Jade, our youngest, didn't like it much. First of all, she never likes being left out of anything; and second, she was a little offended that we were even writing a book called *Empty-Nest Parenting* because, as she frequently pointed out to us, our nest wouldn't be empty as long as she was there—so why were we jumping the gun?

One evening after eavesdropping on one of our brainstorming sessions on "common questions," she said, "You're acting like those questions are so hard, and you're making the answers way too complicated. I'm only fourteen and I already know the answers."

Feeling a little guilty for not having involved Charity more, I (Richard) sat down, took out my pen, and started asking her the questions parents had been asking us.

What unfolded next was an illuminating experience for me. Charity was answering each question with a single, direct declarative sentence! These were questions that parents and older kids were analyzing with hours of discussion and trying to answer with pages of comments. Part of it was that Charity had overheard a lot of the discussion and was boiling it down to a more basic level, but the real factor was the brilliant and candid simplicity that children are often gifted with. ("Out of the mouths of babes . . .") We liked Charity's answers so much that we put them first throughout part 2—right after the questions. We think you'll enjoy the refreshing clarity with which a fourteen-year-old sees the world.

1. When should kids leave home? When should I push them out of the nest?

Charity Jade: After graduation from high school is when they need to learn the independence of being on their own.

Bette T.: I think when they turn eighteen it's really time to go— time to be independent and out in the world.

Winifred R.: Either when they get a full-time job or when they start college.

Carolyn M.: What's the rush? Sometimes it makes so much more sense for them to keep living at home if there's a good college close by. Or even if they're working—they can pay a little rent and keep living at home. I want to keep mine around as long as possible. My mom lives with us, too, and I love having the three generations under one roof. I actually like this "sandwich generation" thing. I don't know where we get this idea that kids need to move out or that parents shouldn't move in. If we love family, why not live together as much as we can—as many as the house can hold? Everyone says it takes away your freedom. On the contrary, Tom and I travel a lot, and it's so great because my mom and our boys are there to watch the house. The place is way too big for just the two of us anyway. We've got three generations living here, and we each live our own lives. We just overlap where it's advantageous.

Peter J.: We couldn't seem to get our girls to move out. Then Bill decided to move back in because his job didn't work out in California, and he brought a roommate with him. So guess what we did? *We* moved out. Now we've got a quiet little condo, and our kids have the house. It's funny because we told Bill we didn't want him to move back in because he'd lose his independence. But he was as independent as ever when he moved back in. We were the ones who were losing our independence. So we moved out.

Alice: I think kids should leave home when they're ready. That means they should have learned how to handle money and make good decisions on their own. Hopefully this "readiness" should come about when they finish high school—but if not, I think parents should get their kids ready—take a few months, if necessary, and help them get ready to face the world before they leave.

Phil: I still live at home and I'm twenty-eight. I'm an only child, and my parents talked me into going to school near home. I ended up getting a job here since all the recruiting at my school was for jobs around here. My parents were always careful about not getting too involved in my life, so things worked out pretty well. My dad died last year, and now I feel like I can't leave home because my mom depends on me. I can't complain about free rent and great home-cooked meals. But I always have to wonder how it would be if I'd gone away to school. There are so many areas of the country I'd like to try out. I don't know what will happen when I get married—my mom will probably want us to live with her! I don't think it's good for her to be so dependent on me, but I don't know what to do about it.

R&L: As we see from these ENP and LTN comments, there is no right answer about when kids should leave. But it's good for each family to *think* about the question and about the individual natures of their own kids. And whatever you conclude, *set it up* so that the rules and expectations are clear and agreed upon.

Saren: I have friends who are thirty-something and still live at home—just because it works well for them and their family. But I have other friends who still live at home and hate it. Still other friends felt "kicked out" by their parents too soon in their lives. Maybe one of the biggest issues to address with your kids is what you need from each other and how you can have a positive relationship regardless of whether you live with them, nearby or far away. After hearing my friend Phil's story as well as Peter J.'s story, I realized that the issue of leaving home doesn't just have to do with your children's independence, it has to do with yours as well. Some of my friends' mothers are very dependent on their kids—their whole identity is wrapped up in being a mother, and they don't know what they'd do with themselves if their kids left home. I think it's so important to encourage your kids to get out on their own and not cling to them or make them feel guilty for leaving! If they want to stay and you can agree on how things should be together, great. But if either party feels at all resentful about the situation, you're headed for trouble! Let your kids leave when they feel it's time! Let them stay if they aren't quite ready to leave, but help them plan when they'll be leaving.

Is going on a mission the best way to leave home for the first time?

R&L: This is a very interesting sub-question. Our experience (both as parents and as mission president) is that missionaries usually start off stronger and are less homesick if it *isn't* their first time away from home. Missionaries who have had a year of college or been away somewhere for a semester or a summer internship or a job are generally a little more mature and a bit more ready for their missions. This isn't the right formula for everyone, but think about it!

2. What emotions will I feel when my child first leaves home?

Charity Jade: You'll feel sad. You should! It's your kid! But I think you'll also feel pretty proud of the person your little boy or girl is turning into!

Fred J.: For me it was bittersweet. I guess I knew I'd feel pretty emotional about seeing her go off to college. What surprised me was that it kind of felt like a celebration, too. I mean, it just seemed to occur to us that this was a happy time. I looked at how beautiful she was, and I could see that she was really ready for this new adventure and new independence. It was better than her high-school graduation. I was choking up, but I felt excited and happy at the same time.

Marilyn J.: It's way harder for me when I see my boys go. The girls are my buddies, and we'll just talk about everything on the phone and have a great shared experience. But my boys still need me to mother them and I won't be there! I think it's just the opposite with Fred. He gets more emotional when our daughters leave.

Marion P.: My daughter didn't leave home until she got married (after her junior year of college), but it was still really hard for me to see her go! It's at dinnertime that I miss Brianne most. That's when we used to talk. She was always hanging out in the kitchen when she was home. Every time I walk in there I have a little pang of nostalgia and worry. I wonder how long this will last!

Jim R.: I'll tell you, it was the weirdest combination of emotions I've ever felt—different feelings I didn't know you could have at the same time. I felt a kind of elation, actually, but right along with it, I felt something really close to despair. This marvelous new young adult was going out into the world, and I had enormous confidence in her. I also felt happy and excited for her. But big pieces of me were going with her—had I done all I could for her and taught her what she'd need to know? And how could I stand it tomorrow when she didn't come down to breakfast?

Shawni: In talking to my mother-in-law about this, she said it didn't really hit her until after her second child left home how difficult it was to let a child go. With her first, it was a totally new experience, and she didn't realize all that would change after he left. When he came home after being gone for quite some time, she realized how much he had changed—matured and grown up. She realized he would never be her little boy again. This made it a lot more difficult when she sent the second child off because she realized she was saying good-bye not only to her child being around the home all the time but also to the child she knew, and life would change forever. Not that this was a negative change—she was proud to have her children grow up and mature. But it was emotionally difficult to say good-bye to those teenage boys and realize that when they returned they would be adults.

Saren: I think my parents had a pretty hard time letting me go. I was their first, after all. But they set up expectations, and that really helped them as well as me. We knew when to expect to hear from each other and see each other. I also think that in my case, my parents missed all the babysitting and housecleaning I did when I was home. Since I was the oldest and took on lots of responsibility, I don't think my leaving home was as much of a "relief" for them as it is for some parents!

R&L: You'll feel a wide range of emotions when a child leaves. The important thing is to talk about what you feel—together with your child—face to face before he or she leaves and by phone afterward. Keep things positive and remind each other that what you're both feeling is normal—and is evidence of your love and concern for each other.

3. What should I worry about when my child leaves? What shouldn't I worry about?

Charity Jade: Worry about their safety and how they're doing. Don't worry or stress too much about what they're doing. You've already taught them all you can by your words and example (or maybe that's why you are worried!).

Fred J.: The real question isn't about our worries. It's about the real *dangers.* And the biggest danger is that we're not *with* them so we don't see the warning signals. There are a million different problems they could have, and we're not going to know enough to even know what to *ask* about, so the big thing is to have enough good and frequent *communication* that we know what's going on!

Kate: I think the best way for you to deal with your worries is to talk to your kids about them. I know lots of friends' parents that seem to worry, worry, worry—but they don't seem to ask many questions, so they don't know if their worries are founded on anything. Before worrying, ask questions. Keep that communication wide open and make sure you are really listening to your kids. If you've taught your kids to make good decisions, you shouldn't have to worry.

R&L: There is a particular basketball coach we've long admired because of his uncommonly calm demeanor during games. No matter how good or bad things are going on the court for his team, he seems to be enjoying the game. We once had a chance to ask him about this, and his answer impressed me so much I can remember it almost verbatim: "Most of my coaching is done in practice, before the game begins. I teach them all I can, and we have a pre-game meeting to go over it all. Then when the game starts, I turn them loose. I hope one of the things I've taught them is to learn from their mistakes in a game, so I'm not going to take a kid out every time he screws up."

This coach does call timeouts to *apply* what he has taught to specific situations in the game, but he doesn't try to teach the players something different during the game than he's taught them in practice.

Parenting is a lot the same. When children move out of the home and into the real game of life, parents have to mostly rely on what the kids have already learned. Some good "pre-departure" reviews are a good idea, and timeouts are the calls and letters and visits, but basically it's a matter of having some confidence in what you've already taught.

Saren: A lot of your worries will go away once you've talked to your kids about the other questions in this chapter and established together some basic principles and agreements about how you want to communicate with each other and help each other as you move into a new phase of your relationship.

4. How will my kids feel as they leave home for the first time? What can I do to help them move into their new life?

Charity Jade: They will feel excited, scared, and nervous. You can help by being there for them when they need you but letting them be independent at the same time.

Bette T.: Probably the best thing you can do is just let them go. It's like jumping into cold water. They've got to do it all at once; they can't just stick their toe in. So I'd say just turn them loose and don't baby them.

Marilyn J.: Well, I think it should be gradual. They will feel so lost and so homesick. I'd say move them out in phases, and in the first phase they still kind of live with you. They come home a lot, and you go see them a lot.

Aja: My mom and dad surprised me with their surety that I would be more than just fine when I moved away to start my freshman year at college. So, I landed in Boston alone, with four big boxes and two big suitcases, not knowing a single soul in the whole city. Some of my mom's friends at home in Las Vegas had a distant cousin in Boston, however, and they all somehow worked it out for me to get a ride to Harvard from the airport. My four new roommates and their parents and sisters and brothers all crowded into our living room for first introductions, and later my roommates told me how bad they felt that I was alone, with no parents to attend opening ceremonies and all the pomp of opening days. But, even though I was alone and a little afraid, I had been prepared for the adventure with years of parents who were also good friends, and who became even better friends as the years continued.

Shawni: I don't think I was really ready to leave home when I left for college. I was always very attached to my family and friends, and although I knew I was making the right decision to go across the country for college, it didn't mean it was easy for me. My parents were great about it, although I don't think they thought I was quite ready either. I guess I was always pretty sheltered growing up, but I got the impression they worried about my leaving and being on my own a lot more than they worried about my older, independent sister. I'm sure it stems from the fact that our family moved to England when I was a freshman in high school and I about drove them crazy with how home-sick I was for home and friends. I literally thought I would wither up and die before we returned to the States six months later.

I have to smile when I think of the moment I made the decision to go to Boston University. I was on a trip exploring the campus with my mom. We had recently visited a school in California that I knew wasn't right as soon as we arrived on campus. But as we passed by the tall brownstones of Boston University on Commonwealth Avenue that bright spring day, the scariest thought secured itself in my mind. I was going to go to this huge, unfamiliar, far-away-from-home school. I kind of blocked it out at first, but I did tell my mom I was feeling pretty seri-ous about B.U. Her reaction is the thing I remember well and have to smile at—she almost gasped. Then she smiled, and I think she told me something to the effect she thought that was great, but I could see in her eyes that she thought I was too naive and would be much too homesick to actually carry it out. I heard her talking on the phone to my dad later, and it was obvious from her voice that she was amazed that I was considering B.U. so strongly. You may think this would hinder my decision—make me question my ability to really leave home and be on my own. But it was actually the best thing that could have happened because it made me that much more determined that I would follow through with what I knew I should. Who knows? Maybe my parents planned this. I think they knew it would be a great choice, but I think I really surprised them when I actually left.

But because my parents knew me so well from when I lived at home, they knew exactly what I needed. They called quite often, sent me packages, and even spent the month of September at a lake north of Boston so they'd be nearby for a while. (This wasn't necessarily for me—it was something they had wanted to do for a while, but I think they timed it well to help their "poor little naive daughter" out.) But most of all, aside from being there for me when I needed it (whether on the phone or in person), they had spent so much time with me when I was at home that they were kind of with me in my heart even when I was all alone. Although they were surprised with my decision, they built me up enough and helped me feel confident and secure enough on the inside before I left that I really could do it. I knew that although they were worried about me and surprised that I was ready to leave them and my friends I loved, they also always taught me I could do anything I put my mind to. I am so thankful to them for that and for their encouragement to leave my comfort zone and their letting me go with all their love.

So what I'm really trying to say is that what I needed when I left home was encouragement from my parents, and a lot of phone contact and visits. I also needed something they couldn't give me after I left, but something they had given me all my life—their time. They knew me so well because of all we did together growing up, and I knew they loved me unconditionally. This meant so much to me. If you still have children at home, take advantage of every moment you can to build strong relations with them! It won't last forever that they are there with you all the time—make it the best relationship you can now, and it will last forever.

Although I must admit I kind of liked how they babied me, I think it would have helped me spread my wings even more had they had a little more confidence in me. Their worry and concern made me want to carry through even more, but it kind of bugged me that they didn't treat me more as an adult. I think it is important for parents to find a balance between still showing their children that they are concerned about them and love them, and that they trust them with adult decisions.

Saren: I felt like I was pretty independent and pretty good at navigating new situations when I left for college. After all, as the oldest in my family, I'd always been the first to do everything. Plus we moved so much when I was growing up that I'd become really adept at meeting new people and adjusting to new situations. But in all the new situations I'd encountered earlier in my life, I'd had my family right there to support me and to hang out with as I searched out new friends. I remember the night before I was supposed to go to college, I had a party with a bunch of friends, and after they left, I sat there thinking, "What am I doing? I've got this great family, all these great friends, why in the world should I be going across the country for school?" I decided I really didn't want to go after all. But with all the money we'd already sent off to Wellesley and all the people I'd told I was going, it didn't look like I could turn back. So I didn't say anything to anyone about my major second thoughts.

I got on that plane the next morning with my mom, full of renewed excitement for this new adventure and totally full of gratitude that I'd have my mom beside me for a few days at least. It was so great to have Mom with me to basically hold my hand while I got registered and set up my dorm room. I'm sure I could have handled things without her, but it made me feel so much more comfortable to have her there. Plus it was just really nice to know that she would know where I was and who I was with and what my life was going to be like to some extent. By the time my mom headed home, I was settled in and excited about my new life. My mom was really excited for me, and that helped me be even happier in my new situation. We both cried when she left, but it was a sweet, soft sadness, not a worried and scared sort of thing. We had learned about and accepted together my new life. All would be well.

R&L: Our LTN kids will feel a range of emotions as wide as those we ENPs are experiencing. The biggest thing parents can do is to ask and listen. Ask about what they're feeling—especially in phone calls where you can hear tone of voice as well as words. Then really listen to the answers. Try to empathize and to remember (and relate) as much as you can about when *you* first left home.

By the way, we're not suggesting that all kids should go away to college at eighteen. Many choose to work, and others stay at home and attend a local college or university. But we do encourage you to *consider* many options and not just to follow the common pattern where you live. For boys (or girls) who are planning on a mission, a year or even a semester away at college can be a great preparation that allows them to enter the mission field more prepared and less homesick.

5. What if they're really homesick? Or, what if they don't seem to miss me at all?

Charity Jade: If they're homesick, let them know that it's natural to feel this way and that you're just a call away. If they don't miss you, tell them that you miss them.

Peter J.: One really important thing is to discuss what a *good* thing homesickness is. After all, it absolutely demonstrates how much we love those we miss.

Pam L.: On the other hand, if your departed child is relatively free from homesickness, take that as a positive, too. Praise him or her for his independence and at the same time prepare him for what might come by telling him that a little longing for home is not a bad thing.

Saren: Once they leave home, one of two things will typically happen to your kids: either they'll have a pretty hard time for a while as they realize how good they had it when they were home with you, or they'll have so much fun trying out their new wings, meeting new people, and living a new life that they won't really seem to miss home at all. Either way, things will be fine. If your kids are super homesick and you call them a lot, send them packages, maybe even go visit them, they'll feel secure about your support, and hopefully they'll get used to their new situation with a little time. Perhaps if you ask your kids a lot about the things they really like about their new situation, that will help them focus on the positive. But they also need you to take their concerns and hard times seriously. Sometimes I'd call my parents and complain and complain—and I really didn't want them to give me an answer or tell me everything was okay. I guess I just needed them to commiserate with me. Sometimes your kids just need you to say, "Wow, that sounds really hard" or "I'm sorry your week has been so terrible. I'm so proud of you for making it through." A lot of times, it was just annoying when my parents tried to reassure me that everything was okay. It didn't feel okay to me, and it felt like they were discounting my worries. I think kids need parents to ask what they can do to help make things better, and sometimes they just need you to listen and agree when they tell you that things are hard.

If your kids are having a great time, be happy for them! Get excited about the things they're excited about and call them to do quick check-ins. They'll really appreciate calls, notes, e-mails, whatever—even if they don't respond right away. Try not to send them on guilt trips about not calling you enough—you don't want to play the role of the whiny parent! Given a little time and confidence, most kids settle into a pretty good pattern of talking to their parents and sharing what's going on in their lives. And given a little time, they'll doubtless hit some bumps and need a little advice, support, and TLC from you. Keep that door wide open so they'll be able to come to you when they need to. You can keep the door open by keeping the calls and notes and packages coming no matter how unresponsive your kids may be at times.

R&L: Saren put it well. Put more mental effort into trying to empathize with what they feel than in trying to fix or correct it.

6. What do my kids need from me when they first leave home? What role should I play in their lives during these first years away from home? Should I be a best friend, a consultant, a manager, a coach, a sounding board, a shoulder to cry on, an observer?

Charity Jade: Your kids need constant support and confidence from you. You should now be both their parent and their friend.

Katherine P.: I like the "observer" answer. That's the *first* role to play. If you really see what they're doing and notice what they're feeling, you'll know what other roles you should play for them.

Jonah: Like a lot of kids, my first real away-from-home experience occurred when I left for college. It was only an hour and a half away, but it seemed like a lot further than that. There was no curfew, and I had to be the one to decide whether or not to get up for church or class. I could have used more phone calls from Mom and Dad just to ask how I was, and that's all. I ended up calling them a lot, and it made me feel like a wuss, but I really needed their support, and I needed to just know that they were thinking about me.

When children leave home, I think they should be able to freely confide in their parents, knowing that the time for punishment is over and that not going to church or getting a bad grade rests on the young man or woman rather than the parent. I recall the first Sunday when I realized that it was completely my choice whether to go to church or not, sans guilt trip or any other bad feelings. I remember knowing that I would go anyway because of how I was brought up. Parents must realize that much of their time to directly influence through guilt or other means is over. They aren't the coach in their kids' lives anymore. They're more like cheerleaders and fans. They can get in there and give advice, but they should just offer or wait for their kids to ask, not jump in there and say what they think their children should do all the time.

Talmadge: For my first year of college I went to a school that is only about an hour away from my house. I didn't struggle with too much homesickness, but the thing I needed the most was for my parents to show concern. For example, when I went home on the weekend, they would ask me about what's going on in life and really keep involved in what I was doing. I wanted my parents to keep being my parents—to care about me and help me when I needed it. But I needed them to sort of back off with some of the heavy-duty parenting things like setting limits and knowing every little thing I did—and they did a good job of backing off. I liked that they seemed more like interested friends than some sort of controlling figures in my life.

Shawni: I think parents have the obligation and responsibility to still be parents once their children move away. That means that although the kids are more adult once they leave, they still need emotional parenting. I love that my parents still looked out for me when I was gone. I could feel that they still loved me just as much and were doing all they could to keep us connected. When I moved to Boston, they came to visit, they called, and they sent tons of letters. Even though I didn't live at home anymore and I was an adult, I felt I was still their daughter, and that they loved and protected me with all their hearts. When I transferred from Boston University to Brigham Young University in Provo, Utah, they were there for me when the transition was tough. Following is a journal entry from when I was having a particularly hard time deciding on a major:

"Today was so stressful, but I think I got most everything worked out. Mom came down and brought me homemade soup and took me to lunch to talk about my major. She came to campus with me and everything, and I went to a ton of classes to figure out what I like. My mom waited for me all day and then brought me back to Salt Lake so we could talk with Dad about everything. I felt so much better after. My parents are so amazing. I love them so much."

Let's face it, when you leave home straight out of high school, no matter how old and mature you think you are, you are only a teenager! Teenagers need protective, nurturing, and loving parents just as much as little kids. So do adults for that matter. Even as a mom with three children of my own now, I still need parents.

Irene: I don't believe a parent's role should be anything other than a parent/teacher. This is the natural state of things, and you don't want your parents to be your best friends or peers. You already have friends, and that is not what you need from your parents. Obviously your parents are not at college with you to establish rules of behavior (you should already know them!), but they should certainly take an active role in the academic life, as that is what they are paying for!

Aja: When I first left home, I could never get enough letters and packages from Dad and Mom. Anything—even just a little note. I especially liked birthday presents and licorice. I think this need applies to anything my parents sent me or said to me that just let me know they were thinking about me as much as I was thinking about them.

I think parents should always provide their grown-up kids with the following:

- A home to come home to, a welcome with open arms every time.

- A telephone number where they can always be reached (with cell phones, this is actually possible).

- Lots of visits, but never too long.

- Lots of conversation and not so much advice.

- Keeping themselves healthy.

- A chance to offer support to their parents, a more even two-way advice-and-support relationship.

- Cash reserves when emergencies come up.

R&L: Actually, you may get a chance to play all the roles mentioned in this question *except* that of *manager*. That's the dangerous one. You're not the manager anymore, and if you try to continue to be, you will either drive your kids away or undermine their independence (or both). All the other roles mentioned are good ones, and ENPs should strive to play each of them well enough to be nominated for best *supporting* actor.

Saren: Gathering from the experiences of the people I know and the information shared by various people above, most kids really need a lot of support (via mail, phone calls, and visits) when they first leave home. If your family is a very tight-knit family, the homesickness your kids experience will likely be harder to deal with in some ways, and easier to deal with in others. As Shawni pointed out in her story, she felt that her family was "still in her heart," even though they were thousands of miles away, since she had so many great memories and connections with them. Strong, solid relationships with your kids before leaving home followed by mutually-agreed-upon regular contact and communication are the best ways to help those who have newly left the nest feel supported, connected, and happy.

7. How will my kids feel about their new independence when they leave home? How can I let them feel independent while staying involved in their lives and making sure they feel my support and interest?

Charity Jade: About half of the time we will feel more scared than excited and half of the time we will feel excited more than scared. Let them know you're always there but don't barge into their lives.

Dick D.: I think, once a kid leaves, we need to get really good at asking questions—not intrusive, interrogation-type questions, but interested, friendly questions that will show support and interest without introducing doubts or lack of confidence in their ability to cope for themselves. They need to know that we respect their independence and have confidence in them.

Aja: Whenever I come back to school after being home, and I have to carry all my luggage and boxes by myself on the subway, I realize I don't live at home anymore. Whenever my roommates go into the bathroom after I've been in there and don't say anything, I know I'm not at home anymore. Whenever I have no cash (and that means I don't have any cash—no sofa cushions, no sister's piggy bank, no benevolent parent)—I know I'm not home anymore. Whenever I'm sick at night from eating only dry cereal for every meal, I know I'm not home anymore. When I came home at four in the morning my first month away from home and my four roommates were waiting at the door looking at their watches, I definitely knew I wasn't home anymore—my parents could never stay up that late! When boys could come in my room—nope, not home anymore. When I opened the mailbox everyday and there was only mail for me—lovin' not being home anymore!

When I could sleep until two minutes before my class and come home after classes and take an uninterrupted three-hour nap, I thought that was the joy of independence! But actually, I don't think moving away from home and independence should be equated. In one sense, I lost my independence from financial obligations, cleaning and cooking responsibilities, and mundane chores and correspondence when I moved out. And, without my parents always watching out for me, I had to impose more rules on myself than they had ever done. The punishments for disobedience just weren't so harsh. There is a certain "feel" of independence, though, when you can go where you want to, do what you please, eat what you want, spend what you want (when you have anything to spend), and talk to all sorts of people. But in a way, though the novelty of the idea and action excited me when I first left home, it made the world seem a little bleak. As I would hop on the subway to downtown Boston and spend my afternoons snacking on roasted nuts from street vendors and window shopping, with no responsibility to come home at a certain time, or tell anyone where I was going or what I was doing, it both excited me and saddened me. Look at me—I was a young woman, surviving on her own, walking around in the big city—watch out, world! But on the other hand, I thought, Who cares? No one. No one cares what I'm doing or if I even come home tonight. I have no one to take care of or be responsible for either. How lonely! When I lived at home, I felt very independent and joyful. It was only when I was on my own that I felt constrained by solidarity and too much self-introspection.

So I don't know what advice I would give parents about independence of kids. Maybe just that parents can help their kids make the most of being kicked out of the nest by helping them still feel secure and lovable even though the kids are trying to fly on their own.

Shawni: When I left home I felt so much support from my family— especially my mom—simply through letters. I lived in a place where my roommates and I all got our mail in one big pile. My friends actually ended up making me my own little mailbox for all my mail because I got so much. It made me feel so loved and still so connected to my family to know they were thinking about me enough to send me so much mail!

Talmadge: When I left home, it was weird. I actually had freedom to stay out as late as I wanted, and my relationship with my parents just got better. They were not always bearing down on me for things, but I had to learn how to manage my time better. My new role in the relationship was to keep them informed about what I was doing in life and take care of myself. I knew that I could do it because my parents showed confidence in me and my ability to make it on my own. My parents' role was to be there when I needed them and to keep up on what was going on in my life. Just recently I overheard my younger brother getting in trouble for getting in late, and it made me glad for my new relationship with my parents. I like being able to do my own thing my own way. But I'm so glad for the values my parents taught me so that I can choose for myself without getting myself in trouble.

R&L: As with so many of these questions, the answer is balance. ENPs need to be constantly aware of the need to balance a confidence of "we respect your independence and have faith in your choices" with the security of "we love you and think of you as much as ever, and we're there for you whenever you need us." These two feelings are not opposites or mutually exclusive. We just have to be *aware* that our LTN kids need both, and we have to work at keeping the two in balance!

Saren: I think most kids relish the idea of independence—and often curse the results of it (not enough money, poor decisions, feeling alone, and so on). But with support and unconditional love from parents, kids can develop a wonderful sense of interdependence with their parents where there is a lot of give and take and a lot of learning from each other.

8. What do I need from my kids once they're gone? What should I expect from my kids when they've moved out?

Charity Jade: You'll need them to keep needing you, but you're not going to be their prime source of everything anymore.

Bill T.: I think there are three things I really *need* from my kids after they leave home—especially *just* after they leave home. First, I need information! The more I know about what they're doing, the less I worry—seriously—even if they are doing some worrisome things. I worry less than if I don't know. My imagination is always worse than reality. Second, I need appreciation. Not a whole lot of it, but just a thank you when appropriate and maybe even some retroactive thanks for things they now realize they didn't thank me for along the way. Third, I really need them to show they need me once in a while. It makes my day when one of my moved-away kids asks for my opinion or, better yet, my advice!

Shawni: I feel like kids are the ones who need to keep the communication open. I've seen so many kids leave for college and feel tremendous freedom in that they don't have to tell their parents anything anymore—they don't have to answer to anyone, and they want to be so independent and on their own. But I think kids have a big responsibility to tell their parents what's going on and what they're thinking if they want to maintain a good, lifelong relationship. They really need to tell parents what they need because parents can't just magically know all the time—no matter how in tune they are with their kids. The other day my dad made me mad in some things he did. It would have been easy for me to just keep it inside and let it bother me, but I'm so glad I just told him it bugged me, because it helped us understand each other's needs and helped us grow closer.

Irene: Parents should expect and give respect and honesty as before but realize that they can't control or make decisions for their children. They can certainly offer their opinions!

Aja: I think parents should be able to expect the following from their kids when they move away from home:

• Lots of visits, and always long enough.

• A telephone number with a reliable messaging device (not room-mates pretending to write down messages).

• A little something, like a job, a boyfriend/girlfriend, a recent trip to Japan, or a half-dozen children, so that the parents can have something to say when their friends ask, "So how is your son/daughter doing?" No matter what little tidbit of information the kids give their parents to use, the joyful mother can answer her friend, "Great! He's got a great job as an international consumption consultant [waiter at a Mexican restaurant] in Boston, and he's dating this great red-headed girl [took a co-worker to get ice cream after work], and he just got back from a business trip to South America [spent a week with friends in Cancun, Mexico]!"

• Phone calls at least once every one or two weeks, on their own phone bill.

• Care and support as the parents get old.

• Taking care of their body and health.

• Grandkids (someday, anyway).

Saren: I think it's reasonable to expect regular communication from your kids—e-mails, phone calls, whatever you decide together works best for you. I think parents should be able to expect as much respect as they give, expect to get their kids to open up as much as they're willing to open up, expect their kids to be as excited about seeing them and keeping in touch as they are excited. Expectations need to go both ways as interdependence replaces dependence. I think the most important thing is to really communicate with your kids about your hopes and expectations and talk things through.

9. What do I want my kids to be to me as they take off on their own? An extension of myself? An accomplishment to be proud of? No longer a burden? A chance to do fun things vicariously through them?

Charity Jade: You want them to be friends, but you shouldn't pressure them to be like you or to be what you want them to be. Be proud of what they really are and of what they want to be.

Pam J.: What a child who's moved out should be, in our minds, is a successful apprentice in life—someone we've tried to teach and to train who is now out learning new things, trying his or her wings, and finding his or her own happiness. I don't think I should live through them, but I love it when what they do broadens my own horizons. I love that with their increased independence and freedom, my own freedom has also increased—not that they were ever a burden, but they did tie me down!

Katherine P.: I think your kids should now be your friends! They couldn't really be that in high school—you were too much of a disciplining parent. But now, with them a little more on their own, you can really feel like friends!

Jonah: Remember that your children will always be your children. The memories that you have made with them will always be far beyond any memories or relationships made with friends. Let your kids help keep you young by involving you in their lives. Advice will move in both directions if you ask for it, and that is what makes everyone feel good.

Jayne: My parents are wonderful about heaping praise on me. They think I'm the greatest—or so they say. Everything I do is wonderful, and they're always bragging about me to everyone they know, which makes me feel great. But it also kind of bothers me. I feel a lot of pressure to always be doing something that they can brag about. I wish they'd get excited about some of their own talents and interests and get their own stuff to brag about! Sometimes I just feel bad for them—they're both retired and don't seem to have enough exciting stuff in their own lives, so they use my life as something to be involved in and talk about. It's sort of like people who watch soap operas all the time—they talk about the characters on TV all the time and live vicariously through them, and it's sort of pathetic. It's not that my parents are pathetic at all. They're wonderful, great people. I just wish they'd do more with their abilities and pay a little less attention to me!

Derek: When I left home, my mom totally redecorated the whole house, threw all my stuff out (pretty much), and made my room into a cozy little sitting room off the master bedroom. She took a full-time job that was really exciting for her, and I thought "Go, Mom! Way to get on with your life!" But she seemed so caught up with all this new stuff—maybe this is selfish for me to feel this way—but it seemed like she was just glad to be done with me, like I was a project she'd successfully finished and now she could move on. She calls me every week, and we are together at the holidays, and she's always so nice to me when I'm home—but I feel like it's all a big duty for her, not something she really likes. My dad's never been a very involved parent, so things didn't change much when I left home. He asks me if I need money sometimes. That's about it.

Saren: I've talked to a lot of people who seem to feel pressure from their parents in one way or another—to be what their parents want them to be, to give their parents something to brag about, and so on. Some people, like Derek, just want a little more assurance that they're still an important priority to their parents. In general, we want to make our parents proud of us, but we need you to be proud of our happiness, not just the select accomplishments that you feel are noteworthy or in line with your vision for us.

R&L: We agree! So we guess we'd better start acting like it. It really is important to let our children become who they really choose to be rather than some preconception we have of who we think they ought to be.

10. How much should I try to influence my kids' college education—the classes they take, the major they choose, and their long-term educational goals?

Charity Jade: You shouldn't do that. Let them follow their dreams and passions. But it's okay to let them know what you think they could succeed in.

Dick D.: Try to think of your influence as that of a consultant rather than that of a manager. Good consultants lay out alternatives, increase awareness, and make nonbinding, no-obligation recommendations. They know it's not their decision, but they have real interest and real concern. They try to divorce themselves from their personal biases and prejudices and try to help their clients see themselves and their options with clarity and perceptiveness.

Kenneth W.: Give advice only if kids ask! Suggest that they take some aptitude tests and see the career counselor.

Tom M.: Don't even go there! Our generation's advice is so outdated! I heard of one dad warning his son to stay out of that "flaky computer industry" and get into something dependable. I don't think we know enough about the future or the new economy to influence our kids. I think they know more than we do about where the opportunities lie!

Irene: My parents definitely had a say in the classes I took, which for the most part I agreed with. Fortunately, they are both aficionados of language, as am I, so we have common interests. Mom said that I couldn't graduate (sort of kidding) without taking a class in art history, and I put it off until my senior year and loved it. I regretted not taking it earlier because I probably would have double-majored. Parents often do know best! They are also paying for your education, so I don't believe in allowing teenagers to decide on their own without any consultation.

Jonah: I think parents need to understand that all people learn differently and that there are a lot of different ways of "making it" in the world. Parents need to really listen to their kids and realize that there are many good paths that are different from the path that the parents took. My dad has always been very complimentary about my abilities, but because he went to Harvard Business School and that worked out great for him, he thinks going to a good business school is the best way to support a family and make a name for yourself. I have always struggled with school and the way that teachers teach, which in most cases is very narrow and with the idea that there is only one right answer. I have never learned like that and have always grown the most when I get out there and experience the world for myself. My frustration with my difficulties with traditional classroom learning is compounded by the expectations of my father.

Recognize and appreciate the differences in your children. Realize that it's okay and even good if they have different abilities and possibilities than you. If they want to take classes that you wouldn't take, encourage them to explore and find what would be best for them. Don't make them feel like you think they're a failure if they don't do well at some of the things you think are important. Just help them to figure out what they are good at and pursue something that will work for them.

Margaret (by Saren): When I was a residence advisor in my dorm at Wellesley, a girl named Margaret who lived down the hall tried to commit suicide. Actually, she didn't try very hard. She took some pills, enough to make her sick and scare everyone, but not enough to do much damage. I felt terrible about the whole thing. Margaret had told me the week before that she'd chosen a major and that her parents were irate about it. They'd told her that there was no way they were investing all their hard-earned money in a degree in studio art that would never result in any sort of decent career. I had suggested that she talk to her parents a little more and try to explain her point of view and really listen to their suggestions to see if maybe they had any validity. I didn't spend that much time with her—I was writing a paper at the time, and it seemed like she wasn't really listening to my suggestions anyway. She just kept saying, "You don't get it, my parents don't talk with me, they talk at me. They don't listen to anything I say, and they don't care what I want. It'd take a lot more than me talking to them to get them to make an attempt to understand me."

Well, Margaret certainly got her parents' attention. The day after the suicide attempt, her mom and dad flew into town. I don't know what went on between them. But I know that she took the rest of the semester off. When I saw her the next semester and asked how she was doing, she said she'd had a wonderful month studying art in Rome while she took off time from school, and she was really excited about all the art classes she was taking. "So you're doing the art major after all?" "Yeah, I know what I want, and now my parents understand how bad I want it, so they've become pretty supportive. They still think art's sort of pointless, but I guess they'd rather have an artist child than a dead child."

Saren: I think it is so important to respect and encourage your children's need to explore many different fields. Most kids start college knowing very little about the range of courses and careers that exist. They know about their parents' and friends' parents' careers, and they've taken courses and done extracurricular activities that have exposed them to potential areas of interest. But there's so much more out there! And there's so much that their parents haven't even heard of. I think it's most helpful to encourage your kids to spend their first couple of years in college really exploring a wide range of possible interests. I've talked with so many friends who regret taking the advice they received to get their general requirements "out of the way" in their first year or two at college. They wish they'd shopped around more—going to at least the first day of any course that struck them as interesting and taken more classes that helped them figure out what they really had a passion for. You can take general classes later. But you're supposed to figure out a major by the end of your sophomore year, in most cases. I'd encourage your kids to use their first couple of years as a time to explore through taking courses and talking to people in different fields. They'll get better grades and ultimately be much happier in life if they pursue their own interests, not yours!

Should I push my kids to go to a Church-sponsored university? Will they be able to stay active in the Church if they don't?

Charity Jade: It's different for every kid, but I don't think they have to go to BYU to stay active.

Kent E.: Well, Church universities sure are great, and they're such a deal financially!

Pam J.: Hey, choosing the right college is hugely important! I think a lot of research should be done, by parent and child!

John: When I decided to go to Dartmouth, my parents (especially my mother) were concerned about whether I would "go inactive." They'd heard stories about kids who go away to college and can't find many Mormon friends and just drift away from church activity. They were also concerned about the peer pressure I might feel to drink or do other things against the teachings of the Church. I was a little offended that they were so worried about me. I felt like I had a good testimony and that their worries showed they didn't have much faith in me. Since I'd spent most of my growing-up years in Utah, I really felt like it would be good for me to go to school where there weren't so many Mormons—I thought it would help my testimony, not hinder it, if I was surrounded by non-Mormons. I would have opportunities to share the gospel and stand up for what I believed. I assured them that I'd be going to church every Sunday and that I would be living by all the standards I'd grown to respect through my upbringing and church teachings. I told them about my plans to be a wonderful example to the non-Mormons who'd surround me.

But I have to admit, things were harder than I'd expected. It was hard to say no when fun activities were happening on Sundays. I often felt sort of embarrassed to refuse alcoholic drinks, and when my dorm-mates talked about their sexual experiences, I didn't know whether to listen or lecture or what. I got a calling at church right away that helped me be sure to be at church every Sunday (I found out later that my mom had called the bishop to politely suggest that he give me such a calling!), and I was grateful for that. I had a small handful of Mormon friends, most of whom were very different from me, but I learned to really appreciate all of them. My testimony really grew as I had daily opportunities to explain my beliefs or the actions that were determined by my beliefs.

I really feel like it's important to let your kids go to whatever university they want—and show faith in their ability to be strong members of the Church in any situation. After their initial worries turned out to be unfounded, my parents became strong proponents of Mormon kids going away to non-Mormon colleges. All of my siblings and many of my cousins and Mormon neighbors have had great experiences going away to school and being part of a Mormon minority rather than a Mormon majority. I do think, though, that it's important that there be some Mormons at any school where your kids go—it's so important to have at least a couple of Mormon friends.

Megan: I got accepted by a couple of really good schools—Brown and Amherst—and I was pretty excited about it. My parents didn't even know that I had applied to these schools. I knew they wouldn't be excited about my going anywhere other than BYU. They were both BYU alums who felt like BYU was the only school for smart Mormons to go to. Anyway, I thought that maybe when I got my acceptance letters, they'd be excited for me and maybe consider the option of my going away to school. Nope. They were mad I'd even applied, and they said there was no way they'd support my going away to school. So I went to BYU and I liked it fine. But I've never gotten over the fact that I didn't really have a choice in the matter. I think that parents should at least entertain the option of sending their kids away to school—if their kids really want to go away. You can be a really good Mormon without going to BYU!

Tom: I just think it's important for parents to help their kids explore all the options of schools they could go to and then support them in whatever they decide. I personally believe that kids who grow up in Utah really need to go away for college. I think it's nice for people to have some part of their lives where they're surrounded by Mormons. But if they've had this experience during their younger years, they don't need to have it again for college. I knew plenty of people at Ricks who went inactive during school or later in life. Going to a Church university is not a guarantee that you'll be a good Church member. You can make your kids resent the Church if you force them to go to a Church school, so watch out.

Saren: I think every kid needs a different sort of educational experience. There's no "one right place" for all kids to go to school, be they

Mormon or not. I'm so glad my parents encouraged me to look at lots of different schools. Going to school in Boston, I had a strong student ward to attend, and that was really important to me. I don't think I'd ever encourage my kids to go to a school where there wasn't a good ward with quite a few single students in it. I spent most of my time with nonmembers, but I also had a tight-knit group of fun friends who were members of the Church. I think parents ought to encourage their kids to explore all the options out there and help them find the place where their own unique abilities, talents, interests, and personality will be best situated.

R&L: We agree with Saren, although we all understand that cost is a factor, and we're grateful that there are also lower-cost alternatives like local community colleges.

11. How should I communicate with my kids, and how often should I do it?

Charity Jade: There's this thing called a telephone. You pick it up and push the numbers. And then you ask questions. And then you listen.

Lonnie P.: I really think you can overdo the communication. Let them call you when they need to talk. If you're always calling them, it expresses a lack of confidence.

Saren: Before I left home for my freshman year, my dad established this idea of writing each other "literature letters" every week. We're both really into poetry and fine literature, and we're great admirers of the day and age when people wrote each other beautifully penned letters that expressed thoughts and described scenes and events in a vivid and lovely way. We decided that every week we'd write each other a "literature letter" that offered interesting and intriguing glimpses into each other's lives. I loved getting letters from my father. They were full of poetry and included some carefully selected advice here and there. I grew to love writing my "literature letters" to my family. I would keep notes all week of interesting people I met, select points made in lectures, thought-provoking stuff I read in books. I'd combine these sorts of observations with updates on the amazing and constantly changing beauty of the Wellesley campus and comments on the events of my week. To this day, I love writing weekly letters to my family, capturing and celebrating all that's going on in my life. The idea has spread to everyone in the family who lives away from home. They now take the form of rather descriptive weekly e-mail updates.

My entire freshman year of college, I received a postcard from my mom pretty much every day. She sent me lovely art-print postcards that offered me great daily glimpses into everything going on at home. We share an avid interest in art, so I loved the prints on the cards and made a collage with them on the back of my dorm-room door. But more important, I loved the fact that she was thinking about me every single day and was keeping me in the loop with everything that was going on. She'd scrawl down a few lines waiting in line at the grocery store, waiting in the car for one of my siblings, watching my little sister's dance class, or sitting in a meeting. She'd start out most postcards by writing about the situation she was in as she wrote, and that made me feel so close to everything going on. My mom's always got a million things going on, so to have her find a few minutes in every day just for me meant so much to me. In addition to all the postcards, she sent me wonderful care packages at holidays. I remember that she sent me this huge Easter basket full of treats and decorations and all these fun little toys as well as a big stuffed Easter bunny. I felt like a little girl, I was so excited. I remember picking up the box at the mail room and seeing all these other students looking at me in envy, and my roommate gasped and said, "Your mom is amazing" when she saw me pull the big basket and bunny out of the box. I had to agree with her.

Jonah: I think the main thing that I needed from my parents right when I left home was for them to call me instead of waiting for me to call them. It's important to just ask simple questions and really listen to the answers—questions that reflect love only, with no judgment passed.

Irene: When I started college, since I was across an ocean from my family (they live in England) and telephone calls were still pretty expensive, I always called home every Sunday at 6:00 P.M., which is when the rates went down. This was a great way to communicate because I was able to look forward to speaking to Mom (she filtered info to Dad) and think about what had happened during the week, academically and socially, and she looked forward to it too. It made communicating special and fun. Mom carried this on with my brother, Allan, when he went to school and still does it now that he's married. Regular, scheduled phone calls make communication more of an event or tradition, and we'll probably always do it this way.

Talmadge: When I first left home, because of the short travel distance between my house and college, I didn't feel the need to talk to my parents every day. I only needed to talk to them if there was a problem or I needed advice on something. I remember many times my parents would call me just to see if everything was okay, and that was nice. Maybe I should have called them more—not just about problems.

I am now into my second year of college, and just last night my dad did something that I really liked. We were talking on the phone because he is in California, and he asked me a bunch of details about my basketball team. He knows each player and how they play as well as I do. During the conversation I could tell that he was really interested. Instead of just saying "How are you?" He says "So, how's Chris playing?" or "Are you having a chance to be a leader on the team?" That wasn't something he just thought up right then. It showed that he had naturally been thinking of me and my situation earlier. Thus it became easy for him to give advice, and easy for me to appreciate and accept it.

Rob: When I first started college, my parents called me all the time, almost every day. I appreciated their interest and concern, but come on, I had a life to live! I started letting the answering machine get it when they'd call. After a while I guess they got the idea and stopped calling. I felt like they were mad at me and like they were acting pretty childish to just stop calling altogether. We went on like that for a month or so—neither of us picking up the phone other than for basic information that we really had to get from each other. Finally they asked me why I wasn't calling them, and we had a big conversation about everything. They had decided that they didn't want to bug me, so they'd just let me take the initiative to call when I wanted to talk to them, and I'd assumed they were mad when they were just trying to give me my space. Anyway, I think it's good to talk to your kids up front about everything. Both parties just get themselves in trouble when they make assumptions.

Saren: Different kids need different amounts of contact and communication with their parents—and what they need changes as they go through different things in their lives. From everyone I've talked to about this question, the best answer seems to be "communicate about communicating"! If you like writing, tell your kids how often you'll be sending them a letter or an e-mail. Definitely plan a regular time to talk on the phone. Don't assume that your best mode of communication will line up with your child's favored mode. I have one friend whose father wrote her e-mails every Wednesday and Sunday throughout college. She loved hearing from him. But she didn't enjoy expressing her thoughts through writing, so she'd just write short replies here and there and do most of her real communication during their Monday-night phone calls. Try out different approaches. Talk about what's working and what's not. Make your communication techniques dynamic and varied yet as consistent as possible once you establish a pattern.

R&L: Most parents need a plan and some sort of a schedule for solid, regular, meaningful communication with kids who have recently left home. Different kinds of communication fill different needs. Letters and thoughtful e-mails can express complex emotions and really describe situations and experiences. Phone calls let us hear each other's immediate feelings.

In our family two strong patterns have emerged. First, a "weekly update" e-mail from each person in the family to everyone else in the family, and second, a Sunday phone call from us to each of the kids. The e-mails just keep us appraised of what's going on in everyone's lives, and each of us takes a certain pride in writing clearly and descriptively—sometimes humorously—about the week we've just experienced. The phone calls are the Q and A of our lives—mostly about how people are doing, what they need, how they are feeling. Other calls happen, of course, but the Sunday ones are the serious ones.

12. How will our relationship and communication change once we don't live in the same house anymore?

Charity Jade: It will be about different things, and it will be a more friendly type of conversation.

Katherine P.: Well, think about it! Everything changes—quantity first of all. Instead of dozens of small interchanges every day, you might have one—or maybe only one or two a week. When your kids were at home, you already knew a lot of what was going on—just by observation. Now you only know what you ask, or what they volunteer. Your questions become *so* important—not only what you ask but how you ask them. If questions sound like interrogation, your kids will resist them. If they make you sound like an interested friend, your kids will welcome them. Also, if kids give you an answer or some information that shocks you, try not to act or sound shocked, or they'll stop talking.

Jim R.: The big difference is, you're not the coach anymore. They've moved off to a higher league, and you're not calling the plays or making the substitutions anymore. You know what you are now—instead of the coach? You're a *fan*. That's what you should be—cheering them on!

Talmadge: I found it much easier to talk to my parents after leaving for college. It seemed like we were on more equal terms. After a while I found myself talking about things that I would only talk to my best friend about in high school. We now talk about girls and friends and situations in more of a casual way, and it's great.

Aja: Although I knew it was sometimes too much for Mom, she very slowly weaned me from talking to her on the phone and e-mail almost twice a day. We talked a lot during high school, and she knew I needed that still, but she also knew it couldn't go on like that forever. Actually, the change for me happened naturally, as I found friends to confide in and became more busy with schoolwork. The great thing I recognize Mom for doing was not being offended by the downplay on talk time but instead encouraging my activities that took me away from dependency. Although the time and amount of communicating was lessened, we still talked about all the important things, and we kept our communication at a level that made me know she was always there to talk when I needed to, and I could still talk to her about almost anything, and she with me. Four years later, even though I'm paying for the phone bills now, it's still something I think we're both very comfortable with.

Lisa (by Saren): When she first started college, Lisa was on the phone with her mother every evening for about an hour. She and her mom had always had a close relationship. Lisa told her mom every detail of her day—what happened in class, how much homework she'd finished and how much she had yet to do, what she had for dinner, you name it. Lisa would complain about how often her mother called, but she felt that her mother would become very depressed and hurt if she didn't fill her in on all the details of her life. She said, "Look, my mom needs to talk to me. Talking to me is the highlight of her day, and I can't just take that away from her." A few months after school started, Lisa met this great guy and started wanting to spend a lot of time with him. Between increasing homework and wanting to spend time with her boyfriend, the talks with her mom started getting shorter and less frequent. Lisa and her mother started fighting on the phone frequently—about how much to talk, how much to share. Gradually, they settled into a pattern of talking that they could both live with. According to Lisa, "My mom really needed to get her own life. I felt bad cutting her out of mine, but I don't think it was healthy for either of us to talk so much or share so much."

Saren: From those I've talked to, communication seems to get simultaneously harder and easier once kids leave home. It often becomes easier to share when you're no longer so intimately involved in the day-to-day happenings of each others' lives. But the question of how much to share and how much to be involved in each others' lives needs to be resolved. Most kids really want to share what's going on in their lives with parents. They welcome and hope for good questions and a listening ear from their parents. But they get really turned off when communication from their parents is primarily suggestions, advice, or probing questions that seem to be searching out bad things that might be going on. Assume the best about your kids. Ask and listen. Offer advice when asked, but encourage your kids to come up with their own answers as you talk things through with them. Share a lot about what's going on in your life—your thoughts and feelings. As parents share, kids are more inclined to share.

13. How often should I visit? How often should they visit me?

Charity Jade: It obviously depends on how far away they live and how much money you have. Not too often if they're close. As often as you can if they're far!

R&L: When both of our oldest girls were in Boston (one a frightened little freshman), we actually arranged our affairs so we could live at nearby Lake Winnipesaukee for a few weeks in September, homeschooling the younger kids so we could be closer to our homesick-prone college kids. This was a rather extreme measure and one that wouldn't be possible in most situations, but it did make their transition a little easier, and hopefully it demonstrated that we would do whatever we could. We also later found that they could endure fairly lengthy periods between our visits to them (or theirs to us) if they knew exactly when the next visit would be.

Irene: Visits home or visits from parents seem to be a great remedy for homesickness. But I think it's all too easy if you're going to college close to home to retreat there when things are tough. I would say that it's important if you live close by to regulate the visits. Otherwise, how has any sort of independence been reached?

Rennie (by Saren): Can you see each other too little? Yes. During my freshman year, my friend Rennie was so homesick she was physically ill. She missed her parents and house and dog and little brother and high-school friends so much—it was all she could talk about. Her parents had both gone away for college, and they'd only gone home for Christmas and in the summer—which worked fine for them and works for lots of people. They told Rennie to just plan on Christmas and summer. But this twice-a-year plan just didn't seem like the right approach for her. Her parents could afford to come visit her or fly her out to visit them for a three-day weekend or something, but they thought that would only make her homesickness worse, and they wanted her to learn to be "tough." Rennie was in such bad shape, though. It got to the point where a bunch of us wanted to call her parents ourselves and fill them in on the full extent of the situation. Finally the Head of House (a woman who lived in our dorm and helped out in crisis situations) called Rennie's parents and told them everything that was going on. They flew Rennie home for a weekend, and she came back doing much better. It seemed like she just really needed a little dose of home to get her through the rest of the semester.

Ellen (by Saren): Can you see each other too much? Yes. I had another friend in college, Ellen, whose parents visited every weekend. They lived about two hours away. Ellen is their only child, and they just missed her a lot. She missed them a lot too, so she was really happy to see them—at least for the first few months. After a while, though, it just wasn't working. She could never do anything with us on Saturdays because she was always booked up by her parents, and she couldn't do fun stuff on weeknights because she was always doing homework and knew she wouldn't have the weekend to catch up like the rest of us. Ellen and her parents would do great stuff together—things that most of us were a bit jealous of. But it was just too much to get together all day every Saturday. We all kept telling her that she should talk to her parents about coming a little less often, but she didn't want to hurt their feelings. Finally she did talk to them, and they weaned their way down to coming once a month, which worked out great. When they only saw each other once a month, it became something they could plan for and look forward to—and my friend as well as her parents had the chance to build up their own separate weekend activities and separate lives.

R&L: Maybe the simplest answer is, "As often as your children want you to visit or as often as you can afford to, whichever is less." A few visits from parents (depending on how far away from home the child is) can not only ease the transition but also give parents a clearer picture and perspective of where the child is and what he or she needs and doesn't need.

Saren: Bottom line, all parents and all kids have different needs. It's important to look at your own individual situations and talk about what's feasible (based on the money and time available) and what everyone's hopes and expectations are. Then work out a plan that feels good to everyone concerned. It may well be that visits will seem much more necessary during the first year than they will down the road. I think everyone concerned can benefit from visits that are as frequent as logically and logistically possible in the first year. Such visits can help ease your kids into becoming more independent. Gradually, visits will become less of an ached-for necessity and more of a nice, fun occasion that happens a few times a year.

How can I make it special for everyone when my children come home to visit?

Charity Jade: Throw a big surprise party for them!

Aja: Always, Mom and Dad got me excited to come home. Not every homecoming was preceded by homesickness, and yet I always longed to come home. It was always a big deal when I came home. My sister, who now goes to school only four hundred miles away from home, goes to see our parents often and usually sporadically, so I don't know if she still gets the same celebration, but it's still a very big deal for her, too.

Irene: I grew up with a wonderful family and was always thrilled to go home. People will feel most happy about visiting a happy home, and since not all are happy, there must be a lot of young people who don't go home. It would be pretty hard to rectify the matter this late in a young person's life, but it seems like a basic concept that if you provide a safe, warm, and nurturing environment, your children will always want to return.

Saren: I remember the first time I came home from college. It was Thanksgiving my freshman year, and I was counting down the days until I could go home practically from my first day away. I was having a great time at college, and my parents had been great about sending lots of letters and calling regularly, but knowing that I'd be going home for Thanksgiving is what kept me going on some bleak homesick-soaked days. I remember the plane ride home. I was so excited that the five-hour plane ride felt like an eternity. It felt just like Christmas Eve when I was a little kid. When we finally arrived in Salt Lake City, I felt like mowing down all those other passengers and racing off that plane. But I waited in that snail-pace line in the plane aisle, my heart racing while my feet shuffled forward. When I finally got off, my whole family was there right outside the door with huge smiles on their faces and holding up a big "welcome home" sign and a bunch of balloons. I couldn't hug them all enough! It was just so amazing to actually be with my family again, after thinking of them and missing them every day for almost three months. I couldn't believe how much my littlest siblings had grown. It was weird to see everyone wearing clothes I hadn't seen them in before. Things change a lot in three months—especially when you suddenly take three months off from people you used to see every single day.

It felt so good to see everyone so excited to see me. It was even nice to hear the little kids fighting—since they were fighting about who got to sit by me in the car on the way home. When we got home, I found everything exactly as I'd left it in my room, except that there was a gorgeous bunch of flowers on the table by my bed—I've always had a special liking for fresh flowers.

Now that I've had about fifty homecomings and now that others in my family have left the nest, my homecomings (and homecomings in general) have become less of a novelty. But my mom still puts fresh flowers by my bed. Quite a few of my family members still come get me at the airport. Everyone still sets aside special time to go on a walk or out to lunch with me when I'm home.

R&L: It's easy to go too far either way on this one. On the one hand, if we treat the LTN as royalty when she comes home, it may make her wonder if you've got a life of your own. On the other hand, if you make no fuss at all, she'll wonder if you even missed her. Strike a middle ground by making her feel special and missed, but also letting her see (and hear) about your own full and busy life.

Saren: I think homecomings should always be special—and just a few little things can make all the difference. But that first homecoming—I'd say go ahead and make it pretty memorable. It's just so nice to be welcomed with joy and jubilation. It's so good to have those you love ask lots of questions and learn all about your new life. It makes you feel so loved and valued and "fills you up" so you can go back to school renewed with energy and confidence. Make sure that whenever your kids come home, you try to make it special for them— plan their favorite meals, some fun family activities, and some good one-on-one time. Be sure to coordinate what you plan with things they may need to do and others they want to see while they're home.

14. How should I handle financial issues? How much support (if any) do I want to provide?

Charity Jade: Have this all worked out before your kids go so everyone will know what to expect.

Marilyn M.: Basically, it's simple. We support them completely until they are married. Then they've got their own family and they're on their own.

Kent E.: Listen, I had to work my way through college, and I'm a better person for it. It made me self-reliant. I want my daughter to have that same experience. She'll thank me for it one day.

Pam J.: I put my college kids on a strict budget. And since it's my money, I get to make up the budget.

Lonnie P.: The last thing I want my son to worry about right now is money. He'll worry enough about that later on. Right now I just want him worrying about grades. If he keeps his grades up, I'll keep his bank account up.

Joel (by Saren): My friend Joel's parents gave him and his brother $50,000 when they turned eighteen. They let their sons know that they'd be getting no more money from there on out—they were on their own. They encouraged their sons to use the money to help pay for school or to invest it and save it to buy a house one day. They'd taught their kids about money management and investing all their lives, so they felt pretty confident handing the money over to their kids. Joel spent a good $10,000 right off the bat on various toys and another $20,000 on his first year of tuition and school expenses. After that first year, he realized he'd better slow down. He transferred to a state school, got a job to help with expenses, and found some scholarships that helped with tuition. He did lots of research and found some pretty unique and unlikely scholarships—one was in the meteorology department even though he was majoring in business! He put as much money as possible into various investments, and by the end of college, he had about $15,000. This kept growing until he put it toward a house a few years later.

Joel's brother went to an Ivy League school, spent all his money on his education and living expenses during college, and took out quite a few loans as well. He got a great job after graduation, so he's been paying off loans and saving money just fine for a couple of years now.

Both Joel and his brother thought their parents' method worked great for them.

Joel said, "I'm not saying this is the way all parents should handle finances. It worked for us because we understood finances and investing pretty well by the time we were eighteen, and we'd been taught to really value education, so my parents weren't worried that we'd just blow the whole thing on dumb stuff. Yeah, they were a little worried when I bought that motorcycle and big-screen TV freshman year. They asked how my money was holding up and hinted around about the fact that it might be hard to pay for the rest of college if I didn't budget more carefully. But they made it clear that the money was mine and that I could do what I liked with it. They also made it very clear that there would be no more money coming from them—and they aren't the sort of people who'd be softies about the whole thing if I ran out of money. You've got to build a strong foundation for doing something like this with your kids."

Bethany (by Saren): My friend Bethany's parents worked their way through school since their parents couldn't afford to help them. They thought the experience of doing everything for themselves was very beneficial, so they decided they wanted the same for their own children. They encouraged their kids to work and save money throughout high school and helped them search out and apply for scholarships. Bethany saved all she could and got great grades in college that helped her get a few thousand dollars in scholarships. But there was no way she could afford to go to anything other than a state school, and since she couldn't afford to pay for tuition as well as room and board, she decided to go to a nearby state college and live at home. She worked about fifteen hours a week at various low-paying jobs to pay for books and spending money, so she couldn't take as many hours as she'd have liked, and it took her five years to finish college. She says she's glad she learned how to make money and budget, and she certainly values her education more than some whose parents just paid for everything. But she says she wonders what it would have been like to go away for college, go to a really good school, or go on study abroad. So many of her high-school friends got to do those things, and she feels like her options were really limited by her parents' decision not to help her financially.

Bethany said, "I really appreciate what they were trying to do. They're such good parents, and they wanted the best for me. But I have to say it was really hard for me that they didn't help me to have more opportunities. It was one thing for my parents when their parents couldn't afford to help them. It's a whole different thing knowing that your parents have the money to help at least a bit, but they just don't believe in helping. It's hard not to feel a little resentful. A couple of thousand a year would have meant nothing to them, and there I was, working long hours as a waitress to make that much money when I could have been taking more classes and learning more."

Saren: My parents believe that it's good for us to pay for our own education, that we'll value it more if we have to pay for it. But they're realistic enough to know that no matter how much we work in high school, saving enough for a private-college education is really not possible. So they set up this plan where they'd pay for our room and board, we'd pay for our tuition via no-interest loans from them, and we'd earn our own spending money doing part-time work or using our savings from high-school and summer jobs. Overall, it's a good plan. It made me feel accountable for the money I was spending and helped me take my education more seriously. But I was always so stressed out about money! I felt like I could never buy anything, and I felt pretty deprived. I did some babysitting to make some spending money, but it didn't go far. I felt like I had this huge burden of debt over me as my loans from my parents increased. I'm sure it was mostly my personality and not so much the method that caused me such stress. But I hated feeling so poor and indebted.

Shawni: It's interesting to read what Saren wrote because I really have no problem with the way my parents helped us financially in college. I don't really understand why she feels so guilty and worried about it. If you can pay it back, pay it back. If not, it's supposed to be fine. I guess different personalities deal with things in different ways. And maybe my parents sort of changed the way they presented everything to me after seeing that Saren was stressed out about it—I went to college two years later.

I would have been in trouble if I had just been plunked down in Boston by myself with no income or financial support. My parents always made a strong effort to help us be financially aware when we were at home. At age eight we had to start buying all our own clothes, and we had our own "family bank" checkbooks. Yes, eight is young, but you must understand that my parents provided every means for us to earn our own money and to have enough for what we needed. We actually had an elaborate system in which we did our household jobs, helped take care of our "tutee" (one of the children younger than we were), got to bed on time, and practiced our music in order to earn money. If we were responsible to keep track of what we did, we reported it to my dad on "pay day" and earned money to put in our "family bank." This is all carefully outlined in another book, but getting to the point, this system ran quite smoothly and was great when we were home. It helped me a lot in the real world of college, too. I knew how to take good care of the things I worked hard to pay for and was well aware of how much money I had.

My parents decided that since they would be paying for our room and board had we stayed at home and gone to a nearby college, they would still pay for that when we left home, which was great. I took care of other things using my savings, but I must admit I still felt pretty attached to my parents for money help. I was so thankful for all the help I could get.

My husband, on the other hand, is really grateful he was much more financially independent. He jokes around with me because he thinks it's funny that I never had a real job until after I graduated from high school. (For some reason he doesn't count my month of gift-wrapping at a jewelry store for the busy Christmas season a real job!) He is so thankful to his parents for teaching him how to work hard and be responsible at a job. He values the fact that he held different, serious jobs every summer because he learned so much from them. He worked hard for his money and was able to pay for a great deal of his college education with his savings. My family was different in that we traveled a lot during the summers and didn't have jobs. I sure wouldn't trade this for the world. But my husband wouldn't trade his experience either, so I guess to each his own!

Stan: My parents provided everything while I was in high school so I could be involved in extracurricular activities rather than working for spending money. At the time this was great, but when I went to college, and my parents expected me to get a job and work for my own spending money (they paid for tuition and rent), I had no experience in getting a job or managing money. I was so indulged during high school that I felt totally unable to deal with applying for jobs and interviewing, plus I lacked any sort of work skills and work experience. I felt shocked! They had set this "giving" mode that I took for granted, and it was hard to go from having everything provided to taking care of myself!

Saren: Wow, there are lots of points of view on this one—and lots of ways of handling finances that seem to work. Parents have all kinds of different ideas, and I saw finances handled in a variety of good ways by the parents of my high-school and college friends. Different approaches seem to work well for different families—and the success of all approaches seems to be connected to the way kids are brought up all their lives and what their expectations are. I'd say the most important thing is to discuss financial support well in advance of your kids' leaving for school. Help them work out how much college will cost and then work out, together, who will pay for what. Put expectations and commitments from both parties in writing.

R&L: We agree with Saren's summary here. But there is more to it than that—much more. We'll present a full-fledged financial strategy in the appendix.

15. How should I be involved in my kids' dating lives? How much should I ask? When should I worry? What about their roommates or friends?

Charity Jade: It's just one area of interest when you're normally talking to them. The two times to worry would be (1) if they're just dating one person while they're too young or (2) if they're not dating anyone at all.

Kenneth W.: Again, give advice only if they ask.

Dick D.: Know all you can. Ask all you can. Just because they're gone doesn't mean you don't still have responsibility for them! They're in more danger now, and you've got less control. There are physical dangers and emotional ones. Be involved! Deep down, they'll appreciate your concerns.

Aja: During college, I got involved with a guy that my whole family (myself and the guy included) thought I would eventually marry. My parents met him when they came to visit me at school. He came home with me for a weekend. These visits, along with the information I gave my parents when I called or wrote home, helped Mom and Dad feel very involved in the relationship. Mom felt very attached to the guy, which pressured me to work to ensure the success of the relationship.

Neither Mom nor Dad had been so involved in one of my relationships before, even when I lived at home, but because of my age, which seemed to them a marriageable one, I think they took this relationship a little too seriously.

As a result, when my boyfriend and I broke up, it hit Mom even a little bit harder than it hit me, I think. I wish she hadn't had to get so involved. But we all learned from the experience, and when I met Jonah, even though I knew my mom loved him immensely, she gave no pressure. I told her just as much about Jonah as I had told her about the other guy, if not more, and I told her about all the things that Jonah and I felt and faced. But this time she played the part of an uninvolved listener. Luckily, I didn't have to test how involved she was with a breakup, because Jonah and I got married. But I know that it was completely my decision to marry him, and my decision was not spurred on, though it was thoroughly approved, by my parents and siblings.

Shawni: I wish my parents had asked me more about the people I was dating back in high school and college. I'm not sure why they didn't, but it seems to me the only thing they asked is whether I was kissing anyone too much. I welcomed even this much interest. I think because I was one of the first in the family to date, they didn't really know how much to be involved. Now I think they are so great with the people my youngest siblings are dating. They know all about every date. I think the communication has just become much more open. Having said this, I definitely think there should be a balance. I had a lot of friends whose parents were much too involved in their relationships. But my parents just seemed to trust whatever I was doing and didn't want to pry too much. As much as some kids may love this, I wished my parents would have been more interested in what I was thinking and feeling.

Sharon: I think it's great to show a real interest in your kids' friends. Remember names and basic information and ask about them whenever you talk to your kids. It meant a lot to me that my parents wanted to take my roommates out to dinner whenever they'd come to visit. My mom was so great about always showing a genuine interest in what was going on with my friends. Friends were such a huge part of my life—like family members in so many ways—so it was really important to me that my friends get to know my family and that my family get to know my friends.

My parents never seemed worried about any of my friends. Sometimes they'd comment about how "interesting" various people were, and I could sense they were a bit uncertain about some of the things my friends chose to do (I had this guy friend with long hair and an earring who played in a band, and a girl friend with maroon hair who did sculpture, and some of her art was a little graphic!). But they knew that my faith and my values were strong and that hanging out with people who chose different lifestyles and different looks didn't mean I was on the road to ruin. They'd say little things like, "You must be learning so much from that Brad. He's so interesting. I bet he's learning a lot from you, too." I love having friends who are really different from me in certain ways and realizing how much we're alike in other ways. I'm glad my parents understand and respect that about me.

Todd: During my college freshman year, I had a girlfriend—Donna—who wasn't a member of the Church. She was a good Christian, shared most of my values, and respected those she didn't share. But my parents were so worried about her! They kept trying to line me up with "nice Mormon girls" who were "more my type." They didn't even know Donna! How could they know if she was my type? They judged her based on one thing—whether or not she was a member of the Church. I'd overhear them talking to each other or to my grandparents or their friends about their worries that I wouldn't go on a mission because I was dating her, and that I'd end up marrying her and going inactive. It made me mad. I was only eighteen, I was not looking for someone to marry, and I was definitely planning on a mission. I was going to school really close to home, and I brought Donna home quite a few times, but my parents weren't interested in getting to know her. They seemed so relieved and almost surprised when I turned in my papers at the end of the school year. Give me a break! I can't believe they had so little faith in me. Donna and I wrote each other quite a bit while I was on my mission. I was able to tell her how much the Church meant to me and how much it could help her life through sharing thoughts and experiences from my mission. She ended up joining the Church and went on a mission herself a few months after I got home. She's now married in the temple to one of my friends, and I'm married in the temple to a great woman. I'm just glad I listened to my own feelings and made my own decisions about my relationship with Donna rather than listening to my parents' unfounded concerns. I'm sure there are some people out there, both in the Church and out of the Church, that your kids really shouldn't date. But don't judge people purely on their religion, and get to know the people your kids are interested in so you can understand what sort of people they are.

Saren: Your kids will have some interesting and tough issues related to dating once they leave home. They may be excited about all the new people to go out with. They may find themselves in a relationship that feels serious pretty quickly. I think it's great for parents to be happy for their kids when they're excited about their dating lives. As your kids get to know people of the opposite sex that they like a lot, they may face some difficult questions about spending a lot of time with one person, keeping standards regarding physical intimacy, and figuring out what sorts of relationships they want now and what they'll want in the future.

Your children will probably be excited to tell you about the people they're meeting—if you have a good relationship with them and if you don't have a history of being judgmental about their friends. They'll really want you to like their boyfriends and girlfriends. It seems like kids get confused and conflicted when their parents don't like someone that they really like a lot. Sometimes parents' disapproval makes kids want to do the opposite of whatever they advise—just to prove that their parents can't tell them what to do. If you meet and like the people they go out with, tell them that you like them, and ask about them whenever you talk. If you're worried about people they're dating, be careful not to judge too soon. Get to know more about them before you decide what you think about them. Ask your kids questions in a genuinely interested way (they can see through you when you ask questions to which you think you already know the answers). When you've given someone a really fair chance, and you're worried that the person isn't good for your child, I think it's good to express your thoughts—explain what you're worried about and why. Your child will probably appreciate your honesty. But you need to recognize that who he or she spends time with is ultimately not your decision.

16. What should I do if I'm worried about some of the things my kids are doing or not doing?

Charity Jade: You should tell them your opinion. But first listen to their opinion—really take it into consideration.

Marilyn J.: Just quit worrying. You've done all you can to teach and train them. Now you just have to pull back and see what happens. Pray for them—that's about all.

Winifred R.: Be open enough to talk about each other's worries. You want to know their worries, so you should tell them your worries. The two go together. Don't just tell them your worries about *them;* tell them your concerns about everything, and ask them to tell you theirs. Just try not to look too shocked if they tell you something shocking.

Aja: When I have confided in my parents, they have been more than understanding and have told me how they had, or would have, handled similar situations in their past. When I was growing up, my parents usually found out about disobedient things I did right away (thanks to my little sister), but when I moved away, when things did come up, they usually found out about it some time after the incident. My mom and dad made the transition well, I think, because they realized they did not need to impose any sort of punishment or chastisement, for if I were to be chastised for the incident, I had already done it to myself. So, those times I felt alone ended up being the punishment I needed to get back on track.

Shawni: I think open communication is so important when kids leave home. If there's open communication, kids will tell parents what they're doing and not doing, and parents can deal with it from there. I think the thing that keeps the communication lines open is total support from parents. This is especially important when kids may confide in parents something that isn't what they expect or what they would be proud of.

I know one girl who is terrified to tell her parents anything that may be a little questionable because her parents would flip out if they even knew she was exposed to something they wouldn't approve of. This is a good kid I'm talking about, but her parents are so overprotective she can't get close to them or have good communication with them because she's so worried they'll freak out if they find out anything that isn't perfect in her life. I don't think her parents realize that the world is out there and you can't protect your kids from everything. All you can do is teach them good things and send them out with your love and confidence, letting them know you'll always be there for them if things get hard.

Saren: Sooner or later, kids are going to see things parents wish they wouldn't. Sadly but realistically, kids will have some pretty negative experiences. But if parents can open the lines of communication and just listen to their kids—even if their kids tell them something that shocks them, they can help their kids so much. A child who confides in her parents—especially something that's not admirable—is reaching out for help and needs understanding, not judgment. If you know your parents love you and trust you, you will tell them what you are up to. You'll feel guilty if you do something they wouldn't approve of, and you'll want to improve if you don't think you're quite up to par with the good things they have taught you. But the relationship has to be good to begin with for this to work. I think parents need to still show their children they care just as much about them (if not more) even when they don't live at home anymore. This includes phone calls, listening, letters, visits—as much contact as possible.

17. How about missions? When should kids go and how much should I push? How about my daughters?

Charity Jade: Simple. The boys should go when they're nineteen, and the girls should think about it and pray about it. But don't be overbearing.

Jim R.: If you push too hard, they'll push back—in the other direction. It's got to be their decision. If they go for the wrong reasons, they may not make it, or they may make it, but it may not do much for them or for those they're supposed to serve.

Carolyn M.: I don't know . . . I'd almost say get a son into the mission field any way you can. Let's be honest, most of them don't know what they're getting into, but once they're there and they feel the spirit of it, most of them thrive. And the prophet did say, "*Every worthy young man.*"

Pam L.: You know, I just wish we wouldn't repeat that so much—like we're ignoring or excluding girls from the experience. I'm told sisters get into more homes and have more converts than elders, and I don't think there's anything stronger or more equal than a marriage partnership between two returned missionaries!

Susan: I wanted to go on a mission really bad but my mom was totally against it. She said that girls aren't supposed to go on missions in general, but if they aren't really marriage material, it's okay for them to go. I had lots of friends who had gone or were going, and I was pretty annoyed by her opinion. I prayed hard about it and decided to go. Ultimately, my mom was supportive, and I wouldn't trade my mission experience for the world. I think parents should pretty much stand back and let their daughters make their own decision about missions. I don't think they should try to influence them one way or another.

Mike: I went on a mission because my parents wouldn't have it any other way. They said I'd never be able to get married to a decent girl if I wasn't a returned missionary. Plus, they said they wouldn't pay for college if I didn't go. I really didn't have a testimony of the gospel at the time, and I was pretty immature and worried about leaving my car and my girlfriend and my nice cushy life. But I turned in my papers, and before I knew it I was in the MTC. I hated the MTC and made life pretty miserable for my companion. I had a really bad attitude when I arrived in the mission field. Luckily, I had a really good mission president, and he helped me get it in gear and have a good mission. But I wish my parents had let me make my own decision. I wish they'd told me about how important they think missions are and then let me know that it was really up to me whether or not I went. I think I would have gone in the end—maybe not right when I turned nineteen. But after seeing all my friends go out and thinking things through, I really think I would have turned in my papers. I would have gotten more out of it if it had really been my decision. I'm sad that I spent so much time in the MTC feeling mad at my parents, making life a big pain for my companion, and trying to figure out how to get out of going on a mission!

Kyle (by Saren): My friend Kyle's parents really didn't push him to go on a mission. He was active in the Church when he turned nineteen, but he really didn't have much of a testimony and had been so caught up in school and having fun and his fraternity and his girlfriend that he didn't really want to go. His parents encouraged him in a loving way and helped him see that it wasn't a "now or never" type of thing. If he didn't feel ready to go right then and wanted to set a date to prepare for his mission, they'd be there to help. After six months of messing around and not taking a mission seriously, he had a girlfriend who gave him an ultimatum—you go on a mission or you don't even think about marrying me or most of the other girls you'd probably be interested in marrying. So he got serious about a mission—got into good scripture reading and praying habits, took institute classes, and prayed about the Book of Mormon. When he left on his mission shortly after his twentieth birthday, he was prepared and ready to serve the Lord. His heart and mind were fully into it.

Saren: I'm so grateful that I went on a mission. And I'm so grateful that it was totally my decision—my parents said they'd be happy if I went and fine if I chose not to go. After finishing college, I prayed hard about it and knew that a mission was right for me. My parents asked whether I was thinking about a mission when I turned twenty-one, but I said I wanted to finish college first (I had just one more year) and then make the decision. When I finished college, they asked me about a mission again—but just in a curious way, not in a pressuring way at all. When I ultimately decided to go, they were completely happy and supportive. For girls, I think it's so important to let them know what you honestly think about a mission but then stand back and let them make their own decision. Then be really supportive of whatever their decision is.

For boys, it really is a little different. The prophet has specifically stated that all young men should go on missions, and there are more serious social and spiritual repercussions if they don't go (Who will marry them? What will they say when the inevitable Mormon topic of missions comes up? How strong will their testimony be?). It's important that parents or other people in their lives (sometimes friends and girlfriends are more effective than parents!) point out that those two years are a small price to pay for all the benefits a mission affords. But young men still need to feel that they are making their own decision, and they'll ultimately be better missionaries if they feel they are out there because they want to be out there.

R&L: Question 17 is a big one, isn't it? It may be the most pivotal question asked so far—and it has so many sub-questions that perhaps it should be treated as a whole section rather than a single question. How much should parents be involved in the mission decision? Is it a commandment that all young men go, or is that just advice from the prophet? How much should we encourage daughters to think about going? What is the hardest part of a mission for most kids? How do you prepare them (and yourself) emotionally? What can we really do for them while they're out there in the mission field? What kind of letters help them most? Is it wise to go pick them up when they're done?

There are, of course, whole books written on this subject. But here are a few candid, personal opinions on aspects you may not have fully considered—questions of *who*, *when*, and *how*.

Who should go? Frankly, for a boy, the decision should be simple because the prophet did say that every worthy young man should go. From our vantage point as former mission president and wife, we understand why. Of the 600 missionaries we had during our three years in London, we sincerely believe there was not *one* who could have learned more, grown more, contributed more, or served God and grown to love Him more by doing *any other thing!* Think about that. A mission does more for God, for fellowman, and for self—far more— than any alternative. For boys, there should be no question. *Just do it!* (We realize we have simplified that—there are many issues, no two cases are the same, and certainly there are marvelous men in the Church who did not serve).

For the same reasons, girls should consider a mission as a serious option, although, for them, it is a more complex decision. During our mission, we were constantly requesting more sisters, because they do get into more homes and teach more families. Each of our daughters has gone and come back far more prepared for life and for an equal partnership in marriage. Still, it is a different *kind* of decision for girls—one of making a personal and individually guided *choice* rather than simply deciding whether or not to follow a prophet's admonition.

When to go? Speaking generally, the best-prepared and "most-ready" elders we received in England had finished a year (or at least a semester) of college. Elders who came right out of high school, or who had never before been on their own or away from home, had a tougher time adjusting. But again, each case is different. Nineteen, with or without any college or experience away from home, is a remarkable age—an age of faith and a time when nothing seems impossible. But young men who are in their early twenties should never think they are too old to go. Some of our best elders were twenty-two or twenty-three when they entered the field.

How to prepare a son or daughter to go? The obvious answer, of course, is to teach and live the gospel. Beyond that, here are aspects that we think sometimes get overlooked:

1. *Teach total commitment and sacrifice.* The missionaries that have the hardest time are those that go out conditionally or tentatively— wondering how much they'll have to give up and how they'll like it. On the other hand, missionaries who are determined to sacrifice and

give up everything except serving the Lord for two years adjust quicker, are less homesick, and enjoy their missions far more.

2. *Have them help finance their missions*. Even though parents usually pay (and receive blessings for doing so), it's a good idea to have prospective missionaries save and pay for at least 10 percent (a "tithe") of their missions.

3. *Prepare them for the MTC*. For many missionaries, the MTC is the hardest part. Wonderful as it is, the MTC is a very regimented place, artificial in some ways because it's not the actual mission field. Prepare your missionary by talking about it and helping him or her understand that the collective uniformity of the MTC will help prepare for the individual challenges of the real mission.

4. *Be totally honest and sincere*. Don't think that by stating your opinion about your child's decision to serve you will be pressuring him or her. Just say exactly what you feel. Bear your testimony honestly and openly. Give your child the benefit of your deepest and truest opinions, but make it clear that you cannot make the decision.

5. *Focus your letters on the mission*. Once your missionary is on the mission, let him or her know all is well at home, but don't dwell or elaborate on things of home. Help the missionary "give it all" by focusing your letters on the gospel, your testimony, any spiritual experience or missionary opportunities you have, and questions about investigators and the mission.

How to bring your child home? If your circumstances permit, go and pick up your missionary when the mission is over. Do some sightseeing, but go mainly to see where he or she has been and to meet converts and members. There is no better way to *feel* and understand the mission. It is also a good beginning for the transition back into regular life. Whether or not you pick your child up, be aware that for a good and dedicated missionary, the adjustment of coming back into normal life is tougher than the adjustment when leaving. What the missionary begins doing after returing home—classes, working, friends, dating—will seem less important, less challenging, and less fulfiling than mission activities. Help your child out with some good discussions of the phases of life and share your assurance that just as God wanted him or her to focus on the needs of others on the mission, He now wants him or her to put some focus on life plans and to work out education, career, and future family.

Phase 1 Review: Conceptualizing and Understanding the Transition

We like the model of the solar system. We've even nicknamed our nine kids after the nine planets (Venus always loved her nickname, but Earth and Uranus were never too fond of theirs). For us, the symbolism is that we want to spin each of our children off into their own successful and independent orbit, self-sufficient and with their own moons. But we still want our own gravity to hold all of us together as an extended solar system or family system. We want each planet to have its own gravity but also to share a common gravity. We hope that we can all stay in the same moral and spiritual proximity within the larger universe, and that each of them can continue to be energized by our warmth.

This is a helpful way to conceptualize the departure of our children. We didn't bring them into the world and raise them to live with us forever or to be appendages of ourselves. The goal of parenting is to gradually work your way out of a job—never to fully retire but to semi-retire—to spin your children off and then watch and enjoy their exciting new orbit. We need to relish that idea rather than resist it.

Keep holding and protecting your children with the gravity of your love. Keep lighting them with the brightness of your confidence and support. Keep warming them with the fire of your loyalty and commitment. But let them spin on their own axis and move out into their own orbit.

What an excellent parenting model we have in our Heavenly Father—particularly as we depart from *our home with him* for the first time. God taught and nurtured us closely in his home, but when we left, his was a plan of agency. He knew that our growth would be facilitated by making our own choices and even by our inevitable mistakes. Yet he is always available, always willing to listen and to guide. And he encourages our close contact and frequent communication. In fact, he repeatedly *asks us to ask* because when his advice or help comes at our initiative, it does not violate our agency. His response to us is always wise and measured. He allows us to work through many of our own difficulties and dilemmas rather than miraculously bailing us out. Yet he is always there when our own resources run out. His love is completely unconditional.

Beyond the example of God's parenting and his plan of salvation, we are also blessed to have the practical, day-to-day help of an expanded family we call a ward, another set of teachers, counselors, and leaders to back us up and support us. And even beyond that, we have the seminary program and the institute program or even a Church university. And still beyond that, we have Church missions, which are the best transition imaginable between childhood and adulthood.

The Church also puts us in the powerful spiritual position that allows us to remind our recently departed children (and ourselves) of who they (and we) really are—part of the same divine family. We are spiritual siblings as well as parent and child, and we are here with reasons and priorities for living, eternally dependent on God and interdependent on each other.

Finally and most important, LDS parents have the overwhelming advantage of knowing who the real parent is and of being able to go to him in a kind of direct-stewardship prayer that essentially says, "Father, please help thy child whom thou has entrusted to my care. Thou knowest her far better than I. Inspire and guide me to be a wise steward and where her needs go beyond my capacities, please intervene." Alma the Elder prayed this way, and so can we.

Chapter 10

Phase 2: Career

Do you cut the purse strings as much
as the apron strings?

This second emotional phase is an interesting combination of relief and worry. We're glad to see our offspring becoming self-sufficient, yet we can't help wonder if they are quite ready and if their choices are quite right.

We often feel that we know more about careers and work than they do, so we're inclined to try to push them in some directions and discourage them from other options. Also, it is so hard to know when to help out financially and when to let them struggle. It's an interesting phase!

So, here are the common questions, with ENP and LTN responses:

18. How much should I be involved in my children's career decisions? How much should I ask? How much should I suggest?

Charity Jade: Tell them what you think they're good at, but respect their own dreams and passions and support whatever they decide.

Bill N.: Here is where we need to really back off. If we give too much advice and they follow it and it doesn't work out, they will blame us. And if it does work out, they'll feel less satisfaction since it wasn't their decision. If we give lots of advice that they don't follow and they end up having problems, we'll say, "I told you so," which is probably the worst thing we could say!

Le Ann D.: I disagree. I say you can't ask too much! Find out all you can and then give them all the suggestions you can. Why let them rediscover the wheel? You've been around the track a few times, and they might as well learn from you! You've got contacts and connections! They don't!

Gregory B.: Well, look, the key here is to give them so much confidence and support that they feel secure. Then they will probably *ask* you for your opinion. Once they've asked, it's their initiative rather than yours, and you can give advice without taking away their independence.

Kenneth W.: Again, give advice only if they ask.

Tom M.: Instead of pushing or making strong suggestions or interrogating, say things like, "What are your two or three best options or alternatives right now?"

Saydi: One of my all-time favorite things my dad has done for me happened a few months ago. I live in New York, and I'm getting my master's degree in Social Work at Columbia. Last summer when I was home, I was having a financial discussion with my dad. I think it was a time when he was a little stressed about supporting the five kids he had in college, and he told me that he thought it was a little unfortunate that I had chosen to go into a career that wasn't an investment. I think he was kind of kidding, and I know he just meant to state the financial facts about the social work profession. But I took what he said right to heart and flew off the handle defending the great investment that learning about social work was in my life and how much it was going to enable me to help people and make a contribution. We patched things up a bit, and he told me that we'd work out my loans but that I had to be realistic and realize that I wasn't in the most lucrative of fields.

A few weeks later, my dad was in New York for business, and he insisted on coming to check out my internship in Brooklyn. I assured him that it wasn't all that important to see, that I just had a shared office full of toys for kids to play with while I talk to their parents and try to help them solve their family and life problems. I told him that my job was at a pretty basic community center in a run-down area of Brooklyn and that he would probably be better off staying at his hotel and preparing for his meetings. But he insisted and came with me. Because we were running late, as soon as we arrived at my work I had to make him turn right around and go back home because I had to go into a meeting. He quickly met my supervisor and some of the other students interning there, and I gave him directions on how to get back to Manhattan and sent him on his way.

When I got home from work, my dad told me that he had some thoughts that he wanted to share with me, an epiphany he had had that day. He took me to a nice restaurant and gave me all his attention while we ate and talked about my life. Near the end of our meal he told me that after I left him to go into that meeting at work, he sat outside the building and just watched people for a while. He noticed the people walking by, the mothers with their babies in strollers, the little kids running around, and he thought about the work I was doing, the person I was becoming, and the people I was helping. He held my hand, looked me in the eye, and said he admired and supported me with all his heart. It meant the world to me.

Tina (by Saren): My friend Tina's father is always offering to pay for things that he'd like to see her do. He thinks her job working for an Internet company isn't a "real" job and continually nags her about going back to school so she can get a graduate degree and pursue something meaningful—which to him is either music (Tina is a gifted pianist and her father worships "the arts"), banking, or law. Every time they get together, he suggests that she go back to school and offers to pay for it as well as give her extra money for books and living expenses. He has no interest whatsoever when Tina tries to explain what she's doing at work and why she likes it. He sees her job as a "phase" that she'll hopefully grow out of soon. He's always holding out his connections and money as if they are carrots that can urge a stubborn horse onto the right path.

Josh: I had a hard time deciding on my major in college. When the time came that I would have to decide or be taking useless classes, I went through the list of majors and started crossing them out. I kept crossing them out until there was only one left—construction management. I had received some valuable advice from a church leader that if you plan on going to graduate school, it doesn't really matter what you study as an undergraduate. Just pick something that you have some interest in. This was from a man who had studied chemistry in undergraduate school, gone on to receive an MBA, started working for Eastman Kodak, and worked his way up to president and CEO. So because construction management was something I had an interest in, I declared it as my major. I wasn't sure how long I'd stay with it, but I ended up making no changes and graduated with a construction-management degree.

After graduation, I got the perfect straight-out-of-school job for a construction-management graduate. I worked for one of the largest, most respected home-building companies in the country. Other companies were always modeling their strategies after this company's. They had a good training program, and I progressed quickly and felt comfortable there. The entire time I was there, I was constantly analyzing things and trying to decide if it was what I wanted to do for a long time. After about a year, after months of thought and prayer, I decided that I wanted to try something else. I was careful to base my decision on my true desires and feelings, making sure that bad days and relationships with other employees didn't influence my decision.

I started looking for other job opportunities but didn't have time to do a thorough search with the hours I was putting in at my job and the commute times. So I decided I would quit that job and put all of my time and effort into a new job search. I know the unwritten rule that you should find a new job before quitting your current one, and I gave that a lot of thought. But I was at a time in my life (perhaps for the last time) when I could take that kind of risk and have it work out to my benefit. I was not supporting a family, and I had plenty of money to live on for several months without any financial problems. I felt that I needed time to think about what I really wanted to do without distractions. For me and the way I think, I felt strongly that it was what I should do. I wouldn't put this out there as a recommendation, but for me at that time, I felt like it was the right thing to do.

I knew my father would have a hard time with my decision, so I wrote him a long letter, explaining in detail how I had come to my decision. As soon as he got the letter, he called me, overreacted, and said that I was a quitter and that I should not quit. I had based my decision on so much thought and prayer that I felt terrible when I didn't get my father's support. I don't think he read my entire letter. There is just no way to know a situation like mine without living through it and making a decision over the course of several months as I had. My father talked me into asking my boss if I could come back after some travel and time off so that I could work until I found a new job. I had a very good relationship with my boss, and he said that would be fine. So I did go back for a few months, but it was an awkward and uncomfortable time. I felt like I didn't belong there and that I should not have gone back. My boss wasn't sure how long I would be there, so it was hard for him to plan accordingly. After a few months, again with no time to look for another job, I finally just sent in my resignation and quit for good. I wished that I hadn't gone back, because I probably would have had another job by then. I didn't tell my father, but when he found out, I could tell that he was upset and didn't agree with my decision.

I found out soon from a brother that my dad had told him I would to regret my decision and that I was going to have a miserable time. He was basically saying that I was going to fail, without even waiting to find out what would really happen. I try to set a good example for my younger siblings, so it was also hard that my father had told my younger brother that I had made a mistake before he knew if it was a mistake. It made me feel that he had no confidence in me and that he was rejecting me because I had gone against his advice. I wished he would realize I was capable of making decisions for myself. It would have felt so much better to hear him say, "I respect your decision. Just let me know if you need any help or advice."

Since then he has changed his outlook, and he says that he has total confidence that I will find what I want. He admitted that he over-reacted, and it made me feel much better. I feel that I made the right decision, and I feel confident now that I will be able to find what I am looking for.

Nancy: My husband, Evan, and I have experienced the two extremes as far as career counseling goes. My father went way over-board with the career thing—he drafted my cover letters for applica-tions, called his friends, and networked for me even if I hadn't said I was interested in his friends' line of work. He also hounded me about how to follow up, how to interview, and so on. It was a disaster. Not only did he jeopardize our relationship, but he also undermined my own confidence in my ability to find a job. I questioned myself at every turn, losing faith in my ability to ever succeed in the workplace since my father was suggesting that I couldn't even get a job without help. I would have gained much more confidence, self-knowledge, and inde-pendence if I were left to enter the work force on my own. On top of all that, the process was wholly unsuccessful, probably because I felt that in applications and interviews I wasn't being myself. I wasn't natural— I was saying what I was told to say instead of what my intuition told me to say.

My dad is a smart man, and it wasn't that he was necessarily giving me bad interviewing advice. It was simply that he was dramatically out of touch with what companies these days are looking for and how business people these days behave and interact. (A simple but illustrative example: On my first interview at a dot com, I wore a formal, tailored suit on my dad's advice but against my intuition. He said that even though dot commers don't wear suits anymore, they'd admire my elegance and sophistication. Instead, my interviewers made cracks about my suit all throughout the interview—which disconcerted and embarrassed me—and I didn't get the job.) My dad stopped working seven years ago and doesn't even know how to turn on a computer. I too was going to become a stone-ager if I didn't get my own act together and pull out of his all-consuming grasp.

The difficult thing about the situation was that I understood the motivations behind my dad's crazy actions, and they weren't all bad: an overwhelming desire for me to be happy in a rewarding, prestigious job; sheer excitement over having me live in the same city, after many years of being apart; and relief from the boredom of retirement, among others. Of course, there were the not-so-good motives of wanting me in debt to him so that I would remain in the subservient, childlike position.

I think that this, although unpleasant, is a primary motivation of parents who exercise control over their adult children. They want to selfishly relive the happy childhood memories, but they also want to maintain their hold on the controlling, parental dominance they enjoyed over reliant and trusting children. If parents can "reign in" their desire to maintain that parental high of being constantly needed, trusted, and turned to, they will more likely succeed across all the challenges of empty-nest parenting. It is a wholly selfless act to give this up, and for my father, whose sense of satisfaction and self-worth in large part comes from my own triumphs, this was and is an impossible sacrifice to make.

For Evan's parents, on the other hand, it seems to have been the easiest thing in the world. I think the difference may lie in the fact that they have four other (younger) children to take care of (whereas I am an only child), and his parents are still very interested in each other (whereas mine are divorced). There are simply other things to occupy them, whereas I'm the only child of an unmarried, retired older man living in the same city. Bad combo.

Saren: A few of us come into this world with a strong inclination toward a particular career. Some of us get pushed toward a certain career from a very young age by overeager parents. Most of us really don't know what we want to do when we start college and have a tough time trying to decide what to major in. Even after we've settled on a major, a lot of us still have a hard time trying to figure out what we want to do for a living. Most people come out of college not really knowing much about many different jobs and careers. Young people typically know a little about their parents' professions and maybe some friends' parents' professions. Life experience has taught them a little about what doctors and dentists and cashiers and policemen do. But there are thousands of careers out there that most young people have never even heard of—and plenty of good careers that their parents haven't heard of either!

Hopefully, you've helped your kids develop and explore different talents and interests all their lives so that they have some ideas about their abilities and likes and dislikes. Hopefully, your kids have taken a good variety of classes and done some good internships as well as worked in some different settings during their college years. If so, they'll have some ideas about what they like and don't like, where their abilities lie, and what sort of environment they might like working in. But regardless of what sorts of classes and part-time jobs they may have under their belts as they leave home or go through college, your kids will probably need to do a fair amount of further exploring as they think about entering the work world.

Encourage them to spend a lot of time in their school's career center, talk with career counselors, and go to career fairs. Suggest that they could talk to some of your friends about their careers. Ask them about their interests and really listen to the career ideas they come up with. Don't try to make them do what you did. And don't try to steer them away from what you did because you didn't like it. Accept the fact that they are not you and that they have their own unique talents and opportunities and dreams. Certainly, ask questions, offer ideas, and suggest connections you have that might be of help to them.

Please understand that we currently live in a world where the average college graduate stays with a first job only a year or two, and most people have three or four different jobs in their first ten years of work. Gone are the days when people picked one career and one company and stuck with it for twenty or more years. Accept the fact that your kids may go through several jobs in the course of finding something they really enjoy—but do what you can to help them make their work experiences positive from the beginning of their career. Be ready to accept it if your kids choose a path that you wouldn't choose. Be open-minded and realize that some of their proposed career paths could well be more interesting and lucrative than you might originally think!

R&L: Right on, Saren! The only thing we'd add is that *parents* might learn a lot by having some "career path" discussions with their kids. Think about holding a little career seminar as part of a family reunion. Invite a career counselor to come. Get on the Internet and read up on career trends. Read through college catalogs on various study programs, majors and minors, and job preparation possibilities.

19. What sort of financial support (if any) should I offer once the kids have finished school and entered the full-time work world?

Charity Jade: It should be a lot less now. So unless they're in a really bad position, tell them it's their obligation and their responsibility.

Kurt E.: None! They've got to be independent and self-reliant by that point. If they have to struggle or scrimp or go without a little bit, it's good for them.

Crystal N.: Well, I think you have to be a safety net. Be there for them if they fall on hard times.

Kate P.: You know, in a way, everything's backward. We're older, and we don't need any big-ticket things, yet we've got money. Our grown children are out there needing to buy a house or a car, yet they've got no money. We should just chip in. Someday they'll probably have more than we do—like in our old age—and maybe then they can return the favor.

Laura: Right after I finished college, my dad sat me and my two brothers down and told us he was no longer giving us money for anything. It was his turn to save for his own retirement and our turn to take care of ourselves. I guess this abrupt approach was the only way to go because we'd all come to feel entitled to what our dad was always giving us. I think all of us felt scared and a bit unsure that we could provide for ourselves. We also were used to having a lot, so it was pretty hard for us to learn to live on a shoestring—not an art we had any practice with! Plus we were pretty annoyed that the purse strings were cut with no warning! So, my advice to parents is to think ahead and prepare your children. It may take time and thought, but it is worth it for your children's future. Let them know ahead of time what their financial expectations of you should be, listen to their concerns, and support them through their anxieties of flying solo.

Saren: My parents made it very clear that once we turned eighteen and left home, we were essentially on our own. They'd give us interest-free loans for certain things (tuition, help with a down-payment on a first home) and they'd pay for room and board while we were in school and plane tickets for us to come home for family reunions in the summer. For as long as I can remember, I knew this would be the case, so I never expected anything different. I think this worked well for all of us that have left home so far. It's good to be independent financially as soon as you can be. It's good to know that you're assured of the chance to go home at least once a year, no matter how difficult your financial situation may be.

Whenever I've visited home, my parents have been really generous about taking me out to dinner, movies, concerts, and so on. It's sort of this unwritten rule that my parents pay for everything as long as we're with them. When you're really counting your pennies, it's just so nice to be able to have a break from that when you go home to visit! Once in a while, it's so nice to order what you want off the menu or go to a wonderful cultural event without worrying that you're ruining your budget for the month. My parents have also been really generous in paying for wonderful family vacations for us. Sometimes they expect us to chip in for airfare—it depends on the situation. But once we're all together, they take care of food, hotels, everything. I've been able to go on some wonderful vacations and build some amazing memories with my family since leaving home thanks to the fact that my parents are willing to plan and pay for these vacations.

Tim: My parents have tons of money and they are such misers! I have a job and I can support myself just fine—but I'm a teacher and that means money's pretty tight. I know I'm an adult, and I'm glad my parents respect my independence—but it sure wouldn't hurt them to be a little more generous with Christmas and birthday gifts or maybe offer to pay for some nice stuff here and there to soften my tight budget. I have this awful old bed, and when my parents came to stay

I had them sleep on the bed and I slept on the couch (which is much worse than the bed). They complained about how bad the bed was and worried that my back was getting messed up. I told them I just didn't have the money for a new bed right now. So there's a simple example of where they could have called up dial-a-mattress or something and had a bed sent my way. The money for the bed wouldn't have made the slightest dent in their fortune, but it would have made a huge difference for me. It's just hard when I know they're rolling in the money and I'm feeling so impoverished. But I guess it's their money and they can do whatever they want with it!

Saren: While it's really important to set clear expectations and be sure that your kids are taking care of themselves after a certain point in their lives, it's also important that your kids know they can always come to you in a time of crisis. I've always felt like my parents would be happy to loan me some money if I was having a hard time. During times when things were really tight for me, my mom has often slipped me a little money or bought me something she knew I needed—just little things, but at a time when it really made a difference. It's good to know that your parents fully acknowledge your financial independence, but that they want to soften things a bit here and there and that they're always there for you if you're really in trouble.

R&L: We'll talk about a "family loan system" in the appendix.

20. How should I help if my kids are out of work?

Charity Jade: Help them not to get discouraged and tell them to look harder. It's good for them to be poor for a while—but if they don't have one thing to eat, help them now and teach them not to let it happen again.

Katelin J.: Help them with a loan. Keep it strictly business. Have them sign a note and pay interest. It's got to be strictly business at this point. Or co-sign with them so they can get a bank loan.

Le Ann D.: Well, the *way* you help them is to show confidence in them and tell them you know they'll find what they're looking for. Then, if they want you to, make some calls for them or give them some contacts.

Jim R.: Get on the phone, call up some of your buddies, and line up some interviews for them! There are always some strings you can pull. You've got to help them get back out there in the workforce.

Joseph: Last year I got laid off. I'd been working hard, getting promotions, and making good money, and my parents were proud of all that. But as soon as I lost my job, their pride in me went right out the window, and they got into this "I told you so" attitude. My dad had never approved of the career path I'd chosen. He kept lining up all these "informational interviews" with all his friends—pushing me toward fields where I had no interest and no expertise. My sister told me that Dad complained to her a lot about how ungrateful I was about these interviews he set up and how picky I was about finding the perfect job. It wasn't like any of his friends were actually offering me jobs. And I don't blame them—my background and experience were a terrible fit for most of the companies where my dad's friends worked. Anyway, I did get a job eventually, and everything's fine now. But I really wish my parents had been more supportive and showed a little faith in me. I wish they'd bothered to listen when I tried to explain what sort of job I was looking for rather than pushing me toward careers they thought would be good for me.

Saren: After graduating from college, I went on a mission to Bulgaria. Then I came back to the United States and expected the perfect job to fall into my lap. Sure, I knew I'd have to do a little research, send out resumes and cover letters and all that, but I had a great education and some good experience, so I had little doubt that something would turn up. I packed everything I could into a couple of suitcases and headed to Washington, D.C., where I had some friends I could live with and where there seemed to be lots of organizations doing interesting things in my field—international development and education.

After living in D.C. for a couple months, I was loving my room-mates, making tons of new friends, and having a blast—but I didn't have a job. I'd spent a good chunk of every day making phone calls, following leads, sending out resumes, going to informational inter-views, searching out job openings, asking anyone and everyone about possibilities. I was really, really doing the best that I could—and I was feeling like a colossal failure. I'd been pretty set on doing this on my own, but after a couple of months with no luck, I asked my dad for some advice and any leads he could think of. He only had connec-tions in certain areas—and they weren't the areas I was most inter-ested in. But as I got more desperate, I asked him to set up any sort of interview he could for me.

With his help, I got a job at an agency in D.C. that supports vol-unteer centers across the United States and helps promote volun-teerism. It was connected to my interests, and I was just grateful for anything at that point. Once I started working, I was able to move around within the agency until I was doing things that I really enjoyed, and I gained lots of experience and contacts. It was really hard for me to ask my dad for help, but I'm so grateful he was able to help me out and that he never made a big deal about the fact that he helped me get that job. He was proud of my accomplishments, and I was able to prove my abilities and gain back some of the confidence I'd lost.

Dana: I was out of work for a year between jobs one time, and my parents were great about offering financial support. Luckily, I didn't need much, because I had some good savings and I did some part-time work while looking for a new job. It took a lot of stress out of the job search to know that I had a safety net to fall back on. It meant a lot to me that my parents wanted me to be happy, and they were always reassuring me that the right job would come along if I kept trying hard.

Saren: Bottom line, when your kids are out of work, I think it's so important to offer whatever help you can, but stand back and let your kids make their own decisions in their own time frame. Help them to feel good about themselves as they go through the often depressing process of searching and getting rejected. They really appreciate your confidence in them, whether or not they accept the job-search help you offer. If you think they're at a point where they really need financial assistance, offer help so that they don't have to come begging to you. Setting it up as a loan helps them preserve their dignity.

21. What if they want to move back into the house?

Charity Jade: Say no. If they come back, it's too easy, and they won't want to be independent. But tell them how much you love them.

Mandy E.: Absolutely not. Worst thing you can do is let them move back in. It's like a defeat for them—like a retreat from the real world. You can't go back into the womb once you're born!

Jim R.: I think it depends on your house. If you've got the space, okay—especially if you've got kind of a separate space where they can be a bit independent. But they should pay rent or cover their share of the expenses.

Carolyn M.: Well, it may make sense—economic sense—if your house is bigger than what you need. You know, most societies have at least three generations living under one roof. I've been kind of encouraging a couple of my kids to come back. And I've got one who's never left.

Aja: Every time I've gone home for Christmas vacation, I've sort of wanted to stay there. My mom does my laundry and cooks for me, and my dad always wants to do fun stuff with me, like go for motorcycle rides or go to the movies. But, as far as moving back home full-time, I've never really been given that option, so I never really thought about it. I have moved back home a number of times since I left. I've spent almost the whole of every summer break from school with my family (even after I got married—Jonah and I moved into the guest room), and I think we're going to keep "moving back home" until we have too many kids to pack into my family's spare room! But I don't think I'd ever go back to living there full-time. I need my own space.

Abigail (by Saren): Abigail, one of my good friends from college, is thirty, single, and living with her parents. She went away for college but then moved back home and has lived there ever since. This situation is great for Abigail and her family. Her parents love having her, their only child, right there with them. She doesn't have to pay rent, so she's saving tons of money (she has a really good job), and she loves being able to spend time with her parents. Both Abigail and her parents have their own separate social lives and do their own thing a lot of the time. When Abigail finished college and found the "perfect job," it turned out to be in the same city where her parents live. Since their house has a bedroom with its own entrance, they all decided together that there was no reason why Abigail shouldn't live there.

Saren: Some people move in with their parents and everything works out well, but it doesn't work for a lot of people. In most cases, parents have a hard time taking on a different role from the one they played when their children were in high school. It can cause havoc in the lives of both parents and kids if parents try to monitor everything going on in their kids' lives, probe their dating lives, set curfews, and do other things that might have been appropriate when their kids were in high school but that won't work now that their kids are adults. For every "success story" of a kid moving back in with his or her parents, there are probably twenty stories of messed-up relationships, hurt feelings, and family disruption that come from kids moving back in.

22. Should I encourage my kids to find a job near me?

Charity Jade: I think they need space from you. If they can get a better job further away—where they can do what they love and get paid for it—they should go for it.

Lonnie P.: Oh, for sure! I mean, they're your best friends as well as your kids. Who would you rather go to a movie with or have over for Sunday dinner? And hey, those grandkids are coming, and you've got to have them close!

Bill N.: You know, I don't think so. As much as I love my kids, I'm glad they live a plane flight away. When I visit them or they visit me, it's so special, and we really talk and focus on each other. I think if they lived right here, we'd take each other for granted, and maybe even take advantage of each other.

Shawni: My parents are almost funny about this because they encouraged us to go to college, find jobs, and live a good portion of our lives away from them. This could be taken in the wrong way—I don't think they really want to get rid of us—they just want us to experience the world. They've seen so much of it out there and have gained so much insight from their travels and experiences that they only want what they think is the best for us. I cannot thank them enough for their "big picture" perspective, because I have learned and gained so much from living away from home and having my own independent experiences. Sure, I have been homesick too, but I think even the homesickness has made me a stronger person. The thing that makes living away so great (and I'm sure the main reason my parents can feel so at ease about sending us far away) is that they love to travel, and they come visit us as much as possible. They love opening their eyes to new things and have helped us love it as well.

Saren: Now that I have a child, I have to admit, it would be so nice to live close to my family. Plane trips get harder and more expensive as our family grows, and I yearn to share my kids' lives more fully with my family. I guess every family needs to work out what's best for them. But it's important for kids to feel that wherever they live, their independence will be respected and their parents will visit!

R&L: Still, there are so many variables here. Go easy on this one, parents. It has to be your kids' decision where they live. If you really want them nearer to you, be the kind of parents they want to live closer to! And realize that you can have great relationships with your kids regardless of where they live. We really enjoy the weekly e-mails and phone calls we have with our kids as well as the visits we make as often as possible. I don't think we'd be closer to our kids if they lived closer. We might have a different sort of relationship, but I don't think it would necessarily be a closer one.

23. How much advice should I offer about how my kids spend their money?

Charity Jade: The only time you'd tell them any advice on this without their asking is if you thought they were spending a big amount on something really dumb.

Kenneth W.: Zero—only if they ask. If you start meddling here, you're on thin ice. It's their money now, and they've got to learn by experience.

Dick D.: Well, the big thing is to help them understand credit. Kids just don't get it about the dangers of credit cards and high consumer debt interest. Show them how to budget and live within their means or they're headed for trouble.

Saren: I wish my parents had talked to me more about financial planning. Growing up, I heard snippets of information that I pieced together to figure out some of what goes on with my parents financially. My dad did a great job teaching us about saving money, always encouraging us to save 20 percent of any money we ever made. I wish he'd helped us understand a little more about where to save this money. For the first five years of my career, I just put money in a savings account. I was very frugal and saved a lot, but the money didn't really grow. I remember hearing the terms IRA and 401K thrown around, but retirement sounded so far off, and I didn't really understand the benefits of such things. After getting married, my husband taught me a lot about investing (his father helped him follow investments all his life), and I realize there are so many simple things I could have done with my money all those years to make it grow so much more! I just wish someone had sat down with me and offered me a few scenarios for how I might want to be saving my money and what sorts of returns I could expect from different scenarios.

If you haven't taught your kids good, solid saving and budgeting habits by the time they leave home, it's a little hard to start now! Once your kids are out there on their own, making their own money, it's really their decision how they spend their money. You can certainly offer advice, but understand that they may not take it well. No one likes to be told how to spend their own money. If you do have concerns or just want to offer general advice, I think it's best to ask questions in a nice, interested way. Ask them how they've decided to handle their savings. Ask what bank they're using. Inquire how their budget is working out. These are all nonconfrontational questions if they're asked in the right way and in the right setting.

Let them know that you're there to help if they want any advice and that they're welcome to talk to your accountant or friends who might offer alternative points of view or other financial advice. It's always great to suggest that they get other points of view from yours — there are many good methods of doing things out there, and the more information they get, the better they'll feel about their decisions.

24. How often should I try to get together with my kids? How often should I encourage them to come home?

Charity Jade: Whenever you can, but no one just starting out is going to have a lot of extra money for travel, so don't expect them to come a long distance too often unless you pay for it!

Bill N.: Hey, as often as you can afford it! And especially for special occasions.

Marilyn J.: I think we should gradually cut it back. As your kids get more and more involved in their own lives and careers, don't expect unreasonable amounts of time with them. You should simultaneously be developing other interests of your own, so you'll probably have less time for visits too.

Peter: I had knee surgery, and my mom took a week off work to fly out, cook for me, and help me hobble around as I got through the worst part of recovery. I hadn't had one-on-one time with her in years, and although we couldn't get out and do fun stuff together, we really had a good time just talking. I have to admit, it was pretty sweet to have my mom baby me like she hasn't in years. Sometimes you really need a mom, and I'm lucky enough that I had one who was willing to be there for me. I think it's great to make every possible attempt to be there for anything important or difficult going on in your kids' lives. Be there if they're really sick. Be there for graduations. Make it to big performances. Also, make a point of visiting when they have a new job or apartment so you can see their new surroundings and learn about important new things going on in their lives.

Jessica: Go visit your kids as often as you can. I loved having my parents come to my work with me when they'd come to visit. I was proud to introduce them to my co-workers and glad to have them see a little bit about what my days consisted of. I loved having them meet my roommates and friends. It was really important to me to have them meet anyone I was dating, so I was really excited to have them come visit when I was getting to know someone new.

Saren: Invite your kids to come home often—but don't pressure them. They won't always be able to make it, but they'll appreciate knowing that you'd love to have them home. They will reciprocate and invite you often, too. Just be sure you communicate about what works best for both of you.

Some people visit home all the time because they live nearby. Some people visit seldom because they don't have the means or it's just really far away or they can't get off work. Every family will go through phases where visits are more or less frequent based on circumstances. But as long as you're keeping in good contact with each other and everyone has the sense that you're seeing each other as much as possible (or as much as is good for everyone concerned), things should be fine. It's important to talk about how everyone feels about the frequency of visits and change things as necessary.

25. How often should we communicate with each other?

Charity Jade: Same answer as when they've just left. But now you'll talk about different things since they're working.

Le Ann D.: Well, that's why I'm glad long-distance rates are coming down. I can call every night. It's almost like they're not even gone. And with cell phones, I can almost always find them.

Katelin J.: I still like letters. They're even better than e-mails because we write them slower and more thoughtfully. It's like reading *Newsweek* once a week instead of reading the newspaper every day. A letter really means something. I try to write one each week. And I save a copy, and it's like my journal. Of course, if there's something more urgent, I can e-mail or call.

Dick D.: Use e-mail. It's the perfect compromise between phone calls and letters.

Tom M.: Our grown kids live so close we have to restrain ourselves a little so we're not calling or going over every day. We're trying to give them a little space.

Valerie (by Saren): Valerie complains about how her parents never call—she always has to initiate any phone conversation they have. They talk fairly frequently, but, she says, "I'm the one who finds the time and pays for the call, and that bugs me big-time. I mean, even though I'm working now, they can afford it easier than I can. I wonder if I just stopped calling if we'd just never talk! Maybe I'll try it." Her parents always seem happy to hear from her, but they usually seem to be in a rush, and they seem to be trying to get her to quickly get to the bottom line. "I feel like they think we should just talk if we have an important question for each other or something like that. I don't think they understand the value of just sort of chatting with each other once in a while about whatever topics come up."

John (by Saren): John's mother calls every day. Mostly she just leaves messages on his answering machine at home or his voice mail at work since John's out a lot, but he's started to not pick up the phone when his mom's number comes up on his caller ID. "It's not that I don't want to talk to her," he says. "We have great talks. But I just don't have time to talk as much or as long as she wants to talk."

Shawni: I've always tried to type up a weekly or bi-weekly update that I send out to all my family members. These updates have become a great journal for me to keep for myself and a good way to let everyone in my family know some of the facts and happenings of my life—without having to repeat things in several phone calls with several people. My mom sends all of us weekly e-mail updates, and I love reading them and getting caught up on everything going on at home. Then my parents and I talk whenever we feel like calling each other, but I wish we had a weekly call that we could plan on. I do miss having good conversations with them, and spur-of-the-moment phone calls seem to always be at a bad time for me or for them.

Saren: Most LTNs I talked to said that they really liked having a set time each week when they could plan on talking to their parents—seems like Sunday evenings were the most popular time. A lot of my friends said that they really appreciated it when their parents asked lots of thoughtful questions—questions about specific events or people that had been brought up in a past conversation or questions like "What's the best thing that happened this week?" and "What was your least favorite thing that happened this week?" With new jobs, they welcomed their parents' curiosity but not their skepticism or criticism.

Several individuals said they really liked exchanging e-mails with their parents, and some said they were frustrated that their parents didn't seem to have quite caught on to the beauty of e-mail yet. E-mail is so nice because it's fast, easy, can be written and received whenever each party has a minute, and doesn't require postage. Since many of us are in front of a computer terminal all day at work, e-mail is very accessible. Many of those I interviewed talked about how much they enjoyed getting e-mail notes from parents asking about their presentation that morning or their date last night. It's nice to know that your parents care about all the little yet important things that are going on in your life.

26. What if my kids' church activity is slipping?

Charity Jade: You should talk more to your kids and really communicate about it and bear your testimony to them!

Katherine P.: I'd think inactivity would be a symptom more than the problem itself. The challenge would be to communicate enough to know if it's a testimony problem or if someone in their ward offended them or whatever. But a parent would just have to find out, because what we're talking about here is where your own child's heart is!

Peter J.: If your child is in a singles ward—well, I guess it really doesn't matter what kind of ward it is—call the bishop there. He's probably the one that can give you some insight, and maybe you can give him some, too. Especially if your child is living a long way from home, that bishop is your best link.

Katherine P.: I'm not so sure about that—it seems like you're checking up on your child rather than communicating. Wouldn't you want to approach something like this face to face, one on one, with your child?

Dick D.: Pray a lot. Sometimes that's the only thing you can do, *and* it's the best thing you can do!

Pam: After I got my first job, I got pretty frustrated with the bishop of my ward at the time. He gave me some counsel that really rubbed me the wrong way, and I stopped going to church. My parents didn't even know that I stopped going to church. I went with them when I was home, and they never really asked about my ward or my church activity, so the subject just didn't come up. I eventually realized that the gospel meant a lot to me and gave up my silly hurt feelings to go back to church. I wish my parents had asked me more about my ward and shown more of an interest in my spirituality and church activity. That might have helped me realize sooner that I needed to go back to church. I think that parents should always pay attention to their kids' spiritual development—whether they're kids or grown-ups.

Joe: I was excommunicated after I got back from my mission. I was stupid and got a girl pregnant. She didn't want to marry me (I realize now that marrying her would have just made things worse—we weren't good for each other), and we decided it was best to give the baby up for adoption. I had a lot of pretty lame friends at the time, and between bad influences and feeling bad about the decisions I'd made and being excommunicated, I fell further and further off the "strait and narrow path." My parents expressed love for me through all this, and they kept fasting and praying that I'd see the light. It took a few years, but all the things they'd taught me all my life were still in me, and I came around. I can't believe how stupid I was. But I'm so grateful that my parents never gave up on me. They had some frank and tough talks with me about where my actions were taking me (I hated those talks at the time, but now I'm grateful for them); they sent me inspirational quotes and scriptures all the time (that bugged me too at the time, but a lot of what they sent really sank in); they talked to the bishop in every area where I lived and asked that he and others in the ward seek me out; they prayed a lot; and most important, they never gave up on me.

Shawni: This is a huge concern and worry. I really think that if you prayerfully raise your kids in the gospel to the best of your ability, you have done an amazing thing, and you can't beat yourself up if a child's church activity slips. Even the best parents have kids that slip and have serious problems with the gospel. I think the only thing you can do in a situation like that is love them with all your heart—just the same as you would otherwise. This doesn't mean you have to love their actions and accept them—you should tell them how you feel— but they need to know that you unconditionally love them, no matter what they decide. I have two friends who decided they didn't believe the gospel and didn't want to come to church anymore. It was inter- esting to see both sets of parents go through so much pain and sor- row, and put their children on guilt trips at first. This did nothing except turn their kids further away from them. When they realized all they could do was just unconditionally love their kids, things were much better, and at least they still had loving relationships.

Christ taught us to love everyone, and I don't think he would ever love anyone less if they didn't do what he wanted. Of course he'd be heartbroken—as most parents would be in this situation—and he wouldn't love their actions. But he would love them! I think parents have to do the same thing. If you love your children and make sure they know how much you love the gospel too, chances are much better that they'll come back someday than if you pressure them, put them on guilt trips, and so on.

Saren: It's important that your kids know that you'll always love them, no matter what. If they go through a period where they're doubting their faith, they need your nonjudgmental love and support more than ever. They need you to really listen to them and to express the fact that you respect them and their decisions. It may help to tell them that you're glad they're really thinking about their faith, encourage them to pray, and tell them you're praying for them. The power of prayer is real. Never give up on them. Always ask about their faith and tell them how much the Church means to you. But don't drive them away by nagging them or sending them on guilt trips. They are adults. They need to make their own decisions, and your respect for their decisions will help them have more respect for your advice and ideas.

R&L: This question looms so large for those who face it that it makes all the other questions seem almost trivial. Most of us trust that if testimony and church activity is intact, other problems will be worked out, but if spiritual commitment declines, everything else is in danger.

The easy answer here would be, "I've taught them all I could and now they have their agency." This might be true, but it is certainly not an acceptable answer. The real answers are never easy, but here are some things to consider:

1. Try to determine the root cause of the inactivity. Three of the most common (and each requiring a completely different approach) are:

a. A genuine lack of testimony—serious and sincere doctrinal doubts.

b. Confusion about the gospel and the culture—doubts or concerns about how something is done and a failure to separate various Church cultural norms from Church doctrine.

c. Some personal offense—someone, often a bishop or ward leader, has offended them.

Actually, *b* and *c* are much more common than *a!*

2. Other than prayer, the most effective thing you can do about any of these is provide deep and trusting communication. Arrange for a long drive where you are alone together in a car for several hours (or some other situation really conducive to talking) and ask questions long enough to understand which of the three you are dealing with. If you determine that it is *a*, the two best things you can do are pray together and bear your testimony. In the more likely scenario of *b* or *c*, try the following:

b (doctrinal/cultural confusion): Try to explain the difference. Predominant Church culture might involve anything from the way people dress to the kind of professions they value or the things to which they afford status. Help your child see that God doesn't attach much value to these things and doesn't control the members of his church regarding them. Explain that the gospel itself and the actual restored truths of the plan of salvation are what matter. Try to think of examples when you have faced similar problems in disliking or not feeling right about something in the culture but retained your doctrinal testimony of the gospel.

c (your child has been offended): If you discover this to be the cause, rejoice a little, because it is both the most common and the most easily corrected problem. Tell your child that and help him or her understand the basic fact that the Church is perfect but its members are not (and some more obviously than others!).

3. Don't expect overnight results and don't ever give up! Patterns of activity can take time to develop (in both directions). Hang in there, and keep communicating and praying. Show *faith* both in God and in your child.

Phase 2 Review: Learning to Be a Consultant Rather Than a Manager

Manager: "A person in charge—with responsibility, with authority; one who decides and directs."

Consultant: "A person who helps another person with his or her goals; one who advises and assists."

What a difference! With small children, parents are the managers. With our growing children depending on us and in our care, the day-to-day responsibility for just about everything in their lives is ours.

With grown working children all this changes—not only in degree but in *kind*. A whole different type of relationship needs to evolve—one where we try to *respond* to their initiative, to help them with *their* goals, to back off and give them space to make their own decisions but always be willing and ready to help.

This is not an easy shift! Our instincts are still to protect and to shelter—to manage. This inclination can undermine our grown children's independence, motivation, and confidence.

Consultant-style suggestions *and* support, on the other hand, complement and enhance their new independence and leave them with the positive incentives that come to anyone who feels entrusted.

But you can't just suddenly announce one day that you are now the consultant rather than the manager. You have to consciously and carefully work into the role. The most effective route is to ask questions. That is the prime skill of all good consultants. Ask (with positive interest and with no judgment) every question you can think of.

Get inside their head and their heart and understand where they're coming from. And learn to wait for the magic moments when *they* ask *you* for advice!

Ask. As mentioned earlier, it's such a critical word and concept in our relationship with God, and it can also be so important in our relationships with our children.

Some have said that one of the great gifts of the Prophet Joseph was his ability to ask the right questions. Virtually every facet of the Restoration (and nearly every section of the Doctrine & Covenants) was triggered by apt and sincere questions. And the whole process of restoration was started by Joseph's response to James's admonition to ask.

In an ideal world (and an ideal parent-child relationship), there would be consistent and considerable asking in both directions. Parents would ask with honest and loving interest about every facet of their grown children's lives. Children would reciprocate and add questions inviting advice and guidance.

And the higher degree of asking—that of asking God and praying for each other—would solidify eternal relationships. Alma the Elder's prayer for his son was answered when all other efforts seemed to have failed. And when children also pray for their parents, the triangle is complete, and God is at the family apex.

Chapter 11

Phase 3: Marriage

Does "gaining a son" or "gaining a daughter" have to be as hard as giving birth?

Your child's marriage may be the biggest emotional peak of all—and the biggest role and relationship change. Nothing marks your child's departure from your family like starting a family of his or her own. Is it time now to really turn them loose? To think of them as equals and peers? If they are to "leave father and mother and cleave to spouse," does that mean we just get out of the way?

Here are some common questions along with a variety of ideas and suggestions from ENPs and LTNs.

27. What's my role in my children's marriage decisions? How can I get to know someone they're talking about marrying? How should I treat their fiancés?

Charity Jade: It's your children's decision, but you should encourage them to think and pray really hard. Ask them and their potential partner lots of questions about why they love each other.

Katelin J.: I think the thing you can do is help them go through the right *process* to make a good decision. Help them ask the right questions about the relationship and encourage them to have a long enough courtship to really answer those questions.

Crystal N.: Be careful not to get too involved. It's got to be their decision. What if you somehow pushed them apart and sidetracked a marriage that would have been great? Or what if you encouraged too much and your child married the wrong person? I'd stay pretty far away in this one. But once they *have* decided, support and welcome the decision with open arms.

Shawni: Being the first child married in our family wasn't the easiest thing. I don't think my parents knew exactly how to deal with it, and neither did I. One thing I really appreciate is that they didn't question my decision of who to marry. They trusted that I had made the right decision (at least they made me think that they did) and were very supportive.

I remember the night I came home late and told them I had decided to date Dave (my husband) exclusively. My dad said, "Just tell me when to start planning the wedding breakfast." They never said, "Whoa, are you sure?" They just trusted my decision. Now I must say that I'm pretty sure in hindsight they actually did worry and pray that I was really doing the right thing just because they love me and it's a huge decision, but the key is that they didn't bring me into their insecurities.

My dad sure wanted to find out everything possible about Dave. We took a family trip up to Jackson Hole with the family right before we got engaged, and my dad insisted that Dave ride in his car alone with him for the first leg of the ten-hour round trip. Well, this ended up including the second leg as well, and a surprise "we got lost!" jaunt to make the trip even longer. By the end my dad and Dave had spent eleven hours in that car alone talking about who knows what. But Dave endured, and that was a strong point, I'm sure. Even though I worried about Dave being questioned to death in that car, I loved that my dad cared enough about me to spend that much time with someone he thought might become my husband.

I think every parent should thoroughly interview anyone trying to marry one of their children. Even though Dave was the one who had to endure the interview, he wants to do the same thing for our kids.

Saren: My decision to get married came as quite a shock to everyone—including myself and my husband-to-be! I was visiting my family for a couple of weeks one summer, and they had the opportunity to spend some time with Jared, whom I had been dating for about a year. With all the time Jared and I spent together that summer, our feelings for each other escalated quickly, and both of us started thinking about marriage—but neither of us dared bring up the subject, and we sort of downplayed our feelings to our families. The day before I was supposed to head back to Boston, we both got pretty frustrated with our somewhat stagnant situation. We drove up the canyon near my house and sat there in the wildflowers, neither of us knowing what to say. Jared finally broke the silence by looking directly into my eyes and saying, "I want to marry you." It was like the floodgates to our feelings had been unlocked, and we were able to get everything out there and decide to be married.

Then we were left with the question of what to do next. We headed back to my house so that Jared could formally ask my dad for my hand in marriage and we could gather everyone together and make an announcement. We were so giddy with the excitement of our recently made decision that we didn't really think much about how our families would take this surprising and sudden news. As my dad and Jared headed out to the balcony to talk, I got this sudden worry that maybe my dad wouldn't be too thrilled. He hadn't interviewed Jared at length as he had my sister's husband before they got engaged. He hadn't really spent much time with Jared—and my dad's known to be somewhat overprotective (I think most of my siblings would call that a major understatement!). I went into my dad's study where I could hear everything and eavesdropped nervously. Jared explained that we'd arrived at the decision to be married. My dad paused just a moment and then asked Jared a single question—why he loved me. I could hear the smile in my dad's voice as he asked the question, and I felt sure that everything would be okay. Jared gave what I thought was a great answer. They talked for a few minutes; then they came inside, and my dad gave me a huge smile and a big hug.

We finally tracked my mom down at the dentist to give her the news—we were too excited to wait until she got home. She was so surprised and excited when we told her that she nearly sent dental instruments flying in her rush to get out of the dentist's chair and hug both of us! My mom had especially liked Jared from the beginning, so I wasn't surprised at her enthusiasm about our marriage decision.

It meant a lot to me that my parents immediately accepted my decision to be married and embraced Jared as a member of our family from that day forward. They never said anything negative about Jared to me and never even asked questions with any negative connotation. Although I was relieved when my dad didn't start grilling Jared when he asked for my hand, I think I sort of expected that he'd pull Jared aside at some point and have a big talk with him, like he'd had with Shawni's husband (but hopefully not for eleven hours!). I remember feeling relieved when he asked Jared to ride with him in his car on the way to Bear Lake a week after we got engaged. I guess I felt like this father-to-future-son-in-law talk was a sort of rite of passage that would give the two main men in my life a chance to get to know and like each other more. Plus, I think I needed to feel like my dad was making sure that Jared was perfect for "his little girl." It sounds silly, but for all my independence and desire to be respected as an adult who makes sound decisions of her own, I wanted my dad to scrutinize my choice and agree with me wholeheartedly.

Jonah (by Saren): When my brother Jonah was getting pretty serious about his wonderful girlfriend, Aja, we all had to hold ourselves back from pushing him toward her. We all loved Aja and could see how happy she made Jonah. She had every positive quality we could imagine that would be good for Jonah. But we knew that he needed to take his time and make his decision without feeling that he was getting any pressure. I remember talking with Jonah about Aja on many occasions, listening as he'd list what he loved about her and as he'd mention his reservations and small concerns. I tried to listen and understand but let him come to his own conclusions rather than jumping in there and saying, "So, Jonah, I think you should marry her!" It was hard to hold myself back, but I knew that he just needed a sounding board and that even if he did want my opinion, this was one decision he would definitely need to make on his own. It would be awful to make a marriage decision and then worry in retrospect that you were unduly influenced by others when you made it!

Saren: While your kids want you to fully respect their decision once they decide to get married, they really do want their parents' approval. They want their parents to take the time to meet their serious boyfriends or girlfriends and perhaps even spend some time alone with them to really get to know them.

As a parent, you'll probably have some concerns that arise—let's face it, no one's perfect, and very few people could be good enough to marry your son or daughter. But keep your minor concerns to yourself, especially once your child has made the decision to be married. Major concerns are a whole different story. But any small, negative thing that you mention about a prospective spouse can really hurt your children's feelings and may encourage them to see you as possessive and petty and even an "opponent" to their loved one. Look for and point out the good in a prospective spouse. Welcome him or her to family activities.

I suggest that you don't push your children too much toward marriage or too much away from it. I'm sure you've noticed this—your kids, no matter how old they get, tend to shy away from anything they feel like their parents are pressuring them to do, even if it's something they're actually already inclined to do.

28. What should I do if I'm worried about marriage decisions my children have made?

Charity Jade: Think about it a lot before you bombard them. But if you feel sure they've made the wrong decision, you have to try to talk it over with them. But no matter what, support them now and also later when they're getting a divorce.

Jim R.: I think about the only thing you could do would be to discuss the *process* by which the decision was made. How and when did they decide? Do they know enough about each other? Questions like this might help your children reexamine their decision without too much resentment.

Betty T.: Quit worrying. You've got to trust them on this!

Dale (by Saren): The other day, I asked a group of friends, "What's the best thing your parents have done for you since you left home?" Without hesitation, my friend Dale answered, "They told me not to marry Tara." He went on to explain that he was engaged to this girl for several months and that the longer he was engaged, the more worried he felt about the relationship. But he didn't say anything. His parents had made every attempt to get to know Tara from the time the relationship became serious; they included her in family activities and shared what they liked about her with Dale. When Dale decided to get engaged, his parents were very supportive, but as time went on, he could sense that they had some worries.

Just as Dale's silent worries about his upcoming marriage began to peak, his parents sat down with him one day and lovingly explained some concerns they had about Dale and Tara's relationship. They didn't say bad things about Tara—which probably would have made Dale jump to her defense. Rather, they pointed out concrete concerns about the way that Dale and Tara interacted with each other and wondered about whether they really complemented each other very well. They said they'd been really hesitant to say anything and that they'd certainly support whatever Dale's final decision was regarding the marriage, but they felt strongly that they should at least share their thoughts.

Apparently Dale's parents' concerns mirrored and confirmed his own worries, helping him to see more clearly what was wrong with the relationship. He broke off the engagement and now says, "I'm happier every day that I didn't go through with that marriage. It would have been a disaster."

Dale writes, "I'd say it's a very good idea to express well-thought-out concerns in a loving and timely manner when it comes to your children's decision about a future spouse. It's probably better to express concerns before an engagement is underway—but late is better than never! In my case, I don't think I'd have listened to my parents if they'd brought up their concerns any earlier. They were wise to wait until I seemed to be having some second thoughts myself."

Paula (by Saren): Sometimes, parents can be too forceful with their opinions about who their children should marry. A parent's pride or preconceived opinions can really taint the ordinarily happy event of marriage and cause all sorts of lasting upset in a family. I have a friend from school, Paula, who met a wonderful man, Doug, and decided to marry him.

Paula was living away from home when she met Doug, and her parents had only met him once before they were informed of the engagement. They were somewhat shocked, as their daughter had not really prepared them for such an announcement.

Paula and Doug wanted to have the wedding soon and were eager to begin their wedding plans, but Paula's parents were really worried about the situation. They started out by saying that they simply needed to get to know this guy better. Paula was initially hurt that they weren't excited for her, but trying to see things from their point of view, she and Doug set up opportunities for everyone to get to know each other better.

But, offended at not having been involved before the engagement, Paula's parents seemed to be looking for bad things about Doug. They seemed set against him. They were just so hurt that Paula had decided to marry without asking their advice or involving them in the process that they couldn't get past it. I knew Doug. He was a perfectly nice guy, clean-cut, a good Church member, a returned missionary, smart, kind, and very good to Paula. Talking to Paula one day, I said, "I don't get why they don't like him." She replied, "It's simple—they decided not to like him, and they decided not to change their minds, and they're mad because everything didn't turn out the way they imagined it, and they've decided not to get over being mad."

Paula and Doug considered delaying the wedding and trying to do what they could to help her parents accept Doug, but they finally went ahead and got married. They decided that Paula's parents weren't going to change their attitude, no matter how long they waited. Paula's parents refused to have anything to do with the wedding plans, and her mom didn't even show up at the wedding.

Doug and Paula are happily married after five years, but their relationship with Paula's parents is still strained. The parents seem quite sure that the marriage is going to fail sooner or later, and then they'll be able to say "I told you so." They have too much pride to just say, "Hey, we were wrong, and we're glad we were wrong. We're glad you guys are so happy." The bitterness, pride, anger, and sadness—they're all very tangible still.

Saren: From every LTN I've talked to about this question, it seems best for parents to meet and get to know any serious boyfriends or girlfriends, and then, in a timely way, express everything they like about each person along with any concerns they may have. Then, most important, completely respect a marriage decision once it has been made. Once your kids decide who they want to marry, they'll expect and need you to support their decision. If you don't like their fiancé, try to learn to like him or her. Your kids are adults, and they'll ultimately make their own decisions. If you're really worried about a marriage decision, your children will probably listen best to your concerns once you've shown and stated that you respect their right to choose. Once they know that you recognize that this is completely their decision and that you trust that they ultimately know more about the situation than you do, they'll be more likely to listen to any concerns you may have.

29. What if my child is seriously dating (or marrying) someone of another faith?

Charity Jade: I think you should really talk to your child about it. If it's an inactive person maybe you can help. But in the end you've got to support your child and never give up on him or her or the person your child is marrying.

Carolyn M.: You should have been warning them about this for years, so now it may be too late. That sounded terrible, didn't it? I guess what I'm saying is that I don't really know what I'd do. My heart would be telling me to discourage the marriage in every way I could, but that might just distance me from my own child.

Katherine P.: I think we jump to conclusions and prioritize the wrong things sometimes. I'd rather have my daughter marry someone with genuinely good character—an honest, honorable, gentle man who may be, for whatever reason, inactive or even wasn't a member than an active member who was two-faced or even abusive. I think if the choice is a truly good person, everything will work out over the long run, even the Church. I'm not saying it would be easy.

Bill T.: I think all you can do is be honest. I'd tell my son or daughter how much the Church has helped in our family and how much eternal temple marriage means to me. I'd just lay it out, but I'd try to respect their free agency.

Lydia: My husband is totally inactive. We got married five years ago, and he went inactive a year after we were married. He was really bothered by the attitudes of many of the members who looked down on us because we have an interracial marriage—plus, he figured he could be a good Christian without necessarily going to church all the time. He is fine with the fact that I go to church, and he thinks that it's good for our two kids to go as well—he wants them to be good Christians and feels that they'll learn a lot at church as they're growing up. I hope and pray that he will become active again one day. It's hard for me that he doesn't have the Church as a priority in his life right now. I appreciate the way my parents have handled the whole thing. They never say bad things about Paul and show nothing but pure love for him. I have friends in similar situations whose parents treat their nonmember or inactive spouse in very un-Christlike ways. It's sad. I think people who are inactive need extra love and don't need to be judged. I think it's important for parents to see the good in their son- or daughter-in-law, regardless of their church activity.

Kristine: When I started dating Raj, my parents were worried because he wasn't a member of the Church. When I decided to marry him, they were really upset. Raj is a wonderful person, but they didn't seem to notice that. They just cared about his church status. They predicted that our marriage wouldn't last and washed their hands of the whole thing, so to speak. They were always nice enough to Raj, to his face. But we both knew what they thought of our marriage—an "accident waiting to happen." Anyway, we've been married for three years now, and Raj and I are really happy together. He respects my beliefs and has no problem with us raising the kids with Mormon beliefs.

Sure, it would be easier if he were a Mormon—but I prayed about my marriage decision and felt good about it. I feel strongly that God approves of our marriage and that he has a plan for our ultimate happiness. I wish my parents could have supported my decision! My sister who was married in the temple is now divorced, and my brother, also married in the temple, is having serious troubles in his marriage and with his testimony (he's got a "little" pornography problem). The other day, as my mother was talking to me about her worries about her kids' marriages, she remarked, "I guess a temple marriage is no guarantee of anything." I agreed and added that Raj and I seem to have the best track record for a marriage in our family. I think that parents should respect their kids' marriage decisions and realize that things aren't always what they seem!

Shawni: This is tough because all parents in the Church want their children to find strong Church members to marry. But the truth is that even kids who have strict rules to date only members and who have grown up with strong testimonies sometimes end up marrying nonmembers. I think it's important for kids who marry out of the Church to be realistic and realize how hard it's going to be for them to do this, but to also realize that not just Church members are good, strong, Christlike people. I have friends with nonmember spouses who have become stronger by being the one to take their kids to church all by themselves and teach them gospel principles all alone (very difficult), and other friends who have gone inactive because they are influenced negatively by their spouse, and still others who are great missionaries and end up helping their spouse get baptized. It's a tough road any way you look at it. I feel so much for those whose relationships suffer because of their beliefs. I just think some kids who get into relationships with nonmembers don't realize the tough road ahead of them if they get married.

Saren: There are all sorts of successful marriages out there.

Having the same religious beliefs is one really good and important part of being compatible within a marriage. But other areas of compatibility are also important, and having the same religion doesn't guarantee that two people can have a happy life together. I think it's important for parents not to judge their children's potential spouse purely on the basis of whether or not he or she is a Church member. There are really good and really bad people both inside the Church and outside it. Look at whether this person complements your child in important ways. Talk to your child about your concerns—such things as how the kids will be raised, how the Sabbath will be observed, how the family will work out on an eternal scope. But realize that not all successful earthly or eternal marriages start with two people kneeling across the altar from each other on their wedding day. Some spouses join the Church and families are sealed years after the wedding. Some spouses never join the Church in this life but provide wonderful companionship and partnership in parenting throughout this life. Obviously, it's easiest in many ways if your child finds a wonderfully compatible spouse who is already a member of the Church—but don't judge potential spouses purely on their church status. Express confidence in your children's ability to do the right thing, and support their decisions. Love their spouse no matter what.

R&L: This is another truly huge question, because most LDS parents sense that if their children make a great decision about marriage, all the other decisions of their life will likely be easier and better.

There is no question that our children's best chance for a happy and lasting marriage is to find someone worthy to go to the temple with. The eternal covenants of temple marriage and the unity that is possible between two people worthy to kneel across that altar amount to an immeasurable advantage! Still, we all know that temple marriage is no guarantee, and its promises are fulfilled only as its commitments are kept. The quantity or duration of a temple marriage is eternal only if the quality of that marriage meets the standards the Lord has set. Thus Katherine P. (above) is probably right when she says she'd prefer her daughter to marry a man of honorable character outside the temple than a scoundrel who somehow got in. The former is capable of progression that may someday be eternal, while the latter is probably doomed to retrogression and failure.

So it's one of those answers that is simpler than it is easy! Strive all your lives to help your children prepare for and find a partner worthy of temple marriage. (In the early dating years, even as you encourage children to date strong members, it is probably unwise to unilaterally and unconditionally forbid them to date people of other faiths or inactive members. Hopefully you have raised them to "influence more than they are influenced," and they will pull their friends toward the Church rather than themselves being pulled away.) Help your children work toward a temple marriage by example, prayer, and discussion (your children should know your feelings and know that statistics are against them if they marry out of the temple and even more against them if they marry out of the Church). If, after all you can do, your child falls in love with a person who can't go immediately to the temple, look at that person's true character and work toward a later sealing.

If circumstances and distances allow, go with your children to the temple for their endowments before the wedding so they can concentrate entirely on the endowment the one time and entirely on the wedding the other time. Encourage the spouse-to-be to do likewise with his or her parents (perhaps together with your family).

Back to the original question: Temple marriage and eternal families are the goal, but if it doesn't happen initially, remember that it is a lifetime goal and that nothing can stop you or your children from working toward it all their lives.

30. What should be my role in my child's wedding?

Charity Jade: Be the supporting actor or actress. Don't try to be the leading role or the center of attention. And just be really happy!

Carolyn M.: Read the books. Those marriage and etiquette books lay out exactly what is expected of the bride's parents and the groom's parents. You've got to follow some higher authority or else there will be disagreements and problems.

Bill N.: To be honest, I thought about paying them to elope. It would be a lot less trouble and a lot less expensive! As it was, I just stayed out of the way and signed the checks.

Le Ann D.: It's the mother of the bride's responsibility, really. I mean, it's mostly our friends who come to the wedding, and I really don't think the kids have the time or the know-how to plan a wedding anyway. I think it should be as big or as little as the parents want to make it.

Fred J.: I think the most important part of weddings is all the new relationships. It's the best chance you'll ever have to meet the new in-laws, and to really talk to and get to know the parents of your new son- or daughter-in-law as you plan your parts of the wedding. Make it fun! Let the kids have the final say on everything, but be on board for the ride! Oh, by the way, give them a budget at the beginning—or at least a bottom line.

Saren: My parents gave me a lump sum of money to use for my wedding and told me I could use it however I wanted. I could spend it all on a nice big wedding, do a simple wedding and save a lot of it, or use it for a honeymoon. I really appreciated their generosity in providing me with ample funds to have a beautiful wedding. I also appreciated the fact that they let me decide what sort of wedding to have without feeling like I'd be forfeiting money or getting less than anyone else in the family if I opted for a small, simple wedding. I'd been out on my own for a few years, and they knew that I knew how to manage money and plan things. Maybe this approach wouldn't work so well if your kids haven't planned an event before or if they aren't good with managing money.

I went with a big, formal yet fun wedding—tons of people, a great swing band, lots of dancing, good food, a gorgeous dress, an amazing cake, and beautiful photography. It was expensive, but it was my dream wedding, and it was worth every penny!

My parents didn't have to do that much. Jared and I found the band, decided on menus, reserved the ballroom, and took care of most logistics without bothering my parents about it. We invited family members to be involved in a lot of ways, and we asked for advice about different options—but it never felt like our parents were trying to assert their opinions or steer us in any particular direction. Everyone in my family helped out with anything I asked them to do. My dad ordered the tuxes for everyone as I'd requested. My mom did some research and put together a short list of the best places for wedding dresses and cakes and invitations—and she went with me on lots of my errands. It was so important to have her by my side as I tried on dresses and decided on the cake and invitations. My brothers and dad stepped way out of their element to help me pick out jewelry and makeup and flowers when I had my bridal photos while my mom and sisters were out of town. Everyone was so supportive of my wishes and determined to help make this day perfect for Jared and me. I wish everyone getting married could have support like I had!

Shawni: Getting ready for my wedding was probably the most memorable time I've had with my mom. I will always cherish the time we were able to spend together one-on-one as we prepared for the big day. I come from a family with a lot of kids, so it was great for me to get so much undivided attention. My mom was so great about everything. This was her first time helping to plan a wedding, and she did so much since I was in school an hour away from home and in the midst of finals the week right before the wedding. With how much work she was doing on my wedding, you'd think she'd be sort of attached to having things her own way, but she always asked me what I thought and made it just how I wanted it. I'd come home and she'd have a big list of things we needed to do, and we'd drive around together and just talk. I loved it.

Jill: I think my mom started planning my wedding when I was born. She's always talked about all these things she envisioned on my "big day"—some of them sounded nice, other ideas didn't line up at all with what I wanted, but I never paid that much attention. I figured I'd work it all out some day when I was engaged. Well, when that time came, my mom was so excited to plan the wedding! She started calling places for receptions and clipping photos of dresses and cakes while I was at school the day after we announced our engagement. I was glad she was so excited, but I wanted this to be my wedding, not hers! It was hard for me to say what I really wanted—my parents were paying for everything, and I didn't want to be ungrateful. I had a nice wedding, but if I had it to do over again, I would have spoken up a lot more and made sure that things were more the way I'd pictured them, not the way my mom pictured them.

Saren: Most LTNs I spoke with agreed that your wedding day can and should be one of the most memorable days of your life. Weddings are about family and friends and traditions—but they're primarily a celebration of the love between the bride and groom, so the bride and groom should really be the ones deciding what they want. Give your kids a budget, be there to help and offer to help in areas where you'd most enjoy helping—then stand back a bit. Make sure your child will always feel that his or her wedding day was his or her day, not your day. Your kids might benefit from various books or websites about wedding planning. Offer them such resources and your advice if they seem overwhelmed. But you should be content to let your kids make the decisions and create what they want while you fill a purely supportive role.

31. What will my children go through during the first few months of marriage? What will they need from me?

Charity Jade: They won't really know what to do. So tell them about how those first few months were for you. They might not seem interested, but they probably really are.

Winnefred R.: There will be adjustments, that's for sure. Your children will probably miss you and appreciate you in some new ways, which is good. Hopefully they will tell you this. I think parents should give a listening ear—but not even that very often. The newlyweds need to learn to depend on each other. If we just support them and tell them we have confidence in them, it will help. We can also tell them that we had a few adjustments to make too, when we were in their shoes.

Marilyn J.: I think our kids just need to know that we approve, that we love them, and that we're happy for them.

Peter J.: The funny thing is, they need just about everything. They need furniture, they need recipes, they need plane tickets, they need a fast modem, they need to go with us on our vacation. And they need money—and more of it now!

Aja: It's hard to fully define what I need most during my first few months of marriage, because I'm still in those first few months right now. I still need and want those same things I needed when I first moved away from home—open communication, an open invitation to always come home (though I bring Jonah now too), and lots of packages to open.

Just a few months ago, we lived for seven weeks at my parents' summer home on an island in Washington State, where I had done most of my growing up, including the big growing up that happened when Jonah asked me to marry him—there on the island. My mom was so excited to have us with her, especially to help her look after my little brother when she had to go back to Las Vegas every few weeks for work. Almost every day I think she told both Jonah and me how excited she was to have us there, and how glad she was that we had found work on the island so we could stay there for a nice, long stretch. Not only did her hospitality and excitement fill those same needs as when I first left home, but I also know that enthusiasm helped ease the tension Jonah and I both felt about parking ourselves in a house that wasn't really ours. We were stuck there on the island for a while, but my mom didn't give us any reason to regret it. It turned out to be a great opportunity for Jonah to get to know my family better and for them to get to know him.

I think it's so important for parents to always welcome their married children home with open arms and to find opportunities to spend some good blocks of time together with their new son- or daughter-in-law. You always need a house to come home to, and even though Jonah and I have our own house together, we both know that we are not excluded from our first homes.

Jake: Those first few months of marriage were pretty rough—wonderful too, though. We had a nice apartment that we'd set up before the wedding, but deciding what should go in the apartment was harder than I would have thought. Mary was really into getting lots of nice furniture that would last a long time, while I thought we might as well sort of camp out since we only planned to be in that apartment for a year. We'd talked about finances before getting married and decided we wanted to combine our savings and checking accounts. It all made sense, and we went through all the processes to get the money moved around. We liked seeing our two names on our new checks. But Mary got freaked out a little about the idea that she didn't have anything of her own anymore, and she questioned stuff I bought, which drove me crazy since I was used to doing my own thing my own way. Anyway, I remember lots of discussions about lots of issues— painful at the time, but we gradually learned how to get things out in the open, and we figured out some solutions that we're always fine-tuning.

Throughout all this, my parents were great. They'd call us every Saturday morning and check in, asking what was new with us and whether we needed anything. They invited us for Sunday dinner as often as we wanted to come. They were really complimentary about the way the apartment looked and the dinners we fixed for them. They made a point of complimenting me on what a good husband I seemed to be, and Mary on how happy she was making me.

I really appreciate the fact that they were interested in hearing about everything going on in our lives, but they never pried. I have a friend whose mother used to corner him and ask him all these questions about his relationship with his wife when they first got married. I'm sure she meant well, but it just made him totally turn off to her.

Mary and I decided right at the beginning of our marriage that we weren't going to say anything bad about each other to anyone other than each other. Does that make sense? Anyway, there were times when I was so frustrated with Mary that I wanted to call a friend or my dad and just vent—but I'm so glad I never did. Instead, I told Mary how I felt, and we worked things out between the two of us.

Saren: Marriage can be hard, especially at first. But I'd say parents should leave their kids alone and let them work things out themselves. Third parties just get in the way. I think if kids start saying bad stuff about their spouse to you, it's good to suggest that they keep those things inside their marriage. If things are really bad, they probably need to get outside help. But as they work out the business of living together and planning a future together and dealing with each other's quirks and needs, it's detrimental for parents to be too involved.

Call regularly, ask sincere, non-prying questions, spend time with them—as much time as you and they are comfortable with—compliment them, and make a point of spending quality time with your new son- or daughter-in-law. Assure them that the first year of marriage is supposed to be hard and that the better they can communicate with each other, the more they'll grow together. I think it's good for parents to selectively share stories of the hard times and great times they had at the beginning of their own marriage.

R&L: Spiritual advice is probably both the easiest and the most important to give with your children's new marriage. Simply encourage them to make their marriage a three-way partnership with the Lord as the third (and managing) partner. Encourage them to pray together over every decision. If they do this, they will succeed—and the pressure will be off you because they will be relying on their true Father.

32. What sort of relationship should I hope for with my married children?

Charity Jade: You should be close and comfortable but not to a point where you take them away at all from their new spouse.

Tom M.: Once they are married, I really think we should try for a horizontal, friend-to-friend relationship. They'll understand so much more about us now, and we'll just have a lot more in common. I really think we should visualize how we talk and relate to a friend, and then treat our married kids the same way.

Kenneth W.: It's like your child has now become the president and you're the chairman of the board. Let your child run his or her own marriage and family, but call your child in for a corporate meeting from time to time.

Shawni: I'm so glad that my parents and I had such good relationships to begin with because it's kind of a difficult transition after you get married. One thing that was hard for me was to lose the strength of the "confidante" relationship I had had with my dad as my husband gradually moved into that role. It wasn't that my husband wasn't good at it—I am so lucky to have a husband who took on the role so perfectly. But I just love my dad, and it was hard to lose some of his deep involvement in me and my life as he loosened his grasp a bit to let my husband take over.

I think my dad has a hard time letting go too, or at least finding a balance. Sometimes I think he still feels like he needs to be in on everything, and he asks too many questions—especially about financial matters. But I think both parents did a pretty good job of letting go enough but not too much. Even though I know they must have been dying to jump in and tell us what to do (especially my dad, who I'm sure my mom was holding back with all her might), they tried to show us they trusted us and let us do it on our own.

My very opinionated dad was obstinate about telling us over and over again how much we should ask for his advice, but he tried to take it in stride when we didn't. I think this is really important. Parents know so much from being through so much before, but I think it's so important that they let their kids figure most of it out for themselves—especially once they're married and have a partner to work with.

Let your children make mistakes—it's good for them. They don't need someone telling them what to do every step of the way, even if they think they do because how else will they learn to cope in the real world. I have some friends who try to make every decision for their children. They read their e-mails, they choose their friends, they control them in so many ways. I wonder about how this will translate into their children's married lives. They may have helped them stay away from some problems, but they have hindered them from learning on their own some very important things.

Jonah: Aja and I have been married for seven months and five days, and there is no doubt that with each day our love grows more and more. I know that she is my family now and that I should "cleave unto her" (as it says in the Bible), but that in no way suggests that my birth family has lessened in importance for me. The support and teaching from my parents is what has made me who I am today and has given me confidence. To this point in my life, I have been away from home full time pretty much since I was nineteen and have come to love the adventure and independence of it, but my family's support will always be important to me.

Even though I'm married, I still need my parents to call me regularly, to come visit me, to show an active interest in my life, to tell me that they're proud of me, and to offer me advice, but also to accept the fact that I won't always ask for or take it.

Saren: Talking with a group of friends about this book one evening, we stumbled onto the topic of how our relationships with our parents should change once we find a spouse. Everyone quickly agreed that parents need to recognize that they should take a backseat once their kids marry. Once we're married, the foremost relationship in our lives should be the one we have with our spouse. Some of those I interviewed said that they had been away from home long enough to begin to see a gradual shift from being under the stewardship of their parents to being their own stewards—and that the next natural step took place quite easily as they entered into a relationship with their spouse and became each other's stewards. Others talked about how their parents seem to have a hard time letting go of the custodial and controlling aspects of their parental role—complaining that parents called them up too often and asked too many questions.

One friend said his mother made his wife's life miserable by constantly comparing everything the wife did to the superior way that she, the mother, had always done things. Overall, everyone agreed that parents need to:

• Acknowledge, verbally and through their actions, that their married child's first allegiance and priority is his or her spouse.

• Regularly express love for and confidence in their child and his or her spouse.

• Talk about what sort of role the child wants the parents to play now that he or she is married.

33. What should I do if I see something going on between my child and his or her spouse that worries me?

Charity Jade: Let them work it out on their own with their own judgment. But if it gets really serious, step in.

Kenneth W.: Bite your tongue! The last thing you want to get into is a marital problem between your kids.

Fred J.: My own mom wouldn't even intervene in a playground fight. If I'd come in and tell her about some kid who was beating me up, she'd say, "Well, you go on back out there and try to talk to him and work things out." And, amazingly, I usually did. Well, if it works that well on playgrounds, the same approach may be good for marriages.

Shawni: My parents have some good friends who are very concerned about some of the things going on in their daughter's marriage. The wife was talking to my mom about some of her concerns—nothing specific, just hinting at the seriousness of her concerns. My mom asked what her friend was going to do about these concerns. "Do?" she said. "I certainly can't do anything. It's really not my place. Well, I guess I'm praying for them, and that's doing something. They need to work everything out themselves, don't you think?" My mom agreed that they certainly need to work things out for themselves—no one else could possibly do that for them. But she tried to politely suggest that talking to her daughter about some of her concerns and asking if she wanted any advice might be appropriate.

I don't know what ever happened with that situation. But when my mom told me about the incident, it made me wonder whether there are a lot of parents out there who feel like they should never say anything at all about their children's marriages. I've certainly heard of parents who go way too far the other way, criticizing their children's spouses or kids all the time and bringing up worries unceasingly. That can be very destructive to both the children's marriages and their parent/child relationships. But I do feel that loving parents should always share any serious concerns and persistent thoughts they have about what's going on in their children's lives.

I think it's a really good thing to regularly notice and tell your children about all the good things you see in their spouses. This helps you maintain and enhance positive feelings toward the spouses, and it helps your children keep looking for the positive themselves.

Saren: I think parents are best off prefacing observations with statements such as, "I want to tell you about some things I've had on my mind. I'm not sure if my concerns are valid at all because I'm just an outsider in this situation, so feel free to totally forget about anything I say that doesn't really apply." It's important to ask your children lots of questions and really listen to the answers. It's extremely important to be open-minded and accept the fact that your concerns may be totally off the mark. And it's important to talk to your children regularly and have a strong relationship so you're not just bringing up concerns about something as personal as their marriage out of the blue to a person you hardly ever talk to.

34. How much financial support (if any) should I offer my children now that they're married?

Charity Jade: None. It's their life now. They don't get an allowance. When they're in big trouble, though, you should help with loans.

Bill N.: I think you've got to just wait and see what they need—and then hope you've got the means to help.

Mandy E.: It's really dangerous to help now that they're married. It can cause more problems than it solves. It can pull them apart from each other. I even think you should talk to the other in-laws and agree together to let them be on their own. Give timely gifts—something for their house or apartment—but not money.

Saren: I was talking to a group of LTNs about this the other day, and they shared some interesting stories about parents helping pay for everything from down payments on houses to family vacations. Some complained about parents giving lots of money to a sibling and less to them for various things. Some complained that parents will say they'll pay for something and then forget about what they said. Some said that parents agree to reimburse them for various things and then forget to send a check, and then it's very awkward having to ask for the money. One person said that he's never asked for or accepted any money from his parents since getting married—he believes in total financial independence after marriage. Most said that they feel like their parents have so much more money than they do right now as they're just getting started, and that they think it's great if their parents want to help out with things. But they get very frustrated when their parents only offer money with strings attached (stuff like "We'll help with a down payment if you buy a house in our neighborhood," "We'd love to help you with graduate school if you want to go for that business degree," or "We'll give you the money if you'll get that ugly green trim painted on your house").

Shawni: How to deal with money after marriage is such a big issue. I feel like it's a continual struggle to find a balance, and I know it's the same with most of my married friends. My parents raised us to understand how important it was to be financially independent. The definition of financially independent to them in no way meant great wealth. It simply meant that when you earn all you have on your own, wholly independently, the joy is so much more heightened than when you have things that are just given to you. My parents (as most parents do) love to talk about the days of their financial struggles (kind of like the walking to school in the snow uphill both ways when they were little). They love to talk about living in Boston as newlyweds with hardly a penny to their name, counting out their coins to buy vegetables at the Haymarket Square farmers' market each Saturday. They always talked about the joy of splurging when they could and not feeling guilty because it was their hard-earned money, not money someone had just flittingly given them. I told my husband before we got married how much I wanted to "struggle" financially. I romanticized about how great it would be to save up and work hard together to make ends meet.

Anyway, with these stories and this philosophy being carefully etched into my brain growing up, I always feel a little guilty when my parents pay for things for my husband and me. Like my parents, we have definitely experienced the "counting-out-our-pennies" days, and to my great surprise, it wasn't as grand as my parents made it out to be! In fact, I didn't like it one bit. My husband had to frequently remind me of my dreams to "struggle" each time I started to feel bad. I didn't like feeling so dependent on parents to help with airline tickets to see them every once in a while, and it was hard to see my husband so worried about financially supporting my dream of having our first baby. It was hard because my parents wanted to help and insisted on helping, but to me it was contrary to everything they had taught us. Of course, we accepted any help we could get, but we still felt guilty about it. In hindsight, just as my parents said, I am glad we struggled so much. We learned so much, and we will understand how to do it better next time if we need to do it again.

I think probably every child/parent relationship has to come to grips with this problem. I know so many parents who almost bribe even married kids with money and trips galore in exchange for a lot of control, and other parents who cut their children off financially the moment they get engaged. One thing that would have helped so much would be to talk much more frankly about financial matters with parents before we got married. I'm not talking about getting financial advice—we got plenty of that, which was great. I'm talking about figuring out exact expectations before the marriage actually took place. My husband and I were the guinea pigs. There was no "formula" for money when we got married. My parents were graciously generous, and we just kind of blindly accepted what they offered (which we so much appreciated) and saved like crazy for the rest. I guess it all comes down to good communication. Kids and parents alike need to be open with what the kids expect help with and what they feel strongly about doing themselves.

Nancy: Financial support from your parents, especially once you're married, can really complicate everything. Part of the reason I let myself wallow for so long in my dad's stifling job-search maze, which I mentioned earlier, was because he was pouring cash into my new out-in-the-world life and I felt like I owed it to him to follow his job-search advice. He did so much for us when we got married. He furnished almost our entire apartment, got his brother to give us a car, got my grandma to buy us a piano, and got his girlfriend to let us live with her for a month when we first moved here. Did I feel indebted? You bet! Although I was grateful for the support, part of the excitement about moving to a new place (newly married) was that we would create our own home, with furniture that we picked and that reflected us. Instead, my husband has to live with heavy, gold, old-man armchairs and a big, poofy bed because that's what my dad picked. I'm so grateful for all he did for us, and I know he mostly just meant to be kind, but it would have worked out a lot better if he'd let us know that he'd like to help, suggested some things he could do for us, and then let us be involved in deciding what would be most helpful.

Saydi: I think my parents have some pretty good ideas on how to handle finances. They have changed their minds about some things here and there, and they've caused some dismay when they've said they'd pay for something and then lost all recollection of that conversation. But we're gradually hammering out a pretty good plan for how they'll help us out with certain things. They'll pay for us and our families to come home once a year for our family reunion in the summer. At other times, when we want to come home for holidays or weddings or whatever, the airfare is up to us. It was two times a year at first when just a few of us had left home—but now that there are so many of us to fly home, once a year seems totally fair. They'll help us with a down payment on a house. They won't "give" us the money to help with a house, but the money they put in will result in their ownership of whatever percentage of the house their money represents. But we get all the leverage. Then when we sell the house, we give them that percentage of the selling price. I like this method a lot. We don't have to feel like we're getting handouts, and my parents simply get a chance to make another investment. I think this is all that my parents have agreed to pay for us. I feel like they'd totally help us out financially if we were ever in dire straits. They've been very kind to slip us a little money or a couple of needed "gifts" here and there if we're going through a hard time, but they never do it in a way that makes us feel guilty.

Saren: It's really important to set up clear expectations about money issues. And it's very important to be consistent—consistent between siblings in a family and consistent in that you say what you'll do and do what you say.

Financial independence following marriage seemed to be a universal value and expectation in most families I spoke with. Kids want and need to be independent financially once they start to create their own family. When times are hard, it's good to know your parents will help out a bit. It's very important to make expectations clear about any financial help you do plan to give your kids once they're married. Among those I talked to, I found that parents frequently help with visits home once a year, down payments on homes, and graduate school expenses. Most people felt grateful and positive about help they received in these areas, provided expectations were clear up front.

R&L: You'll notice how often the "communication and clear expectation" theme comes up from kids. We've stumbled along on some things but now finally have some clarity. We'll explain further in the appendix.

35. What can I do to help when my kids have a crisis with money or have trouble finding a new job?

Charity Jade: Set up an IOU plan where you make them a loan if you can, or help them get a small loan from a bank and then help them set a budget so they can pay it back.

Kenneth W.: Let them work it through. Don't jump in and solve it for them.

Jim R.: Help out, but be sure you use it as a lesson, so they'll learn from it and it won't happen again.

Shawni: One of the hardest times for my husband and me financially was right after we graduated from college. My husband got a job offer from a company in California that we didn't feel good about, and we had a few other leads. But when we graduated, we didn't know what our next step in life was, and neither of us had jobs. So my parents kindly offered to let us stay for free at their little cabin until we figured out what we wanted to do.

The hardest thing for me was to observe how painful it was for my husband to be dependent on my parents; he wanted so much to provide for a family and take the right next step. My parents really tried to be good about it, and not to make us feel bad, but we felt awful. We were stuck. I think it was hard for my dad because he had so much to say about what we ought to do—he kept suggesting people for us to talk to about jobs and telling us his ideas about good careers. Since we were living in his house, completely dependent on him, we felt an obligation to listen and do what he suggested.

It was hard because we didn't have a phone along with not having any money, so we had to be at my parent's house all the time to make phone calls, send letters, and do the things we needed to in order to figure out such an important step. I hated this time because I was trying to be supportive of my new husband at the same time I was trying to heed the advice of my dad and thank him and my mom enough for all they were doing for us. I was totally torn apart about it all. My parents were so nice about it. As much as I could completely tell how frustrated they were for us, they really tried to help us feel better. They even offered us a part-time job at my dad's office while we were there. But it was just horrible for us to feel so dependent.

I don't know exactly what advice I could give to anyone not to get in the same situation. I guess I just want to share with you how newly married kids can feel when they are so dependent. In some ways I felt like my dad was bothered by my husband because he didn't go about getting a job the same way he would have done it. It's just so important to realize that everyone is different.

Denise: My mother can be so pessimistic and unsupportive! One time, I discovered what I had thought was a great home-based business opportunity. I was thrilled at the thought that finally, after wracking my brain and struggling for months, I had found something to support our starving student family while staying home with my two young children. Over the phone, I spilled out all the great details to my mom and told her how perfect a job I thought it would be for me. Immediately she told me every possible thing that could go wrong and "what if this and what if that." My excited, enthusiastic spirit began to suffocate under a thick blanket of skepticism. I just wanted her to be excited—to be proud of me and the challenging yet profitable opportunity I had finally found. I simply wanted some support. Couldn't she stop being a protective mother for just ten minutes and believe in me? Parents don't realize what showing confidence in their children can do for them. If your parents believe in you, you seem to find courage, endurance, and strength to meet challenges and take hold of opportunities. And suddenly you feel intelligent, responsible, and capable. Even if my mom's opinions are almost always the opposite of mine, it would be nice to be supported even a little bit. If parents have real concerns, sure, they should express them, but only after showing support, asking a lot of questions, really listening, and realizing that they are only seeing the situation from the outside, so their concerns may not be valid.

R&L: So, again, find your own "individual-circumstance" balance between assistance and independence. You will find this only together, as you communicate with your kids. Remember that the confidence and trust you show (and your relationship with them) may be more permanently important than any temporary crisis they may have.

36. What sort of relationship should I try to cultivate with my children's spouses?

Charity Jade: Just be their friend. But remember that they've got their own parents, too. Your relationship can't be stronger than between you and your son or daughter or between them and their parents.

Meg L.: I think it's easier, in a way, to have a good relationship with a new son- or daughter-in-law than with your own daughter or son. They respect you more and listen better. And there's not so much baggage.

Marilyn J.: Just treat them like your own children. I think this is what puts everyone at ease. Tell them that's how you think of them and that there will be no secrets or false fronts. Just agree to totally accept them and to be real with each other.

Shawni: My husband has always been so thankful to my mom for how welcoming she was when bringing him into the family. My dad was great too, but from the very beginning my mom has always looked out for Dave and made him feel so at-home and comfortable when he's at our house. She always seems to know what he needs and will even buy extra little things especially for him when we visit. I think this is so important. I was so lucky to marry into my husband's family too. His family has always been so accepting of me. They have a lot more kids married in their family than we do, and they really have the hang of it with the in-laws. It's their family joke that the in-laws become the favorites instead of the kids once they marry into the family. It just feels so good to be so unconditionally accepted and loved.

Dave: I like calling my father-in-law Dad and my mother-in-law Mom. Why not have two dads and two moms? I don't think it diminishes or lessens my love or respect for my own parents.

Rob: Don't ask your son-in-law or daughter-in-law to call you Mom or Dad! My wife's parents asked me to call them Mom and Dad, and I just can't do it. I have a mom and dad—and they aren't my in-laws! I just avoid calling my in-laws anything. It's awkward. Most of my friends call their in-laws by their first names. I think that's a lot more comfortable and appropriate.

Nancy: An issue that has been of great importance to me since getting married is how differently my parents and my husband's parents have viewed the role of our spouses. One of the wonderful things about my parents-in-law is how they've truly adopted me as a friend. They would never counsel me in any sort of condescending way, but they always want to talk with me when we have family calls simply because we enjoy each other. In fact, my husband's mom sometimes calls only to speak with me! I love that. They see me as a true equal, and we can laugh about my husband, Evan, and have that unique bond, but they never assume a parental tone or controlling attitude.

My dad's response to my being married has been quite different. He views Evan as my third parent. For example, at times when my dad has been displeased with my behavior, he has called Evan and complained to him, implying that Evan has disciplinary control over me and seemingly bypassing me because I'm only "the child." On a different bent, whenever Evan is out of town, I get multiple calls from my father daily, because he knows that Evan's not around to "take care" of me, and he feels that he's the default "custodian." He would never dare criticize Evan and treats him on an equal level, as though they are in a chummy, old-boy relationship and have bonded over having responsibility for me. Very weird. I definitely do not encourage this attitude!

Saren: Here is a summary of the suggestions that came up in a discussion I had with several LTNs on this whole in-law subject:

• Set aside time to get to know your new son- or daughter-in-law. Get to know them by doing stuff with them, your spouse, and their spouse (your son or daughter), and also doing stuff with them one-on-one. Examples include going to lunch together, going on a hike together, having them ride with you on a road trip, and taking them to a special event (a ballet, a game, a museum) that represents an interest you share.

• Immediately include new sons- and daughters-in-law on all your family phone lists, e-mail lists, birthday lists, and so on.

• Look for all their good points and be free with compliments. In general, don't say anything bad about your son- or daughter-in-law and his or her family—what's the point?

• When you call your son or daughter, spend a few minutes talking to his or her spouse. Ask about and remember details about his or her job, hobbies, and important events.

• Ask your sons- and daughters-in-law about traditions in their families and ways that their families handle certain things. (Their family may do some great things that you could adopt.)

• Let them call you whatever they're comfortable calling you. Don't insist on "Mom" and "Dad," but welcome it if they are comfortable with it.

• Make a real effort to get to know their parents and families. Point out what you like about their families to your son- or daughter-in-law and to your own family.

R&L: What a joy to get new sons and daughters via the marriage route! As you are gathering through these pages, Dave and Jared are totally like our own sons, and Aja like a lovely fifth daughter. Everything about our family is better and more complete with these three on board. They are true brothers to our sons and sister to our daughters. They are helping to complete our family as well as their new spouses. It's an exciting adventure to get to know each of them and to find the things in them that caused our daughters and son to fall in love!

37. What sort of relationship should I try to cultivate with my child's spouse's parents?

Charity Jade: You're going to be sort of grandparents-in-law with each other—or something like that—so be really nice to each other.

Kate P.: This is really important for your married kids. If you know the other parents well, you can agree on how to do certain things and have a more united front. Also, you can work out (or help your kids work out) how much time your kids will spend with each of you on holidays and such.

Larry L.: Unless you knew them before or live pretty close, it's unrealistic to expect to get to know them very well.

Saren: It's really important to spend time getting to know your child's future in-laws before the wedding. Go to dinner together early in the engagement and work out together some of the issues about who's paying for what at the wedding. Then spend all the time you can getting to know your kids' future in-laws further through inviting them to things, phone calls, e-mails, whatever works for you.

A few weeks before my wedding day, my dad and I made a five-hour drive up to Ashton, Idaho, so that Dad could meet Jared's parents and see the farm where he was raised. My dad's a very busy man, and it meant a lot to me that he'd take the time not just to meet Jared's parents but also to meet them in their element and see this place that was such a part of the Loosli family. My parents and Jared's parents are from different generations (I'm the oldest in my family, and he's the eighth of nine kids). They share a lot of similar experiences in the Church and have both raised very large families. But they've had very different life experiences and careers. I loved seeing my dad so interested in everything about Jared's parents. He asked for and received a full tour of the Loosli farm, asked all sorts of sincerely interested questions about the farm and the family, and showed genuine admiration for this family I was joining. The Looslis were wonderfully hospitable to my dad and clearly enjoyed his company as much as he enjoyed theirs. It was so wonderful for me and Jared to see our parents' mutual admiration for each other and to have them get to know each other.

My mother did a wonderful family dinner and program the night before our wedding—just for my family and Jared's family, so that everyone could casually get to know each other and relax together before the "big day." She made everyone feel so welcome and made sure that everyone got to know everyone else. During the program, she made sure that everyone got a chance to say something about me and about Jared—a great way for everyone to get to know more about us and about everyone else in the room. My mom has made a tradition of having these special night-before-the-wedding parties for both families, and I think it's really helped as two families get linked up.

I've never heard either of my parents say anything remotely negative about my in-laws or my sister- or brothers-in-law. I think it's so important that they've taken the time to get to know the families that we've married into. I think it's vital that they've been so completely positive about the families we've joined.

R&L: Right on! What better way to make good new friends than to have your daughter marry their son. Isn't that how the old kings and queens consolidated and expanded their kingdoms?

38. What should I do if my child complains about his or her spouse to me?

Charity Jade: Say that they should be talking to each other and not to you.

Tom M.: Don't ever talk to one of them about the other one. If one complains about the other, you should probably keep your mouth totally shut. (Maybe your ears, too!) If you do want to talk or try to help, insist that it be with both of them together.

Le Ann D.: Well, you've got to listen, don't you? If they're having problems, they're probably not speaking to each other, so they've got to find someone they can talk to.

Saren: Here's a collection of responses I got from LTNs on this question:

• Don't listen! Cut them off and ask them whether they've shared this concern with their spouse yet. If the answer is "no" tell them to talk to their spouse and then if they still want to talk with you, you'd love to talk.

• Listen, but gently remind them that they chose to marry the other person. Tell him or her that communication between spouses is very important and that marriage isn't a bed of roses, but it can be (and should be) the most wonderful relationship you can have!

• If they have some really serious worries or complaints, perhaps they should talk to a marriage counselor—not to you. They should talk to someone who's really trained to help with marriage problems. You may have some good ideas and advice for them, but you may not have enough information or knowledge to really help them. Plus, you could be perceived by the spouse as messing up the relationship, and things could get sticky. It's better to suggest that they go to a specialist and avoid getting in the middle of things yourself.

39. How do I deal with married kids dividing their time between two sets of parents?

Charity Jade: Make sure you're not demanding more than your share. Try to trade off, and don't bribe them.

Kenneth W.: Well, this always hit us at Christmas and we finally just did the obvious thing: every other year.

Katelin J.: I think the kids have to make their own decisions on this, but it's not a bad idea to talk to the other in-laws before you make invitations. This way you can avoid conflicting schedules and maybe avoid putting your kids in a difficult dilemma where both sets of parents want them at the same time.

Dana: Since we've been married, both my parents and my husband's parents keep "score" of how much time we are spending with the other family. This drives me crazy! They will say, "You spent two weeks with them, why are you only spending one week with us?" Dealing with the demands of a new marriage in addition to new in-laws takes a careful balance and I wish our parents understood that we are trying to be as fair as possible, considering both families' circumstances.

Saren: This is such a hard issue for so many of my friends! Since the issues only get harder for many parents when the grandkids come along, you'll find a lot more information that relates to this question in the next section. Rather than repeat similar information here, I'll put most of my information and comments on this issue in the next section.

40. How often should we communicate with each other now?

Charity Jade: Haven't we had this question before? Nothing's changed. Just keep communicating as often as you can—with both of them!

Jim R.: Probably more than ever. There's more to talk about now.

Betty T.: No, I think less. They've got to "leave you and cleave to their spouse." They need to depend on each other emotionally.

Jim (by Saren): My friend Jim got married a few months ago. Jim's parents and my parents are very good friends, so my parents had dinner with Jim's parents over the holidays, and since I was in town, I joined them. During dinner, Jim's mom, Beth, started talking a little about how she felt about having her first child, Jim, get married. She's always had a special and close relationship with Jim. Ever since Jim left home, Beth had called him almost every day to see what was new in his life and share what was going on in hers. Before the wedding,

Beth had been very apprehensive about how her emotions would hold up once Jim was married and his wife became the "woman in his life."

Anyway, as we talked at dinner, Beth said that she'd called Jim a few times during the first few weeks of his marriage, but when she called and his new wife picked up the phone, Beth sensed some resentment in her voice and worried that she was bothering the newlyweds by calling too much. She resolved not to call Jim anymore, but to let him call her if he wanted to talk. She said this resolution had been very hard for her to keep, but that she'd been really good about it. She hadn't called Jim in almost a month. They'd seen each other a few times, and he'd called a couple of times. But I could tell she was quite hurt that Jim wasn't calling her more and that she really missed their frequent conversations. She said, "This is hard for me, but I know it's what they need right now. They need time to build a great relationship with each other without me calling all the time and butting into their lives. Maybe Jim will call more once the newlywed stage wears off." It made me so sad to see Beth so obviously hurt and sad, and I had to wonder whether Jim had any idea how she felt.

A few days later, I was talking to Jim and asked him how his mom was handling everything. He said it was weird but she didn't seem to want to talk to him much anymore. She was always nice on the phone when he'd call her, but she seemed to want to get off the phone quickly, and she never called him anymore. He was sort of confused by her behavior. "I can't tell whether she's just decided to move on with her life and stop being so involved in mine, or whether she's mad at me for getting married, or whether she just needs some space from me so she can adjust."

Anyway, I suggested that he talk to his mom about the whole thing. But I came away thinking, wow, here are two people whose relationship is being needlessly interrupted because they're misinterpreting each other!

Saren: It's so important to talk about how often you'd each like to communicate and talk about how you feel about the changes going on in your relationship. Don't assume that your kids want to talk to you or don't want to talk to you. Don't assume how often they want to talk or communicate. Ask! There are so many needless hurt feelings and interrupted relationships out there because of misunderstandings and lack of communication about communication!

Phase 3 Review: Backing Off While Staying Close

When your children marry, they're not just under a different roof, they're part of a new and different organization. They're not just playing a road game, they've joined a whole new team. The Bible says it best; they must now leave you and cleave to their spouse. This priority shift, this emotional leaving and cleaving, can be a traumatic transition for your children, even if they have lived away from home for some time. They have just jumped over an invisible barrier out of your immediate family and into their own. You and your children are now parts of each other's extended families.

But that is the amazing thing about families—they expand forever without contracting. They break the law of equal action and opposite reaction because they're always additive and never subtractive. Your children get married and start a new, additional family, yet they are still part of your family, and their spouses are added to your family. Net result: a larger family for you and a new family besides. And so it goes, on and on.

What *does* have to equalize and balance is your time and your priorities. Your family will keep growing, but your time and your mental energy *won't* grow along with it. You'll have the same fixed amount of hours and of effort, and you'll have to spread them thinner and over a larger number of family members. But each of your children will generally need less attention as they become older and more independent, and your grandchildren will have their parents to take care of most of their needs, so although you have more people in your family, you have less day-to-day responsibility for them. And your now-married son or daughter will (and should) devote most of his or her family time to the new spouse and new family.

Once we empty-nesters see this process clearly, and accept it, we can be happy with our evolving role. We can gladly let go of control and responsibility and yet still preserve closeness and confidence. With gratitude and grace, we can step nimbly aside and into the remarkably joyful roles of trusted adviser and friend.

There are a lot of "paydays" or joyous times in parenting, but probably none greater than seeing a faithful, grown child kneeling at an altar of the temple across from a worthy, chosen, eternal companion.

There is a certain relief in our joy—we're glad they made it to this vital place in their lives and in their eternal progression. And along with the relief, we feel a certain release, as though we are released from being our child's closest confidante and most significant eternal relationship. We're never released as parents, of course, and the family kingdom just expands, never divides. Still, this child now "leaves" us and "cleaves" to a new eternal partner and companion. It is about as close as parents ever get to "Well done, thou good and faithful servant."

That unique joy—the deep happiness mellowed by a subtle relief and release—is perhaps the biggest parenting transition of all. We must now support in a different way, respect the sanctity of this new family, and look to our children as respected equals.

If the moment isn't quite that perfect—if the initial marriage isn't in the temple—think of the glass as half full, not half empty. Soak up all the joy that is there and know that no glass is totally full and that the joy is in the ongoing process of filling.

Chapter 12

Phase 4: Children (Grandchildren!)
Can you stop worrying long enough to realize how wonderful this is?

Here is where the vertical or diagonal relationship really seems to become horizontal. Those who made you a parent are now parents themselves. Suddenly they understand certain things and can relate to you with a new commonality. But with grandchildren comes a whole host of new questions.

Here are some of them, along with responses from our ENP and LTN panels.

41. How will our relationship change once our kids have their own children?

Charity Jade: I think you'll be even closer because now they know what it feels like to be a parent. They'll probably turn to you more for advice because being a parent is a scary thing. And they'll appreciate you a lot more!

Marilyn J.: I think you should just be their cheerleader now. They're at the most hectic and busy time of their lives when they have little kids, and they just need to know that we went through it and that it's okay!

Carolyn M.: I think this is the biggest of all the changes. Now our kids are really like us. They understand what we went through with them. It's neat! It opens up whole new areas of commonality and conversation.

Holly: When I had my first child, my parents—and my mother in particular—built on the firm foundation of a relationship they've always had with me. Having a child is a different kind of event from anything else one does in one's life, so some of the things my parents did in our relationship once I had a child were new. But the way in which those things were done was the same pattern they had always followed—giving me complete and total support, sharing in my excitements and anxieties, respecting me as my own person, and trusting me in the conduct of my own life.

Our relationship has changed in that we now have a very strong element of common experience that simply did not exist before. My mother has used that common experience to offer support and encouragement to me as I have tried to settle into my own role of being a mother—a process that has not been easy for me. I am a person who guards and values my personal time, and I found the extraordinary claims my first child made on my time to be a frustrating trial rather than a joyful experience. Instead of telling me to quit complaining or get on with life, my mother listened to me for many hours over the space of seventeen months as I tried to come to terms with what it means to be a mother. She was able to listen and counsel in a way that uniquely met my needs and brought us closer to each other than we've ever been before.

As I've had children, my relationship with my parents has changed, not only because we now have the common experience of raising children, but also because I now understand more what was entailed in raising me, specifically, as their child. Although my mother has counseled me on countless other subjects, such as scholastic and career issues, when she counseled me on mothering, I not only felt like I was going to some specialist in the field of parenting in general, but also to a specialist about me as a unique and individual parent. There is something about my mother's advice on being a mother that feels at once interesting on a general level as well as intensely personal. It's that combination in my mother's advice of both theoretical parenting, and the fact that she has experience in being my own mom, that makes me feel closer to her when I apply that advice.

Aja: Even though I don't have kids of my own yet, I'm sure my mom will answer my questions and give me advice when I need it, but I dearly hope she will give me (for I think I will dearly need it) unending support and affirmation of my potential for being a good parent. It is when I really love myself that I feel most receptive to the positive influences of my life, current and past.

Shawni: Right now I need a fine-line balance from my parents. I need them to continue being the amazing grandparents they are to my children. I have never seen more attentive and more in-love grandparents, which results in grandchildren who idolize them. I can't even describe how amazing it is to watch someone love your kids almost as much as you do. But at the same time, I need them to be aware of me as a separate entity from my children. Sometimes I feel like I'm turning into "Max and Elle's mom" to them instead of their daughter— my own separate person.

My dad recently came out to visit, and we had a great time with the kids as usual. But something started to really bother me. We had decided to take a trip to an aquarium about an hour away, and I was excited for the trip so I could talk to my dad for a little while in the car— I've had some of my best talks with him on road trips. I figured the kids would fall asleep and we'd have a great talk. I was sad when the kids started dozing off that my dad started dozing off too. When we had lunch and the kids were involved in their food, I saw it as another opportunity to get some adult talking in with my dad. But he answered all my questions with one or two words and focused on the kids.

It just made me sad because I still need to have intellectual adult conversations with my dad. I love to talk about his views on politics, on his latest book, on the world in general. Over lunch, my dad talked about the stimulating conversations he had with my single sister he visited in New York before he came to our house, and he went on a long drive and had a long conversation with my single brother who lives close by the night before. I guess I just wanted to have a little time to talk to him too. I'd still choose the "involved grandparents" role over the "stimulating conversationalist" role at the drop of a hat—I wouldn't trade the love my dad gives my kids for anything. But I think it's so important for parents to stay in touch with their children as their children just as much as it is to stay in touch with the new parents their children have become.

Saren: In some ways, once they have their first child, your adult children will need you more than they have in years. They'll have questions about diaper rashes and spitting up and sleeping schedules. They'll want you to be on hand frequently to ooh and ah over the most beautiful children in the world. They'll want you to approve of them as parents, and they'll probably want to help you define your role as a grandparent as that role evolves. They'll ask for quite a bit of advice, and you'll doubtless think of lots of unsolicited advice you could give. You may find that you talk more frequently and have a closer relationship than you have in years. But as Shawni points out, it's also important to continue to show interest in and encourage your children's interests and abilities and activities that are not child-related. When you talk or get together, I think it's a good idea to always ask at least a few questions of your kids that have to do with something other than your grandchildren!

42. How much should I help with my grandchildren? Can we draw appropriate boundaries on our involvement and dependency on each other if my kids live near me and we see each other a lot?

Charity Jade: Offer to help out when needed, but not all the time.

Kate P.: You have to set boundaries. Otherwise you'll be babysitting the grandkids every day, and you won't have a life. Just tell them what days you're available and what days you're not, or set up a schedule in advance. Don't allow the kids to just be dropped off at Grandma's whenever!

Betty T.: Wow, I can't believe I'm ever going to worry about that. No grandkids yet, but I think I'm going to have to fight for my time with them. I want to be there for them whenever they need me. Nothing I'd like better than to be the surrogate mom!

Dawn (by Saren): Dawn recently had her first child. She lives just a few blocks from her mother. When she found out she was pregnant and shared the news with her mother, she was surprised to find that her mother wasn't exactly doing cartwheels. It turns out that her mother had seen a lot of friends really "lose their lives" when they became grandmothers. They started taking care of their grandkids all the time, filling in constantly for the parents when the grandkids needed something and the parents were busy with other things.

Dawn's mother sat down with her early in the pregnancy and basically laid down the law. Grandkids couldn't drop by unannounced; there'd be no spur-of-the-moment babysitting; all babysitting would have to be set up well in advance; and there'd be no more than one babysitting session a week. The kids would be Dawn's responsibility, not her mother's.

Dawn was really crushed by the whole discussion. She feels really guilty whenever she asks her mom to help out in any way—she always tries to get friends to help out and only asks her mom for help as a last resort. She feels like her mother views her baby as an imposition and says, "That's just the saddest thing!" Dawn said she totally understands the need for clear expectations and limits—and she certainly never expected that her mother would do some of the things that her mother adamantly said she wouldn't do. She just wishes that her mother had approached everything in a different, more gentle way. In her words, "I just wish my mom could have been a little more excited about this baby before getting into her concerns about everything. I want my daughter to be a joy to my mother, and I hate to see my mother missing out on her babyhood—but after all my mother said, I just feel awkward about suggesting that she be involved in anything to do with the baby."

Shawni: I think my mother-in-law does a great job with this one. She lives in Mesa, Arizona, and so do four of her children with families of their own. There are so many grandchildren around that she could easily be overwhelmed with babysitting constantly. But she seems to have a perfect balance. Every time we go to visit, I wonder how she divides her time so well among so many. I don't know the details—but she and the families there seem to have an understanding about babysitting that they have obviously discussed and feel good about. Her kids don't depend on her to be there for them all the time because she is really busy with so many other things. I think it would be so easy to have your life just turn into full-time grandchild caregiver in that situation, but she has great hobbies and talents that she works on that are so important for her well-being. I think she has set times each week when she helps out with the grandchildren, which her children appreciate very much, but I think the most meaningful thing she does is plan out specific fun things to do with the grandchildren.

She schedules things like "grandma sleep-overs" and has an annual "Grandma's Christmas party" where she has all the grandkids over to make sugar cookies and go caroling to the neighbors. She makes sure she has individual time with each child and knows them so well, yet she balances her time well enough so that she has time to do the things she feels she needs to for her personal growth as well.

Saren: Again, it's about expectations and communication. After reassuring your kids about how much you love them and your grandkids, explain any concerns you have about grandparenting. Don't get taken advantage of, and don't get taken for granted. But also, don't miss chances to be with those kids! Ask about any concerns your children have about your new role. Decide together what the bounds will be.

43. How can I be involved in my grandkids' lives if they live far away from me?

Charity Jade: Call them if they're old enough to talk, and write them if they're old enough to read. And go visit them whenever you can, or send their aunt to see them (me!).

Katelin J.: That's our vacation nowadays. I don't want to see beaches or volcanoes; I just want to go see my grandkids.

Carolyn M.: I think grandparents have a special license to spoil their grandkids. I try to send them some little thing every month and to write little notes and just constantly tell them how fantastic and perfect they are!

Peter J.: We take grandkids on vacation with us. Their parents can't afford to go some of the places we do, and since we're retired, we go pretty often. We like to take the grandkids one or two at a time so we can really get to know them.

Jack (by Saren): Jack's grandparents have a tradition of taking all their grandkids on a special trip when they are between ten and twelve years old. Every summer, any grandkids who fall into this age range and who have not yet been on this trip meet up at their grandparents house, load up their big RV, and head out on a two-week history trek. For months in advance, the kids work with their grandparents via e-mail and phone calls and meetings at family reunions to choose a part of the country they'd like to visit and map out the sites they will see. They've done the Civil War sites, the Revolutionary War sites, and a Colonial America tour so far. Jack has wonderful memories of the time he spent with his cousins (who've never lived near him) and his grand-parents, learning together, playing games together, planning together, and just being together.

Sara (by Saren): My in-laws are really missing out on my kids' childhood, and it's pretty sad. They live abroad, but they have the means to visit a couple of times a year. When they come, they stay for at least two weeks. So, theoretically, they should be able to spend some quality time with their two little grandsons (ages one and four) and build some good memories with them. They have the money to stay in a hotel, but they always stay with us because they'll "have more time with the grandkids that way." But while they're here, they get up early in the morning, plan out a bunch of things they want to do that day, and take off on their own for the whole day. They play with the kids for a few minutes in the morning and sometimes a half an hour before the kids' bedtime. Last time they were visiting, my four-year-old begged them to take him to the park, and they refused, say-ing they already had plans for the day and that they'd be back to play for a bit in the evening, as usual. I really don't understand them. I don't know what to say to my kids when they ask, "Why don't grandma and grandpa want to play with us?" My husband's pretty bugged about the whole thing too—but he says they'll just get in a fight if he tries to talk to them about it. I hate to say it, but I hate it when they come. More people in the house, more cooking and cleaning for me, but no more attention or memories for my kids or our family!

Shawni: My parents are amazing at being wonderful, long-distance grandparents. We live all the way across the country, but we still see them quite a lot. My parents have to travel a lot, and they've perfected the art of routing every possible trip through Washington, D.C., so they can stop and see us. (Did you know you can get to Dallas from Salt Lake City by going through Washington, D.C.?) I really appreciate their efforts, and so do the kids.

There is nothing better to me than watching how much my parents love my children when we are able to be together. I will never forget the picture in my mind of one night when I was with my dad with my first newborn. He was so sweet with that baby, and so in love with him. I remember that he just sat there and didn't take his eyes off Max for half an hour. He had a big, loving smile on his face and a little tear in his eye—contemplating what sort of boy and man this baby would become. He and my mom watch my children so intently and concentrate on them so much that they really know them inside and out. They give them undivided attention and make them feel so special.

My mom has come to stay with us for at least a week with each newborn baby and she cleans our whole house, stocks the fridge, cooks gourmet meals, and even gets up with the baby in the night. She always sends us the most thoughtful things, too, that make me realize how much she thinks about us and loves us. My kids get so excited when I tell them that "Gamma" and "Gampa" are coming! There's definitely a strong bond between them—and I'm sure it comes from the efforts my parents make to visit as often as possible and to make every visit really special for the kids.

Saren: It's wonderful to see the bond that my parents have with my little one-year-old son. He's just a baby, and we live far from my parents, but when we get together, I can just tell that Ashton is so happy with his grandparents. He'll just sit there in my dad's arms and stare at him with this look of interest and love on his face—I've never seen Ashton look at anyone else that long or that hard. My dad loves playing with him and carefully observing all his little personality traits and interests. I love hearing my dad tell me about his observations after spending a few hours with Ashton. And when we're at their house, Ashton adores the way my mom talks to him and lets him play with all the big spoons and "safe" utensils in her kitchen. She's always giving him a little extra love and attention and buying him great little things that quickly become his favorite things. My parents make the most of every little bit of time they get with my son. Plus, they ask about him all the time, "talk" to him on the phone when they call, and send him nice little things he might like. It's so early in my son's life, but already he's got a firm foundation of a good relationship with his grandparents.

Some grandparents have the means and the desire to do a lot of traveling, so it's easy for them to visit their grandchildren quite often. Some young families (but not many) have the means and the ability (depending on the ages of the children and how well the kids travel) to take their kids to visit grandparents a few times a year. But no matter what the situation may be, everyone I talked to agreed that nothing can replace "face time" with grandkids—especially when they're little. There's an almost magical bond that can develop very easily between grandparents and their grandkids—with even just a few weekends a year spent together.

I guess the biggest suggestions to grandparents that I heard was simply to visit as often as possible (within reason!) and to make visits really count by spending quality one-on-one time with grandkids (reading stories, sharing memories, doing crafts, going on little outings) and planning special, memorable activities to do with the grandkids, both with and without the parents. (A "special, memorable" activity can be something as simple as a trip to the ice cream shop or the zoo.)

44. What sort of financial support (if any) should I offer my children and grandchildren?

Charity Jade: Give them gifts but not money. But you could start a college fund and let it grow.

Tom M.: I think anything you do for the grandkids has got to be in coordination and agreement with your kids (their parents). You've got to support them in their stewardships of their own family. Let them ask for what they need. Or, if you have an idea, clear it with them.

227

Lonnie P.: Vacations are the best idea, if you can afford it. They don't injure your kids' pride or undermine their independence. Nice vacations aren't a feasible expenditure for your kids at this point, so they are so appreciative, and they can use their own funds for more practical things. Plus, vacations are the most relaxed atmosphere to really communicate and to have quality time with grandkids.

Jared: My grandfather put a few hundred dollars for me into some promising stocks when I was born. He did this for all of his grandkids. That money grew and grew. We just used a chunk of it to put a down payment on our first home. I'm so grateful that my grandfather had the forethought and generosity to put some money out there for me! All my life, I watched that money grow. Every couple of months, I'd get a statement showing how my money was growing, and my dad would go over the statement with me. Through this experience, I learned a great deal about the way that saving and investing can make your money grow.

When our son Ashton was born, my dad put some money into some stocks for him. We plan on helping Ashton follow what happens with this money as he grows up. We'll go over statements with him and help him make choices about moving money around. Someday he'll be able to use this money for college or a home or whatever he needs. I think that if grandparents have any resources to put into investments for their grandkids, it's a really good thing to do.

Kristen (by Saren): Kristen has three young children. She works part time, and her husband has a good full-time job, so they're doing quite well financially. So I was surprised the other night when we were chatting with a group about this question and Kristen shared that her parents send her $150 a month. She said she loves having a little "extra" money to spend on "little luxuries like manicures or expensive shoes or a beautiful sweater or a cute outfit for one of the kids." Everyone in the group expressed surprise that Kristen's parents still send her money. She said she's always sort of assumed that most parents send their kids a little stipend every month and was surprised that no one else in the group got money from their parents.

Kristen had to leave fairly early that evening, and after she left, everyone was commenting about her situation. "I can't believe they send her money—sure, my parents sent me money in college, but come on, it's weird to keep sending money forever." "I wouldn't mind if my parents sent me money!" "I wouldn't take money from my parents at this point in my life—it just seems wrong." "I'd feel indebted if I took money from my parents. I like feeling totally financially independent. What I do with my money is totally up to me." "I like it when my parents slip us a little money or send us something we've been needing when they know things are a bit tight for us—but every month, that's too much. I'd feel like my parents had no confidence in my ability to make and handle money." "Hey, it's their money—let them give it out!"

Saren: In talking about this question, most people agreed that kids should be financially independent of their parents once they've established their own family. But most agreed that financial help with the following was helpful and quite common:

- Down payment on a home.
- Trust funds/college funds for grandchildren.
- Help with graduate school tuition.
- Help with plane tickets to visit home.
- Paying for vacations with parents.
- Helping in a time of crisis.

Other than these things, most felt they shouldn't expect or ask for financial help.

45. How can I help my kids be better parents to my grandkids (without offending them or making them feel like I'm forcing my ideas on them)?

Charity Jade: Once again, let them know you want them to call you if they have any parenting questions or problems. But remember, their kid is different than they were when they were your kid.

Kenneth W.: Don't even offer advice unless you are asked. This is such a sensitive area.

Winifred R.: Your kids are going to follow the example you set as a parent whether they want to or not—that's just how it seems to go. So if there is something specific you wish you'd done differently, tell them about it. Then you are criticizing yourself and not them!

Shawni: Each new catastrophe I faced with my children seemed to be something my parents could have done blindfolded with their hands tied behind their backs. I got so frustrated at first, wondering how they just naturally had all the answers. But my parents were so sweet about it when I got frustrated. They always treated me like I was my own expert and like I was just doing a phenomenal job as a parent. They were quick to explain that they have been parents for thirty years and claim to be amazed at what I have been able to do in only three years. Of course, this is pure flattery, because I have so very much to learn, but it sure made me feel better! Their unquestioning approval of me as a parent has meant so much to me. Let's face it, all parents of children with children are going to know much more about a lot of things and are going to have so many answers for their kids in the parenting area. I just think it's so great when parents can build up their new-parent child by not pushing too much advice on them and helping them realize their ultimate parenting potential.

Saren: The other day my dad made a comment that really annoyed me. He said, "I don't think you're feeding Ashton enough. It seems like he's ready to eat a lot more when you stop feeding him. It seems like he's always starving!" Ashton's got to be about the world's biggest eater for a one-year-old. And no matter how much we feed him, he'll always take more, and he'll always act upset when the food is gone. And then when he's thoroughly overeaten, he'll throw up. Over the months, I've figured out how much food seems to work well for him, and I've been trying so hard to make sure he eats right and gets plenty without getting overstuffed. So given this background, it really hurt my feelings when my dad made this comment. It was just a little thing, and maybe he didn't mean much by it, but somehow I came away with the sense that he thought I was a mean mother who underfeeds her little boy, and I felt upset that I'd been judged so unfairly. I think it would have been a lot better if Dad had just asked me some questions about Ashton's eating habits—then I would have told him the whole story, and he'd realize how well Ashton was eating and how hard I was trying to do everything right.

This little example points out a few things. First, your kids can be so easily hurt by any little negative remark you make about what they're doing with their children. Second, it's so important to ask questions before jumping to conclusions. Third, it's good to realize that every child and every situation is different. What worked for you when you were raising your children may not be the right thing for your kids and their kids.

Jackie: My parents grew up in Taiwan, and a lot of the parenting practices that are common over there are not common over here. My mom means well, I'm sure, but she causes so many problems and makes me worried. When my daughter was born, she came over to my house and told me that all the stuff I'd bought for my baby was wrong—wrong sort of clothes, wrong diapers, wrong bathtub. She told me that putting the baby in the baby swing would turn her stupid. She said that strollers were a waste of money and that babies were better off in a baby sling. She insisted that babies should eat ground-up table food by the time they're six weeks old and that bananas and honey would help them sleep (when my doctor said I had to wait until four months for solid foods and told me that honey was dangerous for infants). When she'd hold my daughter, she'd bounce her around so hard on her knee that I was worried about shaken-baby syndrome. All her ideas about baby care and a lot of her ideas about child rearing just don't match up to what I've read or been taught and what my husband and I want to do with our baby. She's very offended that I haven't taken much of her advice. In Taiwan, children are supposed to respect their parents' wishes, no questions asked. She's only visited twice since the baby was born because I think she's offended. I know she grew up with these traditions and that they are ingrained in her, but it makes me so sad that she can't be the sort of grandma I always hoped my daughter would have!

I've talked to friends about my mom, and while they don't have such extreme traditions to deal with, they have shared lots of issues that have come up with their own parents. One friend's mom insisted that her newborn should be slathered in lotion after every bath when the doctor said that lotion was bad and that newborn skin should naturally flake off until it grows accustomed to the air after being in water for so long in the uterus. Another mother accused her daughter of condemning her newborn to misery after refusing to put baby powder on his bottom after changing him to keep him dry. With the stay-dry diapers they have now and the research that's been done on how dangerous it is for babies to inhale talcum powder, my friend didn't want to use powder. There are many more examples of grandparents, especially grandmothers, who insist that their daughters should do things the way they were instructed to do them when they were young mothers—but times have changed, new research has been done, new products are out there. I guess most mothers just want to share knowledge with their kids, but they should realize that there's important new information out there now about babies, and they shouldn't be so pushy!

Denise: I have always done things differently than my mother did, and the way I do things seems either intimidating to her or revolting—I haven't quite figured it out. I feel a great lack of support from her, and often I wonder if she thinks I'm an idiot. I guess having a bachelor's degree, completing a mission, being married, and having children of my own still doesn't make me very experienced or credible. I remember one time when my husband and I and our two-month-old daughter moved into my parents' home for a few months so we could save money for a home. Every time I stepped into the kitchen, it seemed that a smorgasbord of unsolicited opinions was being served. I had shared with my mom that I had some concerns about vaccinations and talked about how I was thinking about holding off on vaccinations for my baby daughter until more research was completed or she was just a little older and more able to ward off any side effects. I had really felt worried about the vaccinations and was doing lots of research. Anyway, before I could even explain my concerns, my mother began to tell me horrific stories of children she grew up with who contracted polio or whooping cough. She used statements like: "You'd better ———" or "If you ——— you'll regret it for the rest of your life" or "Boy, if I were you . . ." I just cringed and felt like screaming: "Who do you think I am? Don't you realize that this is my baby, and of course I want the best for her? I'm not eleven years old! I'm not an idiot!" It just would have been nice to have a few words of caution along with a few words of support. It's a lot easier to listen if your parents express confidence in your abilities and assure you that you are doing a good job and that you are obviously trying to do the best for your kids before throwing out their advice and opinions.

Saren: Ask questions a lot. As you ask and listen, your kids may ask you for your ideas and advice. The best time to offer advice is when you're asked! Assume the best of your kids—they're probably trying to do the very best they can for their kids, just as you tried to do your best for them. Praise your kids for everything good you see in their parenting. Model child-care techniques that you think might help them while you're with them and their kids. Respect the fact that they're the parents, and they have the final say. Realize that what worked for you may not be right for them and their children.

How much can I help with the spiritual development of my grandkids? What if the parents don't want me to be involved this way?

R&L: There is nothing sweeter than teaching the gospel to grandkids. Telling them Bible and Book of Mormon stories, teaching them principles, asking them questions, and getting them in discussions—what could be better?

The only caution is to coordinate what you're doing with the parents and make sure the child knows that his or her parents are their *main* teachers and that you are just helping out.

If one of the parents is inactive or not a member, be sure you discuss what you want to do and have their support for it. "Tone" what you teach whatever way you need to so that the parent doesn't feel undercut, left out, or bypassed in any way.

46. What is the biggest difference between parenting and grandparenting?

Charity Jade: Parents influence their kids every day. Grandparents just come in and out and spoil the kids. You can do grandparenting, but don't try to do parenting, too.

Peter J.: The biggest single difference is that you can send the kids home!

Kate P.: One big difference I'm hoping for, although it hasn't happened to me yet, is that grandparents have more time and don't have to be in a hurry. I want to be able to sit down and just be with my grandkids—really listen to them and not have to rush off to the next thing!

Shawni: Parents should provide for all their kids' basic needs—physical, emotional, mental, and so on. Parents should be the ones who make the major decisions for their kids—from what they should eat as a baby to when they should be potty trained to what school they should attend to what lessons they should take. Parents are the primary caregivers, educators, and decision-makers in their children's lives. Grandparents should be sort of like the "icing on the cake."

Grandparents can add so many wonderful "extras" to their kids lives—more outings, more fun, more love, more support. They can also help reinforce the things that their children are trying to teach their grandkids, encouraging them to listen to their parents, sharing personal stories that help kids understand why they should do or not do certain things, listening to them when they just need someone else to listen, offering them more of an "outsider's" view on issues going on in their lives or with their parents.

Saren: Many of the LTNs I talked with vehemently stated that grandparents should never disagree with something that they (the parents) have said in front of the children. They should do everything they can to be on the children's side and on the parents' side when there's a disagreement, helping kids to see both sides of an issue and understand what their parents are trying to do. If grandparents have issues with the way their children are handling or not handling certain things, they should bring up these issues by asking questions in a caring way and in a private setting.

Most LTNs also agreed that it's great if grandparents want to help out with some of the needs and wants of their grandchildren (i.e. paying for lessons or college, buying them clothes sometimes, setting up a trust fund for them), but they should always coordinate any help they offer with them. The parents are in charge. The grandparents are loving helpers who step in as needed and requested and desired.

47. What should I do if my kids don't want me to do the things I'd like to do for their kids?

Charity Jade: Try to lay off on the stuff they don't want you to do but I think presents should be okay.

Kenneth W.: Clear everything with your kids. If they don't want you to do it, don't!

Carolyn M.: Like I said, I think I have a license to spoil my grandkids, and I just can't help myself. I guess I'll just keep doing it and repent later.

Karen (by Saren): My friend Karen was complaining to me the other day about her in-laws. Karen has three kids, ages five, three, and one. She and her husband, Dan, are really health-conscious people—they exercise a lot, and they try to eat right. They limit the amount of sugar and empty calories their kids get in their diet—focusing instead on whole grains, fruits and vegetables. On Saturdays or on holidays, the kids can have candy. Karen was saying that it's really hard when they visit Dan's parents because his parents love candy and treats. They always stock their house with candy—especially when they know the grandkids are coming. Dan's dad always has pockets full of butterscotch candies and loves handing out candy every time a kid gets near him. Dan's mom puts candy dishes full of treats on every available surface in the house and offers the kids candy whenever they do something for her or whenever she wants them to read a book with her. After a day at Dan's parents' house, the kids are on serious sugar highs, and it's hard to get them to settle down and go to bed. Plus, it really bothers Karen that Dan's parents seem to be using candy as a way to "buy" the kids' affection and bribe them to do things. They want their kids to spend time with their grandparents because it's fun, not because they get treats for doing it.

Karen said that she really doesn't know what to do. She wants the kids to spend time with their grandparents, but she's really uncomfortable with her kids having all that sugar and associating their grandparents so strongly with candy. Dan did try to talk to his parents a while back. It was a short conversation because Dan felt that he offended his parents right off the bat by even bringing up the subject. His parents said they felt it was good for kids to get special treats when they're with their grandparents and that the candy made their visit more special. Besides, "a little sugar can't really hurt kids, Son."

After recently coming home from a four-day stay with Dan's parents, the kids kept on begging for candy every day. Karen said, "It really bothers me that we've worked so hard to help these kids be healthy and enjoy healthy foods and do things without bribes and all that—and Dan's parents just don't care. They're so set in their ways!"

Dallin: I was so mad the other day! My eight-year-old daughter, Marissa, came up to me and said, "Grandpa said I can take gymnastics and I might even be in the Olympics some day!" She was so excited. Her grandpa (my dad) had told her he'd take her down to sign up for lessons next week as long as my wife and I said it was okay. Several of Marissa's friends have been in gymnastics since they were three, so several of them are excellent gymnasts now. Marissa did take one gymnastics class when she was four, but she didn't like it much and didn't seem to have a lot of talent in that direction. Marissa has lots of talents, but even though we put her in ballet and jazz and tried the gymnastics thing, she just has a hard time making her body do anything complicated. Okay, so she's not the most coordinated kid. Who cares? She's a great little flutist, she's been in plays and choirs, and she excels in school. We've tried to get her over disappointments about dance and gymnastics by helping her excel in other areas, and it's worked great. Sure, she mentions from time to time that she wishes she could dance like so-and-so or do gymnastics like so-and-so.

Anyway, I've told my parents about all this—but I guess they weren't listening. I'm sure Marissa just mentioned something about how cool it would be to be able to do gymnastics and my dad jumped in there and offered lessons. I'm sure Marissa said she wasn't good at it, and I can just picture my dad saying, "Sweetheart, a beautiful, smart girl like you can do anything she sets her mind to do," and then he probably went on about her being in the Olympics. I know my dad means well, but I wish he'd talk to me about stuff like this before getting my daughter's hopes up. What am I supposed to do now? Tell Marissa that her grandpa's wrong and no matter how hard she tries, she'll probably never be an Olympic gymnast? Let her take some lessons and be in the class with all the three-year-old beginners? I'm sure that'd make her feel just great. This is just like when he bought her a kitten without talking to us. "She just wanted it so much, Dallin! Who can say no to that cute little face." My wife's allergic to cats. The whole thing was a mess. Parents need to ask their kids before they do anything or offer anything to their grandkids. It's just safer that way!

Saren: From these stories, it's clear how important it is to talk to your kids about virtually anything you want to give your grandkids. Your kids have the final say about what's best for their children. Don't assume that anything is "no big deal." It's much safer to ask.

48. How often should I talk and write to my grandchildren?

Charity Jade: Often! As much as you can. You should play a really big middle-size role in who they become.

Carolyn M.: In many cultures of the world the grandparents teach and influence children more than the parents. This is not a bad idea—grandparents are probably wiser and more experienced. Just communicate and coordinate with your kids about what you'll each do for the grandkids.

Shawni: It means the world to them and to us. I think it's good to set up a regular time every week when you talk to your kids and grandkids—that way everyone has their expectations straight and it really happens.

Saren: When I turned five, I started receiving letters every other week from a character called "Ellsworth Elephant." Ellsworth wrote me all about his family and how excited he was to be starting school soon. He told me what he was scared of and what he was excited about. I wrote back to him (with help from my parents) and had so much fun corresponding with an elephant just my age who went through so many of the same things as me! It was my grandma sending me the Ellsworth letters. She's done that with every grandchild once they turn five. I still remember the joy of finding a letter from Ellsworth in the mailbox and having my mom read it to me! I think it's wonderful for grandparents to think of something like this—something sort of magical and special—to do for their grandkids. When I grew out of the Ellsworth stage, my grandmother continued to write me, always telling me how special I am to her and pointing out what she appreciates about me. I've always treasured these letters. There's nothing like getting a special letter in the mail, addressed just to you, when you're a little kid. Whether your grandkids live close or far away, write to them regularly—they'll be so excited to get your letters! Reading your letters and writing back to you is a great way to help your grandkids work on their reading and writing skills in a fun way. (By the way, all of this applies to e-mail too—but letters are especially exciting for little kids!)

John: My grandparents never seemed to want to talk to me. They'd always try to get off the phone as quickly as possible, and I thought it was because they didn't want to talk. But now I realize it was because they were worried about the expense of long-distance calls—they were very frugal people. When we'd get together, they had all the time in the world for me, and I loved being with them. But we only got to see them a couple times a year, and it would have been nice to be able to talk to them and connect with them on the phone during the many months we were apart.

Now that I have kids of my own, I want them to be able to talk to their grandparents on a regular basis. My wife and I have set up a time every Sunday evening when we'll talk to her parents and my parents and have the kids talk to them. Just before the call is due, we talk to our kids about what they want to tell Grandma and Grandpa this week and have them come up with some good questions to ask them. I think these calls have been great for the kids—they're sharing their lives with their grandparents and practicing good conversation skills.

Saren: Set up regular times to talk to your grandkids. Ask your kids what's going on in their lives so you can think of appropriate questions to ask them. Write them regularly. Getting mail or e-mail can be such a highlight in a child's life. Coordinate with your kids about how often you should communicate so that everyone's comfortable and knows what to expect.

49. How often should I get together with my married kids? How often should I encourage them to come home? How should we handle family reunions and holiday get-togethers once our family gets bigger and more spread out? What if they want to have Christmas on their own with their spouse and kids?

Charity Jade: Your grandchildren are cute and you want to see them. But remember, they have other grandparents and another side of their family.

Peter J.: As time goes by, the only reliable way to get them all together is to make the reunion so compelling and attractive that they choose to come to it over their other vacation or holiday alternatives.

Pam J.: You've got to try to be flexible here and to leave a lot of initiative to the kids.

Shawni: Your family is always your family. No matter how many other people join the family (in-laws, grandchildren), there is still a family unit to prioritize. Now that I am married with my own family, I feel I need to put their needs as my top priority. I need to be in tune enough with them that I know what they need from me, and I need to look out for them for my entire life. When my children grow up and have their own children, I hope I will understand their need to put their new families as their first priorities. I think it will be my husband's and my own responsibility to set up family reunions, visit our children, and keep in contact with them as much as humanly possible. But it will also be important for us to respect their freedom as their own families too. No matter what happens, I will continue to nurture and love them in every way I can. I think that is the role of a parent in keeping a family intact. I think that is exactly what my parents have tried to do for us so far. They gather us together twice a year and make sure everyone can make it. They make sure we have time to discuss life and really connect once again after being apart for a while. I have friends who are frustrated because their parents have dropped the ball on that, and they are stuck with the logistics of making sure reunions take place. I really think this should be the parents' responsibility.

Saren: Wow, holidays get pretty hectic when you have two families to juggle! Since my parents and my husband's parents live within a five-hour drive from each other, we feel like we should really try to get to both families for holidays. This is okay over Christmas, when we typically have a week or more—but Thanksgiving is tricky, and so are other quick weekend trips. We try to keep things even, visiting each side of the family as equally as possible, and so far, we've been successful. Our families seem to have had a pretty equal number of special events and reunions, which makes it easy to be fair. We try to trade off visiting our different families for the major holidays, and our families have been understanding about these trade-offs.

I have lots of friends whose parents can be very demanding of their children's holiday time and very hurt if their kids don't visit as often as they'd like. I think it's important to realize that your kids typically have about two weeks of vacation from work out of the whole year. If they go to family reunions with both families during the summer, that can eat up all their vacation time right there—without saving any time for their own Christmas or their own little family vacation. It's great to invite them home all the time and make sure they know they're always welcome for holidays, but be understanding if they can't always make it for everything you'd like them to come home for.

Susan: My parents and my husband's parents both live within an hour's drive from us. A few years back, my parents decided that the 26th of December would be Christmas for them. They saw no reason why they couldn't just move Christmas back a day so that all their loved ones could be with them every year and still be with their in-laws or have their own family Christmas on December 25. The holidays have been so much nicer since then! My husband's parents have this major feast on Christmas Eve and love doing special stuff with the grandkids on Christmas morning. We tried to trade off going to see my parents and my husband's parents on Christmas Eve and morning, but we felt that we were running all over and never really pleasing everyone. Now there aren't any conflicts, and my kids certainly don't complain about having Christmas twice every year!

Debbie: We live near almost all of my family members and almost all my husband's family. We see each other a lot, and my kids are great friends with their grandparents, aunts and uncles, and cousins, which I love. But sometimes I feel like all I do is go to family events! It seems like pretty much every week we have a baptism, a graduation, a track meet, a basketball game, or a Cub Scout court of honor that we're supposed to attend for some family member! We really want to be supportive of everyone's important events, but we don't know how to juggle it all. I don't really have a solution, but we have to do something pretty soon. I don't want to offend anyone. Maybe we need to get together with some other family members and talk about this issue so we can see how people feel about everyone making it to everyone's important events. Sometimes I think my little nieces and nephews don't even notice that we're there for their special events, which is sort of sad since we have to make such colossal efforts to get to some of these things!

Mark: My family is really close, and we seem to get together all the time. We have big-deal reunions—usually a cruise or a trip somewhere great. My wife's family, on the other hand, is smaller, and they're content with getting together every couple of years. She has two brothers who are much older than her, and her parents are a lot older. She's never felt like she has a whole lot in common with any of them. When they do get together, they like to go to movies and play silent games like chess or Scrabble. Frankly, neither I nor my wife really cares to get together with her family—and the kids complain about visiting them. "It's so boring." "What are we going to do there?" "Do we have to go for three whole days?" It's pretty sad, I guess.

My wife says sometimes that she feels bad that we're so uneven in how much time we spend with our families, and she wonders if it bothers her family—but they've never said anything. I know it's really important to them that we visit at least once a year. They do try to plan some things that the kids might like—but they're pretty out of touch with their needs. Last year they took us to this petting zoo—obviously designed for toddlers—and my kids are eight and ten. The kids thought it was pretty lame, although they were nice about it (we threatened them). Anyway, I guess we'll just keep things the way they are—we don't know what to do. I hate to admit it, but deep down, I guess

I'm glad that we don't need to visit Marie's parents more often—it means we can use all our vacation time doing stuff with my family!

Saren: Here are the top responses I got in a discussion with LTNs on this question:

• Talk with your kids well in advance about dates for weddings, reunions, and other family events. Try to accommodate their schedules when possible. Be understanding if they can't make it to every family event.

• Decide together how often you will all be able to count on seeing each other. Will you have a reunion every summer? When? How long will it be?

• Make expectations clear and be consistent about helping to pay for airfare to get them home.

• Well in advance, invite your kids to everything important—extended family reunions, graduations of younger kids in your family and cousins, and so on. It's important that they feel included and informed. Understand, however, that they will not be able to attend many of these events, even if they live nearby. If they know about things in advance, though, there's a better chance they might be able to come even if they live far away. You never know when your kids are going to be able to get some time off, or when they may have other things going on with friends or business in your area. Don't expect them to be there for every extended family event! Help them figure out which events are most important, and don't hold it against them if they can't make it to everything. Just because they live nearby doesn't mean they should be able to come to everything!

• Acknowledge the importance of their spending time with their in-laws.

• Acknowledge the importance of their having their own family time and vacation time with just their spouse and kids.

• When they do come home, make it special for them. Plan

favorite meals and activities. Don't just sit around together in the same house and make them wonder why they came. Always ask them in advance about some of the things they hope to do while they are home.

• Understand that they will probably want to spend time with friends and other family members in the area when they come to visit. Don't expect them to spend every minute with you.

• Try to set a time every year when everyone will do their best to get together (often summer reunions work best since most families trade off which parents to spend Christmas with).

R&L: Have a schedule and an agenda so your time spent together really counts. If possible, have a special, traditional place to gather each year. Isn't it interesting to see how much the grown children want the identity of an extended family reunion!

50. What is my role in teaching the gospel to my grandchildren and helping them build their testimonies?

Charity Jade: You need to be a good example, share your testimony, and teach them about the gospel whenever you're with them. It will be fun!

Lonnie P.: Well, this is the best question of all. That's my vision of grandparenting at its best! Reading a Bible or Book of Mormon storybook to my grandchildren—I can't wait. It's the best role of all.

Kenneth W.: Don't take the stewardship away from the parents, but help where you can. I think just letting grandkids know you have a testimony is the key thing.

Pam J.: You know, I have an even more specific answer—something I've been trying. Tell them stories about you when you were their age—and about any of their other grandparents or ancestors. They love it, especially if you have pictures or maybe even a family tree with pictures so they can see where they came from and who they look like. If you tell them a true story about an ancestor's testimony or mission or conversion or an act of courage or honesty, they just internalize this kind of stuff. I think it makes them feel connected and important.

Joseph: My parents gave me a wonderful set of books full of illustrated Bible stories to use with my kids during sacrament meeting, and I really appreciate that. They also give all the grandkids their first set of scriptures when they turn eight, at their baptism. My mom made a baptism outfit for the grandsons and one for the granddaughters that all the grandkids have used. My parents are always there for baptisms and confirmations, and I'm sure they'll be there to see the grandkids get their Eagle Scouts and their Young Womanhood Recognition awards. I think it's great for grandparents to do whatever little things they can think of to help their grandkids get excited about special gospel milestones—that's one very important role a grandparent can play in helping a grandchild's gospel growth.

Noel: I think that grandparents should be really careful about trying to impose what they see as their "values" on their grandkids. For example, my parents talk a lot about how we should be careful about associating too much with "nonmembers," and they are worried that my family lives in an area where there aren't many Mormons. They're always pressuring us to move back to "Zion." My kids are having great testimony-building experiences all the time as they grow up here in the mission field, and we're helping the missionaries teach a couple of families right now. I'd hate for my parents to express to my kids that they think it's "dangerous" for them to be around nonmembers. They have the cutest little friends who aren't members! I know my parents mean well—but I'd rather they keep their opinions about how to live the gospel and what to think of other people to themselves! My husband and I can teach our kids what we want them to know about the gospel, and my parents can teach them about other subjects.

Shawni: I think grandparents should try to teach their grandchildren everything they've taught their own children if they get a chance. I think any parent would love to have their own parents reinforcing the most important things they try to teach their kids. I love that my parents help my children pray, teach them more about Christ, encourage them to bear their testimonies, and so on. I couldn't ask for better helpers to teach my children the most important things in life.

Saren: In talking to other LTNs about this question, there didn't seem to be much concern about parents doing too much in the realm of supporting their grandkids' spiritual growth. Most people shared stories like Joseph's—their parents did simple little things that helped support their children's testimony development and celebrated their progress in the Church. As well as buying grandkids church materials and attending special church events for their grandkids, some grandparents wrote out their testimonies for their grandkids, and others told great stories about ancestors and got their grandkids excited about family history. Some told Bible and Book of Mormon stories as bedtime stories, and others went on missions and wrote their grandkids special letters about their experiences. My friends pretty much unanimously said they appreciated all the help they could get in reinforcing gospel principles in their children's lives. They did say that they felt it was important for their parents to respect and support their role as their children's most important teachers regarding the gospel. But extra help was more than welcome! The only complaints I heard were about parents who never talked to their grandkids at all about the gospel, parents who had slipped in their own church activity and weren't setting very good examples for their grandkids, or on rare occasions, parents like Noel's, who were self-righteous or judgmental in their beliefs or actions. Everyone agreed that they should observe and listen in on the things that their kids' parents were teaching their kids—both to be sure that their kids were learning appropriate things and to learn from their parents' good examples of teaching kids about the gospel.

R&L: First of all, don't think of teaching the gospel to grandchildren as an obligation or responsibility. It is a joy! What could be better than the opportunity to transfer parts of the most valuable possession to yet another generation.

Essentially, there are two ways to do so: (1) Individually—with just one or two grandchildren at a time—discussing, asking, listening, telling stories that teach principles—especially stories about yourself—and even more especially, stories about yourself at their age. (2) In groups or "meetings." Many of our cherished memories (and still one of our favorite traditions) is a family testimony meeting after we get home from church and before we eat on Fast Sundays. We sit in a big circle in our living room—in the same place and the same circle as when someone is ordained or confirmed or blessed—and bear our testimonies to each other. All our kids are rarely there at once, but several always are, on any given Fast Sunday. We're often joined by a close friend or two, and by one or more grandchildren. Feelings are expressed in these meetings that don't come out as deeply in any other place or at any other time. The Spirit witnesses our love for each other and testifies to each of us of what each other knows and believes. We have begun to feel that the best way to strengthen the testimonies of the next generation is just to get them to this family testimony meeting as soon as they are old enough.

Oh what a special and unique testimony we can bear to our grandchildren when the opportunity permits—individually or in a group. We can tell them what we believe and the experiences we have had that helped us believe. We can promise to be examples for them and we can extend to them a pure and spiritual love. We can give to them our spiritual heritage and inheritance. We can tell them things we learned the hard way so they won't have to make the same mistakes.

In the long run, our grandchildren will revere us more for what we have taught them of the gospel than for what we have left them of the world.

What should I do if my grandkids don't seem to be getting the church upbringing that I think they need? What if my kids are less active and don't regularly take my grandchildren to church?

Nicole: My husband, Tim, and I went through a period when we were really questioning our Church membership. We chose to "take some time off" from going to church. My parents respected our wishes but offered to take our two kids to church with them while we figured out what we wanted to do. We didn't see any harm in letting the kids go with them. We didn't have any issues with good things the kids were learning in Primary, we just needed some time to figure some things out for ourselves concerning some of the points of Church doctrine—or so we told ourselves at the time. We're now very active in the Church, and we're very grateful to my parents for being nonjudgmental as we went through a hard time. We're also very grateful that they were willing to drive all the way across town and get the kids for church every Sunday for almost a year. The kids really would have missed out if they hadn't been going to church during that time.

Saren: Most of the people I talked to about this question were very active in the Church, so it was hard to get much from the child's perspective on what an ENP should do for grandkids if their child is inactive or not teaching correct gospel principles. I would suggest that if you're worried about your kids' testimonies or church attendance, talk to them directly about it. Talk about their hopes as far as their kids' faith and gospel knowledge. Hopefully even if they don't choose to go to church, they'll recognize the importance of their kids' learning basic

Christian principles and will agree to let you teach your grandkids stories from the scriptures, reinforce positive values, or take the kids to church with you. It's important that you respect their role as your grandkids' most important teacher. But it's also important that you do all you can, in a loving and patient way, to help ensure that your grandkids get a good gospel education.

Phase 4 Review:
Your Three-Generation Family

Nowhere in the scriptures is the word "family" used to describe a two-generation household. "Family" always means more than that—three generations or more. As an empty-nest parent and a grandparent, you are now the patriarch or matriarch of a real three-generation family. You have the opportunity to create a beautiful family culture that will bless and enrich your own life and the lives of every family member.

The time and mental energy you used to use to read bedtime stories or pick up car pools or help with high school homework can now be used to plan family reunions or to visit new grandchildren or to orchestrate family e-mail updates or family chat rooms where you develop an extended family mission statement.

The point is that if we think of families as two generations only, then your grandchildren replace you as the other generation in your children's family. It's like odd man out or a game of musical chairs with only two chairs. And you are the one left standing, left out, labeled as redundant or past the point of usefulness or relevance.

But if we learn, together with our children, to think of families as three or four generations, then we are the respected matriarchs and patriarchs, useful and important in countless ways, enriching the lives of our children and grandchildren by our advice, assistance, and support even as they enrich ours by their respect, love, and friendship.

The perspective of the premortal existence is such a powerful prism through which to see more accurately the whole process and flow of expanding families.

Our children came to us as stewardships from their (and our) true Father. They were, in the premortal world, at least as mature spirits as we were, and their entrustment, as helpless infants, into our inexperienced care was a great act of faith on their part as well as a profound gift from God. They could have just as well been our parents but for the birth order that heaven ordained. So we try to respect them and to raise them the way their true Father would want them to be raised.

Then they themselves take their turn as parents and we watch them welcome their own little stewardships. What a joy to now see more clearly how it all fits together. And what a privilege to be there on the sidelines, getting into the action when we are asked or prompted, watching their family expand within ours, even as ours expands within His.

Chapter 13

Conclusion to Part 2:
It's All about Asking and Listening

When I (Richard) was a mission president, I once had a young missionary who, in an interview, asked me a most interesting question: "What do you think," he said, "is the most frequently repeated admonition in the holy scriptures?"

"Do you mean the thing God tells us most often to do?" I asked.

"Yes," he said. "What advice or counsel does God give the most often, the most repetitively? What's number one?" (This elder was quite a scripture student and also something of a trivia expert and statistician.)

"Something to do with love or loving," I guessed.

"Nope, that's number three."

"Then how about something to do with repenting."

"That's number two."

"Okay," I said, "I give up. What's number one?"

"To ask," he said. "God's most frequently repeated admonition is to ask."

I've thought a lot about that. Linda and I have thought a lot about it together. If we are God's children, and if He has placed us here on the earth to learn and progress through our experiences and our choices, and if God respects our agency by letting us take the initiative rather than Him, then our asking is the key to everything. God wants to bless us, to help us, to guide us, but He waits for us to ask so it is our choice, our initiative, our learning and progress. This is the point illustrated by the great Christian painting that shows Christ on a doorstep, knocking on our door, willing to come in to our lives. But there is no latch or handle on His side of the door. We have to open the door from inside, from our side, by asking.

There are three powerful ENP applications or adaptations of this principle of asking, and if we understand and implement all three of them, we will meet every challenge and succeed at every opportunity that has been suggested in part 2.

1. *Make asking your prime conversational approach with your adult children.* Hold off on the advice, judgment, and criticism that jumps into your head. Ask questions instead. Don't ask like an interrogator or a cross-examiner. Ask like an interested friend. Ask about feelings and hopes. Ask about day-to-day activities. And when you really feel like you know what's going on (and they really feel like you care), ask what you can do to help.

2. *Ask them to ask you—and thank them for asking when they do.* Really discuss the important difference it makes when your adult children ask you for your advice. It automatically makes you a helpful consultant rather than a bossy manager or a nosy superior. When they ask, you can respond with love and without that uncomfortable feeling that you might be interfering or imposing.

3. *Ask God for help.* Most parents who have any kind of faith or belief in a higher power eventually come to two conclusions: First, parenting at any stage is a super-human task where we need all the help we can get from a higher source; and second, our children are really God's children, so it is appropriate and natural to ask for His help. Parents, especially in times of intense worry and crisis, often find a level of faith and prayer beyond what they have known. Rather than waiting for crisis, we should learn to pray more often and more consistently for help from our Father in wisely caring for His children.

Once you get the asking going, there's one more thing: Listen! Listen and then ask some more. Ask and listen. Listen and ask. Make it your mantra and your motto.

Establishing a Family Strategy for the Rest of Your Life

Having a plan for the Emotional, Social,

Financial, Mental, and Spiritual aspects of

Empty-Nest Parenting is so much better than just

figuring it out as you go along.

Here is our case study . . .

A Long-Term Plan or "Offense" for Your Family: The Dangers of a "Defense"—of Just Reacting to Situations as They Develop

Stop Now or Read on

This appendix is certainly not "required reading." You may have found what you needed (or at least plenty to think about and work on) in the body of the book and the exhaustive list of questions and answers. If so, now is a good time to stop reading.

But if you are interested in a full-blown ENP strategy—based on a case study of our family—then read on.

Two Ways to Fail—Abdicate or Arbitrate

There are two perfectly predictable ways to fail at empty-nest parenting, and most of us are headed directly for one of them. Ironically, they are the exact opposite of each other, yet each is a virtual guarantee of a deteriorating relationship between you and your grown children. One way to fail is to abdicate—to simply quit parenting once your kids leave home, to have no strategy or plan about how you will or won't help, to step totally aside and give them complete independence unless they come to you with a problem, hoping you'll find a way to help. The other way is to arbitrarily lay down a pattern or set of standards—how much financial help they'll get, what responsibilities they'll take and what ones you'll keep, all without their suggestions or agreement.

We're thinking of one family we know who had a little send-off party each time one of their three children went off to college. It was like a celebration, a bon voyage, a good-bye party for the child and a retirement party for the parents. The tone was, "Okay, we're done. Good luck! Try not to bother us, but if you really need something, call and we'll try to help."

Another family was the complete opposite. With the help of his attorney, the father drafted a document that laid out not only a trust account and a precise schedule of when his children would receive what funds, but also a schedule of when they would visit home, when and how they would communicate by phone and e-mail, how he expected them to budget their time and their money, and where he expected them to be in their professional careers by the end of the decade.

Most parents don't do it this distinctly, but most do gravitate gradually toward one or the other of those two extremes—to abdicate or to arbitrate. Once again, both courses are guaranteed to drive parents and children apart! What is needed instead is a carefully planned and communicated middle course involving a well-discussed and agreed-upon strategy of how the relationship, the independence, and the assistance will evolve as the child goes through the phases of moving out, going to school, working, and starting his or her own family. It is like a spectrum where we need to pull ourselves to the middle rather than be sucked to one end or the other:

Abdicate	Consult and Communicate	Arbitrate
Back off and just wait for needs and problems to arise.	Develop an agreed-upon strategy that balances growing independence with gradually decreasing assistance.	Lay down the rules according to what *you* want.

We hope that you will be attracted to the middle possibility, that you will see the opportunity and the joy of communicating and working with your kids to develop a plan for your ongoing relationship with each other. We also hope that you develop a real fear of the two extremes and realize that abdicating or arbitrating can erode family relationships and eventually cut off parent from child and child from parent.

The Middle Course

Because we have been through the consulting and communicating process with our children that the middle course requires, our family can serve as a case study or an illustration of what the process is like. We will present the pattern of what we went through, the conclusions we reached, and the strategy we established for our own empty-nest parenting and for the relationships we hope to maintain and build with our adult children and their families.

You will not necessarily follow or copy our conclusions or our solutions. Rather, they can serve as a stimulus (along with the other alternative approaches and examples from other families) for the development of your own unique strategy based on your own unique situation and your own unique communication with your own unique children. We've done the research and sifted through the ideas enough to save you some time and to push you ahead in creating your own approach.

The Case-Study Method

When I (Richard) attended Harvard Business School, the classes were taught entirely by the case-study method. Instead of a lot of theory and instruction, students are just presented with a situation—a story to follow—and asked to think about what the characters did and to see where they agree and disagree and what they would have done differently. I found that the case-study approach made me think and drew out my own creativity in my effort to find my solutions. That case-study method is basically the approach we will take in this appendix. After some opening discussion and stories about each aspect of empty-nest parenting, we'll use our own family as a case study, laying out some excerpts from our own discussions and communication with each other in our struggles to reach agreements about how we wanted to relate to and help each other as our children moved out, went to school, entered careers, got married, and had children of their own.

The evolution of our case study is probably more complicated than your own situation for two reasons: First, we have nine children and, strangely enough, no two of them are alike. And second, we were writing this book at the same time we were trying to figure out and restructure our own family, so we wrote down and documented everything. Please don't feel that you have to go to quite the lengths we have to figure out your empty-nest parenting. Just glean what makes sense to you from our case study, and use the parts you like as a head start on your own strategy.

We are convinced that parents have an open channel to inspiration from a higher source when it comes to the divine stewardship they have over their own children. Our case study and the other points we make in this concluding section will hopefully be the "prompters" that will cause you to think (and to pray) about your own family, and as you do, we promise you that you will find your own answers and your own strategies!

Remember that what follows is not intended to be a model for you to follow. A case study is different from a model in that it merely brings to mind points to think about and directions you might consider rather than laying out some formula for you to follow. This appendix is highly personal because it is an honest account of what our family went through. If it seems a little overwhelming at times while you're reading it, remember that it was a process that evolved over many months. As we were going through it (and you'll probably feel this as you read it), we often felt like it was just too much and that maybe we should quit trying so hard to figure everything out and just let life happen. When we felt like that, we would remind ourselves of the reason we were doing it: Because of our belief in our eternal family, we must throughout life maintain and improve our relationships and our unity, for in them lies the core of our joy in this life and in the next. Thus, a "defense" (wherein we try to fix things as they break) is not enough. We need an "offense," a working strategy for how our family is to preserve and expand our relationship during the empty-nest years!

Process over Product

You'll notice, throughout this case study, how our approaches and agreements evolved through our process of communicating with our children and gradually developing a family constitution and extended family mission statement along with some plans or principles that would get us there. It's this process—some kind of communicating and collectively developing your approach and your united sense of what your family should be and how it will operate—that really draws family members together and gives them all "ownership" in and commitment to the final product.

Oliver Cromwell said, "I wouldn't give a fig for the simplicity that lies on this side of complexity, but I would give my right arm for the simplicity that lies beyond complexity." What we did was go through a fairly complex process (and a lot of drafts and discussions) to figure out how to get to simplicity. We wanted to discuss and think about our growing, evolving future family in all its dimensions and complexity—getting everyone involved—and then distill diversity and complexity back to certain simple principles and basic strategies and agreements that every one of us had ownership in and commitment to.

So first we talked. We talked at family reunions and on conference calls. We talked through e-mail and family chat rooms. We came up with ideas and e-mailed them to each other. Finally Linda and I started trying to put things in writing—sending out memos to our far-flung kids and asking for their responses on each of the five facets of how we wanted to function as an empty-nest family:

1. Emotionally (how we would love and encourage each other).

2. Socially (how our roles and relationships should evolve and how our communication could stay open and positive).

3. Physically (financial and temporal guidelines and policies).

4. Mentally (sharing goals and dreams and keeping each other mentally stimulated and educated).

5. Spiritually (how we would remain united and serve and support each other in the Church and the gospel).

These memos and responses evolved from ideas to agreements. It was, we think, a good example of gradually moving toward the "simplicity that lies beyond complexity." Simple ideas led to the fairly complicated memos that you'll see in this section, and then progressed beyond that complexity to the much simpler sets of principles, practices, and premises in each of the five areas or facets.

By the way, if you're thinking, "my kids wouldn't take the time to read or respond to memos or to get involved in this big process," let us make an admission. We believe in bribery! Knowing how busy our adult children are, we offered to pay them for the time they would have to put in to read and respond to the memos. After all, they would be helping us with our empty-nest parenting. Of course their prime motivation would be love and their own desire to preserve our family. But sometimes a little secondary motivation helps to get things done when there are so many other things competing for our time.

If they had lived closer to us, our process would likely have been meetings rather than memos, and maybe a big Sunday dinner could have provided the secondary motivation. We did manage to get everyone together (except missionary Noah) for our annual family reunion a few months after the back-and-forth e-mails you'll be reading—and Saren suggests later in this chapter that maybe we could have simplified the whole process and done it all at the reunion. Perhaps that just underscores the point that there are many ways to do it, but the important thing is to do it.

Results!

The results of our own efforts to figure out empty-nest parenting were:

1. A "family constitution" consisting of agreements in the five areas mentioned above.

2. A general "vision statement," which is a declaration of purpose about what we want our family to be and how we hope to connect and relate to each other as we separate: the purpose or goal of our family.

3. A boiled-down "mission statement" that serves like a motto.

Case Study

Once we had decided that we really wanted to get serious about the whole business of creating solid agreements between ourselves and our children regarding what our empty-nest family should be and how it should function, we decided that the first step was to try to write some kind of memo about the process we would have to go through to figure it all out.

So we started with the following note sent out by e-mail to try to capture a lot of what we'd been talking about within our family. (By the way, we call our family "Eyrealm.")

> To: Eyrealm
> From: Dad and Mom
> Re: Eyrealm Evolution
>
> Note: Please read this carefully. It reflects a lot of what we've talked about and tries to provide the basis for how we'll try to structure our ongoing family. Read this with your pen out! Edit it and mark any questions you have or changes you'd like to see.
>
> 1. Raising each of you and having you with us full time for eighteen years has been by far our greatest joy and privilege as well as our most important stewardship. The traditions and rituals that were developed in our family, our ways of helping and showing love for each other, our family rules and family economy—these are the very heart and substance of our lives, and we know that we have learned more from you (and from being your parents) than we have taught you. As we have tried to raise you, you have completed us as people and opened within us capacities for love far beyond what we could have otherwise known. Since you are the source of so much joy (joy defined as challenge as well as pleasure), it is only natural that we have such apprehension and anxiety about your departure and that we miss you so much once you're gone—so much that we're actually somewhat comforted when you tell us that you miss us too.
>
> 2. Perhaps it's partly because of what you've taught us about where real joy comes from that we want to continue to be active, involved parents (albeit in a different way) after you've left home. We don't want to lose any of the joy (or the security or the pride or the challenge) when you don't live here full time anymore—nor do we want you to lose any of it. That's why we're so anxious to redefine our relationship now that you're gone—in ways that are helpful and useful to you without being overbearing or overprotective—in ways that increase your independence even as they preserve our interdependence—so that we can have the strength of depending and relying and counting on each other without the weakness of being too dependent on each other. This transition, from the dependence of your childhood to the independence and interdependence of your adulthood is the subject of this draft memo, which we will

finalize with your suggestions. If we have the right strategy and approach to the transition, it can be a progressive thing of beauty and power. Together with you, we want to develop and create our family's approach to the progression of this transition so that we're acting on a well-conceived strategy rather than reacting to circumstances as they come up.

3. The transition can be diagrammed to help us conceptualize it better:

childhood _____ adulthood

childhood _____ adulthood
the security,   the security,
identity and pride _____ identity and pride
of our nuclear family   of your nuclear family
                                                              and our extended family
Your dependence on us
          Your growing and evolving independence
                    Our chosen interdependence on each other

As a baby and a child, you were almost completely dependent on us, and it was our stewardship for you that taught us so much of a deeper love. Much of your early security and larger-than-self identity hopefully came from being part of our family. As you grew, you became, usually with our encouragement, more and more independent in various ways—from learning to walk and talk and dress yourself to learning to make good choices, to think for yourself and to develop and follow your personal values. Although the transition was gradual, parts of it became rather abrupt when you moved out of the house and into your own world as a college freshman. Separation can enhance the transition, hopefully without breaking any family bonds. Gradually the transition takes on additional financial and social dimensions and eventually leads to marriage and to a family of your own, refocusing your security, identity and pride in your own nuclear family. As the transition progresses, we hope the emotional and spiritual support and connections between us never weaken. In fact, we hope they continue to grow into a marvelous and chosen interdependence where your family cares for ours, and ours for yours.

4. Practically speaking, this transition probably has four key parts or phases, each adding new levels of independence and self-responsibility.

A. When you first move out. In our family this means the

freshman year—new bed, new environment, new life. Dramatically increased mental, physical, and social independence.

B. When you first go to work full time—generally after graduation, perhaps before graduate school. Big changes in financial independence.

C. When you get married. Now your emotional dependence shifts to your own family.

D. When you have children of your own, the cycle starts over. You start learning, as we did, from life's greatest stewardship, and we start enjoying the greatest privilege of all—grandparenting.

5. Nothing about the transition or its stages is predictable or necessarily sequential. Everyone of you will live a unique life and do things and learn things in your own way. Given that uniqueness and unpredictability, it is even more important to have as much stability, reliability, and predictability as possible in the way we will help each other and relate to each other within our family. How much better it is if we've agreed in advance on some things—thought through a pattern of financial assistance for different phases, for example, or worked out a strategy for staying emotionally in touch. Your lives are increasingly busy, and, strangely enough, so are ours, and since day-to-day necessity doesn't force us to interact and communicate anymore, how important it is to have well-thought approaches for ongoing communication and helping and sharing between us.

6. This whole business, which from our perspective we are calling "empty-nest parenting," should be a process of thinking together and agreeing together with you. There should be nothing arbitrary or unilateral about it. Our strategy should be composed of a series of agreements about how we will handle certain things, how we will balance our assistance with your independence, how we will give advice enough but not too much, how we will communicate and get together and preserve family traditions. These agreements will take some thought and some discussion (and hopefully some creativity) and need to accurately reflect each other's needs as well as desires.

7. One way to look at the whole transition is to try to analyze the various facets of the change. What changes emotionally as you move away—and how should these changes be handled? What changes socially? What changes physically (financially)? What

changes mentally? What changes spiritually? How can each of these changes be dealt with and built on positively so we can each learn and grow from them? As we think about these things together, we can anticipate a lot and have some approaches and strategies in mind that will keep our family together in the ways we want it to stay together even as the circumstances and time lines of our lives pull us apart.

PROPOSED AGREEMENT ON AGREEMENTS:

Since we're the empty-nest parents (and still the stewards though in a very different way), we'll take some of the initiative by putting together a series of memos—draft memos—on these various aspects of our long-term relationship with you and on the various parts or phases of the transition. We'll get these drafts to you one at a time so you can respond and revise. We'll work at being clear on each other's needs. We'll develop together some strategies, some standards, and some systems that will maximize our individual and collective happiness (which we think is the basic reason we were put together in a family in the first place). Hopefully the end product will be something like a "family constitution" and out of it we can draw a family mission statement.

Love, Mom and Dad

We received varied reactions to this first memo from our children. Here is a sampling, some excerpts of what they e-mailed back to us:

Saren: I totally agree that as we "spin off" into our own lives and families, it's important for us to figure out how we can best increase our necessary independence and build great relationships with new family members while maintaining the enormously beneficial relationships we have with everyone in the family. I think that basic principles are important in order to do this. Systems such as we had when we were at home won't work with this new phase of our family. There can be formulas for financial support and regular plans for family reunions. There can be agendas and meetings when we get together. There can be established methods of communication and advice-seeking and giving. But we need some basic principles that we all agree to, and individual approaches that suit each person's needs, rather than a bunch of new "systems." I think you realize this—I'm just stating it clearly for us all.

I really like paragraph 3 and wish that more parents understood the principle of dependence leading to independence, leading to interdependence! There are way too many parents out there who try to keep their kids safely tucked under their wing for too long, or who very abruptly cut their kids off too soon in their lives.

On paragraph 5, I think that while we should definitely have these strategies and expectations, we need to all accept that they should be subject to flexibility and change (as long as everyone agrees on a proposed change). Situations will arise that none of us can anticipate right now. Plus we all have very different needs on some issues—so I think it's important that we all understand the basic "principles" but we're all willing to accept that there will be exceptions.

Shawni: I feel that communication is definitely the bottom line. It has to be there to make good relationships and build a strong family. It's so important to keep working on our relationships and to be open with what we expect and want so we can continue to be close.

On paragraph 2, I think we can all function okay on our own, and don't die if we can't talk every single day, yet we yearn to talk to each other and we consider each other best friends. I don't know what I would do without each of our family members. I want to tell you guys things and want to share my life with you and I want to know all about what everyone else is doing. And I am so glad we are all doing such different things because we learn and gain so much from each other.

In paragraph 3, as much as I love my own amazing new little family now, I would feel so much loss if I didn't have the emotional and spiritual support from you guys that I've always had. It is so strong and it completes me.

Josh: I think that, in a way, the transition is complete before we move out to college. Then when we actually move out, we implement many things that we have learned, that up until that time were just ideas about how we would act when we left. It's like we were developing our own values and choices for eighteen years.

Just a comment on paragraph 5: A lot of the interaction and communication we will be doing will be totally spontaneous. While it is good to have approaches in place, they will be ever changing as we continue to learn and grow.

Saydi: All families are going to be different, with their own strengths and challenges. However, all families have the same basic needs and structure and power to hurt and to heal. Thus, it is essential that parents and families engage in the struggle. I see so many families in my work as a family counselor who just kind of float through their lives, they don't give solid thoughts to what is happening, what forces they are letting take control. They just live, floating where the wind and current take them.

I love it that Mom and Dad want to stay active in our lives. It makes sense. If they didn't have this great urge to stay connected I'd be sad. I believe that these memos will be good and that we need to find a good balance.

But, Mom and Dad are essentially saying, "We need to come up with strategies, approaches or formulas." I don't think that I really agree with this way of thinking of it at all. We are all so different, I think that it would be amazingly hard, if not impossible, to come up with precise strategies to use in different situations. I think the thing that would work best is to come up with a list of principles that we can all agree to live by. I believe that we need to commit to principles that ring true to our hearts and then we can act straight from our hearts. Something about reading the memo just seemed a little too strategic to me for dealing with human emotions and experiences. It is good to analyze things, but it's also very important to consult your heart and live by the Spirit so that our relationships and communications can be led and directed by that which is higher and all knowing and all understanding.

Aja: I respect the fact that "acting on a well-conceived strategy rather than to circumstances as they come up" is a very stable and good managing technique. But I believe that part of the uniqueness of families in comparison to other organizations is their potential to deal so individually with their members and grow and change with time, all the while maintaining complete unity. Any plan to facilitate communication through and around an empty nest must be as dynamic and flexible as the present and future members that make it up.

Talmadge: It's interesting that as I read this, it dawns on me that there are so many social problems in this world because people don't have families or responsibility enough to raise kids correctly. Therefore they get caught up in "other things" to please them and keep them excited.

I've always thought—you leave home and just find out from there. Your family is still a nice support when you need it but you're on your own. I guess I thought that because I've seen it on many occasions. It's a norm. But I think our family can be a deviant and break into a new and higher perspective where we've thought it through and know in advance how we'll handle some things. (These words norm and deviant I just learned in my social problems class.)

In the kids' responses it became clear that many of them were a little wary of "strategies" and "systems" and wanted instead to think more in terms of basic principles and simple, flexible agreements that allowed them all to be themselves and do things their own way.

Still, we all agreed that it was a process and that we might have to start by laying everything out and then simplifying it and boiling it down.

Emotional Empty-Nest Parenting: Finding the Balance Between "Hanging On" and "Letting Go"

In Ecclesiastes 3:1 we read, "To every thing there is a season." For most empty-nest parents it is autumn, or at least Indian Summer, in our lives. Our children have grown up and have left or are beginning to leave home like leaves falling from the trees.

So how do we think about fall? Is it a time of loss and decline, or is it the most glorious and colorful time of all? Is it a time when our family separates and dissipates, or a time when it reaches its full richness and maturity? For us parents, is it a time when we retreat or retire from family life, or a time when we redefine our role as advisers and mentors and grandparents and patriarchs and matriarchs of three-generation families?

As we make these fall decisions and set our autumn priorities, we ought to also be thinking about winter. When real old age comes, do we want to be alone or to be emotionally surrounded by our children and grandchildren?

Studies on longevity have shown that those who retire earliest die soonest, and that those in the most engaging and creative vocations live longest. Orchestra conductors lived the longest of all professions surveyed. That bears some thought. Maestros are always creating, always mentoring, always orchestrating, always conducting. Can we, in the fall and winter of our lives, become the maestros of our families?

Pain and Gain

The best decisions are made and the best goals set when we carefully analyze both the long-term pain and long-term gain that are likely to accrue from various alternative directions. If we make choices for the fall of our lives that allow the emotional bonds of the family to fray or weaken, a lot of pain will result, both in the sense of what our children and grandchildren will miss out on and in terms of our own loneliness. If we make the choice and take the steps to keep our families emotionally close despite the departures and distances, we will gain security and connectedness and motivation for our children and involved usefulness and perhaps even longer lives for ourselves.

The beginning step in the active, involved, family-prioritized approach to the autumn of our lives is to have a plan for the all-important emotional facet of our empty-nest parenting, a strategy for continuing to give love, confidence, identity, and emotional support to each other.

What a tall order! Once kids are gone—away from your daily

observation and interchange—how do you even know when they are emotionally up or down, and how can you gauge what kind of emotional support they need?

The simple answer is that you can never give too much love or support, so long as you couple it with confidence in them and respect for their adult independence.

Case Study

In our own effort to figure out this first facet, we again started with a memo in order to try to crystallize our own thoughts and get a discussion going. We weren't trying to be formal or businesslike, we just needed an organized way to get all of us, living so far apart from each other, to focus on the emotional needs we could help each other with.

> To: Eyrealm
> From: Mom and Dad
> Re: Finding Balance Between Our Two Common Emotional Needs
>
> 1. When you were little children, all of us living together, thinking more about Little League or being popular at Indian Hills Elementary than about choosing a college major or planning for families of your own—back in those good old days, we felt like there were two things which would, if we could instill them in you, give you a happy life. First was a solid emotional foundation of family identity, security, and pride—a safe harbor of acceptance and inclusion so that whatever went wrong outside the home you would be comforted and sustained by the unconditional love from within our family. Second was an emerging, growing sense of individual confidence and uniqueness—so you could gradually begin to strike out on your own, find your own gifts, your own niche, your own way of becoming your truest self.
>
> 2. Now that you are mostly grown and mostly gone, we find we still have exactly the same two hopes for you, although perhaps reversed in their emphasis: First, that through your own growth, with God's help and the occasional bit of advice from us, you find and enjoy your own unique foreordination, building your own family and your own life in your own way, flowering and broadening into the person (and the family) that God intended you to be and contributing in the directions to which you are particularly suited.

Second, that the ongoing love and support of your extended family helps you to magnify it all, to go through the hard times with less pain and through the good times with more joy.

3. There is always a certain dynamic tension between these two most basic emotional needs (the need for the security and identity of being part of something bigger than self and the need for the confidence, individuality, and freedom of being on one's own). We're so aware now, as you leave, of the need to balance the two—to balance continuing care with having your own life: It's an issue on both sides of the table. You "nest leavers" deserve and desire your new freedom and independence, and yet you want our ongoing interest and involvement. We "empty-nesters" want to "get a life" in terms of new freedom to travel and do other things we couldn't while you were our chosen, in-home priorities, and yet we deeply want to continue to help and parent you, and to continue to give and receive love and support.

4. *Proposed agreements draft:* It seems to us that there are two agreements we can come to that will help if not ensure this balance.

A. That we each cast ourselves as "supporters" rather than as "critics"—that we build up rather than tear down, looking for the positive in each other's choices. What this does is to prioritize each other's emotional needs above what we might judge to be their mental shortcomings or errors. If we have misgivings for example about a career choice or professional decision one of you is leaning toward, we ought to first express our support for you, our love for you, our respect for your agency and our confidence that you ultimately know more about yourself and your destiny than we do. Then, within the warm cocoon of that positive confidence, we should tell you our misgivings and you should consider them. In the other direction, if you question some choice we are making, perhaps to sell a house or to take an extended trip, you ought to take the time to understand our thinking and reasons and then express support before you raise any concerns or objections.

B. That we all recognize the need for balance between support/security and individuality/independence and communicate about it, on the one hand, asking questions like, "How much do you want me to be involved in this?" and on the other hand saying, "You know I want and respect your opinion, but after all is said and done, I'm going to have to do what I think is best." Inherent and implicit in all the communication is the unconditional love that supersedes any and all differences of opinion and says that, no matter what, we are always there for each other!

Here are some of the reactions and responses we got from our kids:

Saren: It's interesting—as we've left home and developed our unique abilities and personalities, we've grown so much closer to each other in so many ways. We've found bonds and similarities that were hard to see when we were all living on top of each other, fighting for space and attention, and separated by age differences that become less and less important as we grow older. At certain periods of time since I've left home, circumstances have led me to draw extra close to each of the other kids in the family.

I think it's important that love and support become more and more a two-way thing. When we were little, we needed and got a whole lot more acts of love and support than we gave. But as we get older and learn more and understand new things, we're more and more in a position to give you more. I think it's so healthy and positive for all of us to be helping each other in a more and more equal "give and take" manner. It always makes me feel good when you ask for my ideas about what can be done to help someone else in the family.

On paragraph 4: Dad can say that he respects our point of view and our ability to make a good decision—but he seems to really, truly believe in his heart that his point of view and assessment of the situation and ideas about what we should do are better than ours. Dad's like me—he really thinks he's right almost all the time—and if you really think you're right, it's very hard to genuinely accept someone else's decision if it isn't what you think is right. I guess the key is really convincing yourself that you do not know the whole situation and you are not really the person involved, so no matter what seems right to you, you could really, truly be wrong.

I think this memo leaves out a few important things about emotional ENP.

I think we should add some specific stuff about how we want to help each other during times of intense emotions—ending a relationship, deciding to get married, losing a job, making career changes, going through identity crises and mid-life crises, trouble with friends, dealing with the death of a loved one. How should parents help their kids when they're going through something involving intense emotions? How can kids help their parents? To me, a big part of the meaning of family is the knowledge that there are people out there who will rejoice with you and weep with you and love you no matter what.

Shawni: I sure felt this "safe harbor" of acceptance and inclusion. I wonder how you guys did it now that I have kids of my own and want to duplicate that feeling for them.

On paragraph 3: This sure is a tough balance to achieve. Sometimes I miss being "under your wing" but at the same time I am so glad you let Dave and me be our own unique family and you let us make our own decisions and never even question them (at least not to us). It's interesting to hear you say you want to "get a life" because it's so weird to think of it that way. Yet we need to understand that you need your personal space as a couple just as we need ours and I just think that is so important—something I don't think us kids think about that much and need to focus on more.

Josh: Emotional needs are very important. And because we do know more about ourselves than anyone but God, understanding what we want to do or decide to do should come before any misgivings are shared.

I feel that it needs to be stated again here, that if we continue with what we were leaning toward, and choose not to follow your advice, that decision needs to be accepted and respected.

Jonah: There does need to be a distinguishable difference between the advice that you give now compared to the advice earlier in our lives. Hopefully you do feel confident that we will make right decisions because of the way we were raised.

I know that we all want to feel less pain and more joy and you give us advice to try to save us from the pain, but some of the pain that we feel is essential to our growth. Try to imagine how you and Mom would be now, had you not slept on the floor in Peabody Terrace and struggled through those first years. I know it is hard to think that we are going to have a hard time but I think that we need to go through these things ourselves.

Let us always look for the positive in others' choices even if the statistics and our own judgment say otherwise. Let us, once a person has made a decision and especially if they have received confirmation from God, totally stand behind them and try to see things from their level and realize that we never have all of the insights into each other's lives because we are all so different.

Whether or not we ever get these memos all ironed out, let's always remember that we love each other and that love will never fail. Emotional support is all about really loving each other, not just when it comes to giving advice.

Aja: I appreciated its emphasis on the strength of individuality as a partner with the strength of unity. The strength of unity may be given too much attention though, and that strength is typified as coming only out of Eyrealm and not out of other families that a person will build in their lifetime.

Paragraph 1 says that two gifts of Eyrealm should be acceptance and inclusion and individual confidence and uniqueness. I think that both of these gifts and the goals that are behind them lead to a contract of listening and support rather than how we can critique and consult. In other words our emotional agreements should not have an underlying motive of correcting one another but of admiring and sharing life with one another.

I really like 4A and what it's trying to promote. The line about the warm cocoon of "positive confidence" is good, but let's be sure it doesn't become a way to introduce a family-friendly tactfulness when dishing out "misgivings," rather than a way to allow opinions. I think a tact that works in close relationships of this kind would mean things like the following: the giver always strongly presents misgivings as what they usually are—just opinions (except in the case of maybe life- or soul-threatening decisions or actions); the misgivings are expressed more of a questioning session, rather than a telling session (that is, how does this whole thing make you feel? Do you have any worries about your decision?); the giver offers help in pursuing that and alternate paths in order to make other options more feasible; or perhaps tact might even just include waiting until an opinion is asked for.

I think a great thing to elaborate on would be the meaning of the phrase, "We are always there for each other." This is not implicit to everyone, and it doesn't mean the same thing for everyone. It would be helpful maybe to even sketch how and what this means. For example, a list might include: we can call each other anytime, anywhere and just be able to talk, or if I was starving, my family would feed me, or if I were going astray, they would help, or when I experience joy, my family experiences it with me, or if I have a heartache, they will listen, if I need a ride to the airport, they are there for me, and when I need a bed to sleep in, they'll pull down the sheets and tuck me in. The list would be different for everyone, but I think it's a great thing to think about.

Talmadge: I like this stuff. I love that you guys are involved and the question shouldn't be, "How much do you want me to be involved in this?" The question should be from us: "Mom or Dad, can you help a little with this decision?"

Again, I think the ideal scenario is if the children ask for the help and advice. We need to be the aggressive ones in this. We need to be the ones who take the initiative. When we get offended, it's because we probably know that we should be the ones figuring out our lives.

After reading the kids' responses, we realized we had been a little bit off in the focus of our memo. Emotional needs and emotional empty-nest parenting is not about advice or correction on what someone is doing. It's purely and simply about love and support and empowerment. The reason for creating the "warm cocoon of positive confidence" is not to soften our misgivings or criticism, it is an end in itself!

We decided we should leave the questions of giving and receiving advice to the social empty-nest parenting strategy which is more about our roles and advice-giving communication with each other.

Emotional empty-nest parenting is the first facet because it is about giving each other the kind of unconditional love that makes each other facet of empty-nest parenting possible. It is about making sure your family is an emotional safe harbor (a metaphor they all seemed to appreciate) where you know you are always loved and accepted no matter what. It is about creating what Stephen Covey calls an "emotional bank account" into which you continue to make such large "deposits" that every other kind of parenting you do can never overdraw it.

Also, once again, the kids' responses were saying that on this emotional level we needed something simpler—something less like a contract and more like a set of principles we agreed on and promises we would make to each other.

The Eyrealm Emotional Safe Harbor (giving love, confidence, identity, and emotional support to each other)

After much discussion, mostly by phone and e-mail, we finally came up with a metaphor and a format and a set of simple emotional principles that we all agreed on and "signed off" on.

Dear LTNs:

Thanks for your feedback and ideas. It seems what you're all saying, and we totally agree, is that Eyrealm needs to be, first of all, an emotional safe harbor where we all know we are unconditionally loved and accepted for who we are. Here is a summary of what we've come up with together. It has turned out to be a short and sweet emotional agreement for Eyrealm.

We're glad you've helped us to see that our emotional empty-nest parenting, and the agreements and commitments we make in the first ("emotional") facet of our adult Eyrealm "constitution" shouldn't be about advice-giving or correcting or changing each other. On the contrary, they should be about loving and accepting each other for who and what we are. That's what the safe harbor is safe from—from second-guessing, guilt, the uncomfortable turbulence of people trying to improve you. Questions about those things are best left to other parts of the constitution.

Our "emotional agreements" are now simplified into some very basic principles, practices, and promises.

Principles of the safe harbor:

• What people need emotionally from family is unconditional and even irrational (not tied to performance) love, acceptance, approval, and confidence.

• In the adult Eyrealm, this works in all directions: kids need it from parents, parents from kids, parents from each other, kids from each other, and grandkids from all of the above.

• The purpose of the love is not to change each other but to nourish each other.

Promises of the safe harbor:

• We will love each other unconditionally and consciously strive to make each other happy.

• We will always be there for each other, night or day, to laugh or cry, to rejoice or commiserate, to share each other's emotion.

Practices of the safe harbor:

• We say "love you" instead of (or in addition to) "good-bye" whenever we talk, and we think about it and we mean it.

• We e-mail and call each other regularly (so we're all "updated").

• We "listen and lift," developing our gifts of empathy and genuine compliments—and giving these gifts to each other.

Social Empty-Nest Parenting: Sorting Out the Evolving Relationships and Changing Roles

We "adopted" Eldar Maximov, a nineteen-year-old Ukrainian boy, at the behest of our missionary son Jonah, who had taught and baptized Eldar in London. We sponsored his entry to the U. S. as a student and helped him as required with living and college expenses. He became like another son to us and has blessed our lives in many ways. One way that Eldar has probably exceeded any of our natural-born children is in his desire to seek our advice on everything—and to implement that advice almost unquestioningly once he has received it. On almost every question—from education to dating—I (Richard) could count on Eldar asking "for our advices," taking careful notes on everything I said, and then implementing it to the letter. I always had to be pretty careful what I suggested he do, because he would do it!

Until one particular day . . .

His call came on my cell phone while I was traveling, and in Eldar's typical, get-right-to-the-point style, he said he had something very important to "get advices" on and that he first had to "explain something to me for about ten minutes." He told me about a girl he'd met at school three weeks ago, seen every day since, and was totally in love with. It was his first real experience with love, he said, and hers, too. She was everything he'd ever wanted. He felt that he'd known her forever, and the "advices" he wanted was about where he could get the best deal on a diamond.

"Whoa! Hang on a minute," was my reaction. "Aren't there a few other things we ought to talk about first—like how well you really know each other after three weeks and what the big rush is?"

But the usually deliberate and careful Eldar didn't want to hear it. "Well," he said, "I'm going to go meet her parents next week and I want to get engaged first. We're totally in love and we're perfect for each other—I just know it. Besides, we'll have a long engagement—three or four months—where we can really get to know each other."

I called him back when I got to a land phone and it was a two-hour telephone call, consisting mostly of me repeating the reasons he should take it all a little slower and him repeating the reasons he shouldn't. I brought up every experience and story I could think of and Eldar listened politely, frequently telling me that he respected my suggestions and advice, even if he didn't think he'd follow them. Probably the one thing I did right was to avoid getting completely exasperated with him, instead reminding him throughout the conversation that I had faith in him and would support whatever decision he made.

To make a long story short, Eldar and Courtney are now married and they're doing just fine, although it was a rocky road at first. They've been coming to us for advice, and we've had some great talks. They think, and we agree, that the toughest part of the marriage is probably behind them. We've even wondered if the only way the Lord could get them married was on the "fast track" because if they'd had some of their problems prior to the commitments of marriage, they might have called it off. I'm so glad now that they made their own decision, that I didn't undermine it, and that we kept our communication channels open.

As we have discussed with other parents the issues surrounding communication and relationships with grown children, a sort of spectrum has developed. At one end of the spectrum, parents say, "We're still the parents. They're still our stewardship even though they've left home. There's so much they don't know and of course we should continue to help, advise, and guide them in whatever ways we can. If they're off course, we need to help them get back on. If they're about to make a mistake, we have to try to help them avoid it."

At the opposite end of the spectrum, other parents say, "We've got to give grown kids their independence, to back off, to let them make mistakes and learn from them, and to be sure we don't offend them or undermine their confidence by giving too much advice. And when we do give advice, we've got to be sure we're not offended if they disregard it or don't follow it."

It's the classic argument (and dilemma) between "staying involved" and "backing off." Those on one end of the spectrum fear conflict and contention and being hurt or offending each other. Those on the other end fear not knowing what others are truly thinking and feeling, and they fear the consequences of not doing all they can to help their kids.

We have experienced the trickiness of finding the right balance within our own family. One night I was sitting with Saydi and Tal and Eli at dinner, and we were talking about Josh and some issues we knew he was facing. Eli said, "We've all just got to leave Josh alone on those things. He knows what he's doing. He's worried enough about it. He's sick of all our advice. It just bugs him if we bring it up." Talmadge responded that if it's a concern then we should be talking about it—"That's what families are for." Eli countered that it offends people if you bring up things that might be shortcomings or worries. Tal said, "Maybe not," and reminded us that when he was having trouble reading, everyone in the family gave him advice, kept it an open subject, and that motivated him to work at it and improve. Saydi sympathized with both sides, saying we certainly need to avoid being critical, but that if you feel or believe something in a family, you need to bring it up. She said she sometimes feels like she's walking on eggshells around Josh, being so careful not to mention any subject that he's sensitive about. She said she hated that feeling and that she's learned in her social work profession that if you really care about people, you have to be able to talk to them honestly and candidly.

That same night, Jonah told me that my advice and my personality are too strong and there have been times he's done just the opposite of what I suggested to prove his own independence (to himself and to me)!

Even advice-advocating Tal said to me another night (when I suggested something I thought he should say to his coach): "I think I would have had that idea, but now you suggested it so it can't be my idea."

The questions of social empty-nest parenting strike right at the heart of our changing relationships with our adult children. How much advice should we give? How forcefully should we give it? How much should they accept? Where do our strong opinions undermine their ability to develop their own? How often should we communicate? How open and candid should we be? How involved should we be in each other's lives?

Case Study

We knew the social facet of empty-nest parenting had to do with transferring our relationship from "vertical" to "horizontal." This was reflected in our first "social" memo:

> To: Our children
>
> From: Mom and Dad
>
> Re: Eyrealm Social Strategy Draft: Your Transition with Us from a "Vertical" to a "Horizontal" Relationship and Our Transition from a Management Role to a Consulting Role
>
> 1. When you were born, you came to us as a precious stewardship from God. Our commitment, as we understood it in bringing you into this world, was to love you unconditionally, to educate you and teach you correct principles and values, and to help and motivate you in every way we could to reach your full potential and happiness.
>
> 2. Now, as you leave home to live under another roof for the first time, we feel an exquisite combination of sadness and joy. We

also feel the importance of understanding and defining the ways we want our roles and relationship to stay the same in this new phase, and the ways we want them to change.

3. As we have discussed, when you were a child, our relationship was "vertical." We were responsible for you. At some time in the future, when your own family and your own life is thoroughly established, our relationship will be "horizontal." You will be completely responsible for yourself. During the transition, our relationship is sort of "diagonal." This can be a difficult time, with the danger of us trying to be too intrusive and controlling (or the opposite—of backing off so completely that we're not there when you need us). You, at the same time, might try to be too independent too soon on the one extreme, or too dependent on us for too long on the other.

4. Another related danger, during this transition, is for either of us to become "offended." If you are offended by advice we give you (or by the fact that we give advice at all) then (a) you won't follow it even if it's good; (b) you won't ask for it even when you need it; and (c) you will in essence say, "I'll show you" and become locked into a contrary position. If we feel offended that you don't want our advice or don't follow some advice we have given then (a) we might stop giving advice even when you need it; (b) we might argue too vigorously for our position in a power-grabbing attempt to prove we are right; and (c) we might say, "I told you so" when something doesn't work out. Each of these six possibilities can drive us apart.

5. On the question of advice, clearly your dad is prone to lean toward the "over-advice" side. Your mom, while she is as strong-willed and opinionated as anyone, tends to lean correspondingly (balancingly?) to the "careful not to push or offend" side.

So, where do we want to be as a family? Where do Mom and I want to be on the advice spectrum, and where do you, as siblings want to be in terms of how much you share with each other, and how much opinion and advice you give each other? How much do we share? How much do we say? How brutally honest should we be with each other?

6. Moliere's *Le Misanthrope* (*The Misfit*) is about a man who is always totally honest and candid, expressing literally everything he

thinks and feels, regardless of the circumstances. He constantly embarrasses and offends people because the society in which he lives just doesn't operate so openly and honestly. The message is that caution, tact, and discretion in what you say and what you don't say is necessary to function well in the broader society.

7. On a more personal note, when Mom and I were in college, there was a bit of a fad going on called "T Groups" or "Encounter Groups." Basically it was a group of students getting together, sitting in a circle, usually late into the night, and being brutally honest with each other. One person at a time would be focused on and everyone else in the group would tell that person exactly what he or she thought of him or her. The idea was to not sugarcoat anything—what's wrong with his nose, his clothes, his personality, "what I thought of you the first time I met you," "what problems I see with you that you probably don't see in yourself." I went to a couple of sessions that were just brutal. One girl left in sobbing tears and was absent from campus for a week. There was a rumor that another participant attempted suicide. Clearly, too much blunt openness among friends and acquaintances can be counterproductive.

8. In a Sunday School class once, the teacher read some passages where Christ seemed to be harshly and bluntly critical of His apostles, particularly Peter. Then she reminded us of how totally and unconditionally Christ loved His apostles. Then she reread the same words, but in a tone that reflected one who cared enough to correct. Her point was that when love is strong enough, there is no need for tact or for mincing words or for walking on eggshells.

9. We remember an old mouthwash commercial that had the tag line, "Even your best friend won't tell you" (about your bad breath). So the question is—who will tell you? Who will tell you about something you may not be able to see for yourself, about something that might keep you from having to rediscover the wheel—from having to learn from mistakes that someone else has already made, from getting hit by the truck instead of going around it?

10. We've talked with some of you about the staying involved vs. backing off spectrum:

Staying Involved	Backing Off
Advice, openness, let it all out "Unexpressed feelings never die, they just fester and come forth later in uglier forms."	Don't intrude, don't ask. "Some things are better left unsaid."

11. What occurs to us is that the only real justifications for the right end of the spectrum is that we don't want to offend or to be offended and that we don't want to infringe on anyone's independence. It's a defensive position. It's about what we don't want to do. Don't offend. Don't antagonize. Don't push away. Don't try to control. The left, on the other hand, is about what we do want to do. We want to help, to support, to advise, to motivate, to give perspective and insights. It's an offense rather than a defense—but the problem is that the offense can be offensive.

12. Now, as we make our transition toward horizontal relationships, if we could come up with something that would take care of the defense, that would ensure against anyone being offended or losing any independence . . . some strategy or agreement that just took care of all that, then we could concentrate on the offense, we could eliminate the fear and just get on with loving each other openly, with sharing all that we feel about each other, and with each other. No secrets, no sacred cows, no fronts, no facades, no taboos, no off-limits, no eggshells.

It didn't work in *Le Misanthrope*, and it didn't work in T Groups, but it worked for Christ. Could it work in a family? Could we create a family "bubble" containing the pure oxygen of such unconditional, unquestioned love that offense is never given or taken and that independence is never compromised or undermined? Christ did so with His apostles. Can we approach some similar level within our family?

13. It's a high-risk, high-effort strategy. Harder and more dangerous than just backing off, skirting issues, saying nothing, avoiding friction or feelings. But isn't that what we learn from the premortal existence and the war in heaven—that risk and effort are why we came? That "hard" and "danger" are good? That helping and mutual interdependence is what it's all about?

14. But how do we create that bubble—that family in which the very atmosphere is different from the world around it? How can we create an atmosphere within Eyrealm where no offense exists, or control or manipulation, where independence and uniqueness flourish and grow right along with advice and opinion and candid suggestion from each other?

15. We think the answer is that we have to carefully and consciously build that bubble. It won't come about by chance or by luck, and it won't grow spontaneously just because we love each other. We think we have to plan it and build it and maintain it. And we're going to go over now some of the things we've talked about and some that we haven't for your review and suggestions, in the hopes that we can refine and complete it and thus have the eternal blessing of being able to communicate all and share all and give all.

Proposed "Congruence" Agreement (Draft)

i. Let's define *congruence* as complete honesty, openness and candor—too complete for use within society, but desirable (though difficult) within our family. It allows (indeed encourages) us to say what we feel and what we believe to each other and about each other individually and collectively.

Thus we commit that we will stay open and communicative with each other about our transitional roles—telling each other what we feel, what we need, and what we don't need. Particularly we trust that you will try to be aware of areas where advice might be helpful and take the initiative to ask us. When the initiative comes from you there is less chance of offense from either side.

ii. In order to achieve congruence, each family member agrees:

(a) to trust each other and to trust our love for each other, to believe and remember that we have each other's best interests at heart;

(b) to seek time together in groups and one-on-one, to prioritize opportunities to talk and to share;

(c) to pray together—all together or two together, remembering that with God's help and with the Spirit present, we can never hurt or misadvise (or even misunderstand) each other.

iii. As parents (or siblings in the advice and opinion-giving mode), we agree:

(a) to listen, ask, and try to understand first;

(b) to give suggestions and advice in the "consulting mode"—objectively, without guilt, knowing that it is not the only advice going to the receiver and acknowledging his independence and decision-making control;

(c) to not be offended when advice is not followed.

iv. As offspring (or siblings in the advice-receiving mode), we agree:

(a) to be neither offended nor diminished by opinions, suggestions, or advice given.

(b) to strenuously avoid overreaction either toward or against suggestions given, and to take them as additions to our own broader knowledge, and decide and act independently.

(c) to ask parents and other family members for suggestions and counsel, thus keeping the initiative and allowing ourselves to feel ownership of the ideas (we asked for them, they were given, and they are now ours).

The responses, as usual, were a mix of the expected and the surprise:

Saren: I think it's good to have a sense of what to say and when. I don't think it's necessary to "let it all hang out all the time" in order to be an open and honest family. I think that tact is a valuable trait for all of us to hang on to. But, with a little tact, I think we should all have the courage and the desire to say anything that we've thought over and decided is important and worthwhile.

I don't think we need to say everything that's on our mind, but I do think we need to say everything that is persistently on our minds and that we think could really help someone else. I had a good talk with Josh over Christmas—I just laid out all my feelings on the table (I was having similar feelings to those Saydi mentioned—feeling like I was walking on eggshells around Josh). I was totally open and honest and shared things that had been on my mind a lot about Josh—directly to him. He seemed to really appreciate my directness and we both learned a lot during our discussion. I realized that I'd been making some assumptions about Josh that crumble when you talk directly with him. This brings me to an important point: We should all agree that it's okay to talk about other people when they aren't there—as long as we share what was talked about in the discussion with the person who is the subject of the discussion right away. Whoever we're talking about has a right to know that they're being talked about and what people are saying—plus hearing what was said can be very helpful to them as they deal with whatever situation is at hand.

Dad, you can be overbearing with your advice sometimes—and I know you don't want to be. I'm way overbearing with my advice a lot. I think that you and I are alike in that we honestly think we're right the vast majority of the time. If we think about someone's situation and come up with an idea about what they should do, we feel quite certain it's the right idea. So if they don't do what we suggest—they're doing it wrong. I'm trying to learn to really believe that other people's ways of doing things and their decisions that are different from what mine would be are okay.

One important way to make advice less overbearing is to always ask questions before giving advice. You do ask questions, but maybe if you ask more, we would come up with ideas ourselves rather than you having to outright offer them to us. For example, if you'd asked Tal what he was thinking about saying to his coach, he might have said what you were about to suggest. Or he might have said, "I'm having a hard time figuring that out. Do you have any ideas for me?" Then he's asking your advice and anything you say, after he's asked, will be more welcome. When I was doing all these training sessions to prepare to be a residence advisor at Wellesley, they suggested that whenever someone has a problem or tells you about a problem, or even asks you for advice, you should ask lots of questions and ask them what they think about everything before you share what you think. Maybe helping people figure out what to do isn't really about making the right suggestions, it's about asking the right questions until the solution comes out.

It would really help if you'd always encourage us to ask other people for advice as well. We don't ask others enough and you're so willing to jump in and advise, that we get all "adviced out" and don't often enough look for further insights. I think it would soften any advice you give and keep people from thinking you're overbearing with your advice if you simply routinely asked who else they've talked to about this.

If we want to be like Christ, I think we should seek to understand situations and people very well before offering advice. I think we should express confidence in them and make sure they know that they make their own decisions in this life. I think we should say anything that we're inspired to say in a loving and kind and timely manner. I think we should do all we can to help people come up with their own solutions rather than suggesting whole ideal scenarios to them. I think we should be very careful to let go of our advice and let people do with it what they will, fully respecting their free agency.

I think it would be good to be a little more specific with these commitments. Maybe we should commit to stuff like monthly interviews with Mom and Dad, making a point of asking for advice every time we possibly can, expressing our feelings through e-mails or conversations as soon as something comes up between us that is worrisome. Dad and Mom could always use some preface phrase that everyone agrees with before starting to give advice (something like: "I have a few ideas on your situation that might help you out. I don't know everything about this situation, so maybe my advice won't work for you. I know that you will ultimately make your own decision and I'm sure you'll know what is right for you. Do you want to hear my thoughts?")

It's hard to "let go" of a piece of advice you've given and totally feel fine about it when your advice is not followed. It's hard for me, and I know it's hard for you. I think we all need to learn to truly give advice—when you truly give, you let go and you allow the person who now owns the advice you gave them to do whatever they want with it. Usually, when we "give" advice we're really holding on to it—holding it out in front of our advisees and feeling quite sure that they must follow it or things will not go well.

Shawni: I'm not sure I agree with the thought that we would ever be truly "horizontal." I understand what you are trying to say—as I've become a parent I do feel that we have become more and more that way. I love that I can share things with you that you may not have thought of and that I can relate so much to being a parent now, too. But I think a parent should always be a little bit on the "vertical" side of things just because they are a parent. I don't think a parent should ever just discontinue the nurturing relationship because I feel that the kids will always need that—no matter how old they are. I know that even though I am older now it still feels like velvet to me when you guys care about my emotional well-being and ask questions and are still my parents that way.

Yes, you were more obtrusive in my decision-making processes when I lived at home, but I really think you've stayed out of it since I left home. You've always been positive and encouraging to what I decide to do, but I don't think you've tried to push me to do anything—especially since I've been married. Dave and I really appreciate that. We really have felt that you trust us in our decision-making and have really stayed out of it.

With three of us in the family married so far, it seems like you've stayed out of what Saren and I do much more than you have with Jonah. I think it's just different with daughters. It shows you trust our husbands to make important decisions with us—their wives. This has really meant a lot to Dave. He feels a lot of trust from you and really appreciates that. I'm sure it's much easier not to get involved though when it's not your own son—even if you may not agree. It's easier to draw the line on how much advice to give since you didn't actually raise these men in your own home and you don't know them inside and out like you know your own sons. I think since you know Jonah and Josh so well you want so much to push them and mold them in a way you see so clearly would help them and benefit them. I see you wanting to get involved purely to help them and let them see things from an experienced eye. But in some cases this may be the hardest thing because they need to figure out so much of it on their own without you.

Josh: The analogy to the vertical and horizontal relationships makes sense, and I guess the big question is how far diagonal the "diagonal" relationship is. I think that in different stages it changes. I think it starts moving from the vertical position sometime in high school. It gradually moves from vertical toward horizontal, and on the very day that we leave home, it immediately drops below 45 degrees to a more horizontal position than vertical. Then it gradually moves all the way to horizontal.

The root word "offend" is used so many times in this memo. Sometimes it doesn't feel like the right word. I think that true advice in itself is never offensive, but that the way that it is given or the reaction of the person on the receiving end can be offensive.

I think these are good commitments. The only thing that I would add would be that when we don't ask for advice, that decision should also be respected. There are certain times when I am in a situation when only God and myself understand. There are some things that are impossible for other people to understand, because the only way to understand it is to have lived through it or to be God, who knows everything. So I think that understanding and not being offended when we make decisions without asking for advice should be added.

Sometimes I don't want to hear advice, for fear that it will be what I have already decided, which makes it look like it wasn't my idea. Sometimes I have done the opposite of what I have been advised to prove my independence. Other times I have followed advice that I later wished I hadn't. And there are times I don't want to hear advice because I know exactly what it will be, and it is sometimes hard to go against someone's advice, especially when they are very assertive when they give it. I value my independence so much. I feel it is very important to live my own life without being pushed into doing things I don't want to do.

When two members of our family are communicating, advice doesn't always have to be given. I just get the feeling from some of the things said here that the only times we're going to help each other out is when we are giving each other advice. I think it is just as important, and sometimes more important, to just be a good listener. And to ask good questions. So many times this leads to the person genuinely asking for advice and appreciating so much more the advice he does receive. When two people meet just so one can give advice to the other, the advice is not as valuable. Sometimes we need to just talk about fun and exciting things, and enjoy each other's company. Then it becomes more natural to ask for, give, and receive advice.

Give advice on only two conditions. First, when the advice is asked for. And second, when it is clear that a big mistake is going to be made, and that avoiding the mistake completely is better for the person than learning from the mistake. Because learning from mistakes is sometimes the only way to learn something. This may sound strange, but I am actually grateful for some of the mistakes I made in my life. If I had been advised to avoid the mistake and had followed that advice, I wouldn't have learned as much as I did by making the mistake and learning from it.

Saydi: While I was home for Christmas Dad and Mom and I were talking about all this "relationship, advice" stuff and Dad (on the verge of his guilt trip approach) said that maybe he'd just stop giving any advice at all. Maybe the solution should be to just work on his books, to just give advice to people who'll buy it in his books and send him great letters of praise, who'll even want him to personally address and sign the advice! Although it was kind of just a point Dad was making, I could tell that part of him really wondered if that was the solution (whether it was to make us realize what we're missing, or just to not put so much energy into thankless work—I don't know). We all know that despite this passing thought of Dad's, he'd never really stop giving advice—and thank heavens for that! But Dad's comment really got me thinking, and I felt panicked for a minute. I'd feel so sad if I didn't have Dad and Mom to look to for examples and advice. Yeah, sometimes Dad's advice might feel a little controlling, but we are old enough to not let that affect us. We are old enough to see the value and wisdom in Dad and Mom's advice. (What Mom is speaks so loudly that sometimes she doesn't need to say anything. Dad too—but he likes to say things.) Let's all keep that in mind, okay?

Within the family there is the power for complete renewal, salvation, joy and completeness. At the same time, there are powers to destroy, pull down, crush and hate. Because we are biologically, emotionally, and socially tied to our family members, they can have tremendous power in our lives. You can be helped or hurt the most by those who are closest to you. That's why love is so important. I like what it says a little later in the memo: Christ showed a perfect example. He loved so completely that he was able to scold, to be honest, to reproach, because people felt loved and accepted. I think we have that safety in our family, so we need to use it to help unlock the powerful influence of family and help one another progress. It's true, we can be more honest with one another because we love one another. I know that I need to use this obligation in two ways (both encompassed by mutual love that should be reassured and restated before doing either). First, I must ask for the honest opinion of my siblings and parents. They see me perhaps more clearly than anyone else and thus they can help me see what I cannot (bad breath). I need to be humble and open to really regarding and considering their advice, critique as well as compliments. Second, I need to be open with my siblings and parents and not keep thoughts that could help them to progress to myself because I fear their reaction. I need to be more prayerful in really being a powerful force in my family's life. If I can see things and help more powerfully than others then I feel obligated to put in the energy to do so. I can already think of some things that I should say (like to Dad that he really shouldn't wear those jeans with the white back pocket that he's had for years [ha ha ha!]).

Again, I don't like the "strategy" terminology. We need basic principles that we can act by when situations come up. All situations will be different. I don't like the idea of one proposed strategy; it would feel fake.

Sometimes the reason we become offended when we are offered advice or when our advice is rejected is because we don't feel the safety of complete love and confidence and support. Perhaps when Mom and Dad offer suggestions it would be good for them to surround them with a net of love and support and confidence in our abilities to make good choices and do what is right for us. They have taught us correct principles and part of letting us govern ourselves is showing their faith in our abilities and the truths that they have taught us. So perhaps it would be good to preface any advice by statements like, "We know you will do what is best for you; we know you will think it all through well and pray and know what it is the Lord would have you do. We also are confident that you have strength, talents, abilities, insights beyond what we have to do that which the Lord requires of you. So here's the advice; take it or leave it." Something like that would provide a buffer and make advice easier to give, accept, or reject.

Key element: Without the help and guidance of God through the Spirit, all of our efforts to work this out are futile.

Jonah: I feel great about the relationships that we all have but I am feeling like this is all a business and it can all be planned and mapped out to the point where smoother is better.

I don't think that there can be a "consulting relationship" between family members, at least not in a family like ours. A consultant by definition is totally free of obligation to the person receiving advice because there are certain contracts written and things signed to put the consultant out of harm's way.

Because parents know their children much better than a consultant knows his clients, parent is the term that should be used, so as not to confuse people.

The business model is great to illustrate points, but the term parents is so much more fitting to the role. God chooses the title "father" above all others.

What I am saying here is that the advice that parents give is always strong to me because I know how much they love me, but many times there is an urge to start making my own choices.

I hope that parents would sometimes allow their children to make less-than-perfect choices because that is how we learn. They are not forfeiting their stewardship by allowing their children to make their own decisions; they are enhancing it. By writing this I am not saying that there should be some huge decision to be made that parents should not offer suggestions, but I think that the suggestions that are offered should be asked for. If parents feel confident in what they taught their child then they will trust that they will choose right and if they choose wrong that they can learn from it. I think that sometimes the right choice is the wrong choice because we learn from it.

Talmadge: I wonder if any of the kids who have left feel like you parents are holding on too much or staying too involved in our lives? I don't think you two have the ability to "hang on" to them as much as you hang on to the kids at home.

It seems to me that those of us who live away just naturally become more independent and ask Mom and Dad for help and advice where needed. It's almost like M & D are the car batteries in our cars. It almost seems that you are ahead of us in our lives. You think about our problems and solutions before we do. You (parent batteries) keep trying to start our cars and the alternators (us) are not putting out the effort. Soon enough the battery will wear out because the alternator never pre-charged the battery. We need to take initiative!

With strong parents, it is harder to take initiative. I think it should be the other way around. We should be the batteries, and you (parents) the alternators. If we are constantly trying to fulfill our destiny, we will learn and you will help when you can.

We, the children, need to get going!

On paragraph 8: This is a part that I feel is very important. In Parley P. Pratt's description of the Spirit he indicates that "someone who has the Spirit doesn't get offended." If we take advice from someone with the Spirit, we will be better off and not be offended.

Our family isn't a business. We're an eternal unit and that means we will function the best on gospel principles (based on the Spirit) and not on man-made principles.

The way I keep seeing it, Mom and Dad, is that your example should propel us to want to excel in our lives. Thus we will naturally want to ask for your help on our decisions. We as kids just need to step it up and do better.

An ideal comment could be, "Dad and Mom, I've been thinking and praying about something in my life and I'd like to know what you think."

Eli: This is really good stuff. I agree with Sar and Tal's comments. It is true, that we need to have a good balance between brutally honest, and tact. If this were all to work out, especially between me and Charity, I would be the happiest kid around. But it is all of our faults when it gets screwed up. No one person can be blamed. We need to recognize our shortcomings, and pray and set goals to overcome them.

Aja: The problem with this memo is that it introduces the concept of fear and offense as a motivator of communication. In this way, the advice perhaps takes on a more defensive tone and suggests that parents gauge communication in order to avoid offending their children or "undermin[ing] their confidence by giving too much advice." Thus, those who "disclose everything" are pitted against those who "don't intrude" and "don't ask" on opposite sides of the spectrum. Are these really two distinct sides of the coin? The two sides are described as harsh extremes, and yet the rest of the memo seems to side with the far left.

I think that siblings' advice is more easily seen as just suggestions instead of "consulting"; there's less weight tied to accepting or rejecting the advice, so it's easier to listen to in the first place.

There should be cases where a parent can ask a trusted sibling to offer the advice rather than an authoritative parent.

Christ, I believe, could and does listen in a moment to the intent of someone's heart. I think that pinnacle of "unconditional, unquestioned love" is not being able to freely say what you think and have people freely take it or leave it, but instead loving someone so much that you know what they need from you, not just what one thinks they need. The greatest example of this is prayer—sometimes we need an answer and sometimes we need to go ahead on our own. We don't know which is which, but Heavenly Father knows us well enough to practice restraint and to give freely.

I disagree with the extreme lean toward the left of the spectrum—both sides have their equal merit, which makes me question whether there should be a spectrum at all. And does there need to be an agreement? Is there perhaps a flexible agreement that could actually work across family members and across time so that it could work for the other in-laws that will be coming into the family and the families they are going to start? We must not promote individual understanding and intense listening and conversation (instead of consulting). I do believe that a static agreement is possible, but would be too impersonal, too formulated. We didn't grow up all our lives with a family and spend countless hours together and learn to understand one another only to throw it out the window with one scheme to fit all.

The beauty and uniqueness of families is that unlike the world, there can always be love and support and people who understand you. I get enough advice and correction and formulas from the world, from school, from work, from friends, even from church. When I am home, whether it is in my mind, my heart, or in actuality, I need and look for that unending, uncalculated, effervescent love. That love corrects my shortcomings only because it loves the good parts of me so much, I feel like they can overtake the bad, and they do.

I would like to see more of a positive, simple statement of principles than this long contract.

The Eyrealm Social Grove (charting the evolution of our roles and relationships with each other and establishing enduring patterns of communication and advice, asking, giving, and receiving)

The feedback from our children helped us understand how dynamically and dramatically our roles and relationships with each other were changing and how important it was to have some basic agreements about how we would communicate and give advice to each other.

They all wanted to stay in close touch and to preserve the friendship and enjoyment we feel from each other, yet they all wanted their independence and agency to be respected. They wanted a special kind of trust and openness that was removed from the "norms" of the world, but they didn't want such complete openness that there was no tact and no sensitivity.

Beyond their e-mails, we had numerous phone chats, and it seemed like everyone in the family talked individually to everyone else. I (Linda) got together with all five girls in New York, and we discussed it further still. Finally, we came up with the simplified concept of the Eyrealm "social grove." Here is the e-mail where we tried to summarize it:

Dear Eyrealm LTNs:
Your feedback and ideas and suggestions on the "social" memo were fantastic. You've all seen each other's responses now, so you know how much agreement there was, and how many common suggestions. It helped us realize that we can never be (nor should we

want to be) "mere consultants" to you. Even as our relationship becomes more horizontal, we will always be your parents, and our advice and opinion, if not given in the right way, can be dangerous. Because of its emotional weight, it can cause overreaction (either in accord or in resistance) and can even undermine your free agency and independence.

We need to remind ourselves that each of us existed as individual unique spirits long before our family was formed. We are each who we are, and only God knows us fully. The family's role should not be to mold us into some stereotype or some copy or extension of our parents, but rather to help us each discover more who we each truly are and then to nourish and magnify that core into the best reality it can be.

The best metaphor we've been able to come up with together is a young grove of trees. As seedlings the new trees look very similar. They begin to differentiate as saplings because each is a different kind of tree: an oak, an elm, a poplar—but even more than that— each tree is unique, the only one of its exact kind, and that uniqueness is in the spirit seed which comes magically from afar rather than just dropping off of the older trees. The two parent trees, and indeed the whole growing grove itself, offers protection and community, and the roots of the trees even intertwine and draw and share the same nourishment. But, the trees don't try to change each other's identity and the parent trees are not disappointed when the saplings don't turn out to be just like them. Rather, they appreciate each other's diversity. As they grow, they shade and shield each other and eventually the young trees become fuller than their gradually and gracefully aging parents.

We seem to all like that image, and, with it in mind, we've worked together with all of you to boil down our "social agreements" into some simple principles, promises, and practices.

Social grove principles:

• Each individual's uniqueness must be discovered and appreciated.

• Each person's agency must be protected and respected.

• ASKING each other is the key to this discovery, appreciation, protection, and respect. Asking about needs and about dreams, and asking for opinions and advice.

Social grove promises:

• We will become "masters of the ASK," seeking each other's opinions and ideas and feelings and within this context we will each be both givers and receivers of advice.

• Even if the ASK principle is not followed, we will neither overreact (pro or con) to advice or be offended by it. Nor will we be offended if our advice is not followed.

• We will communicate openly and honestly and fully, using tact not as a devise but as a way to build each other and be sensitive and positive.

• In-laws (new sons- or daughters-in-law) come into the grove as complete equals both in our trust and in our sharing.

• We will seek time together and spend time together and prioritize time together despite all the other demands.

• If two or more Eyrealm members talk about a nonpresent member (an observation, a situation, how we can help) it will be kept positive and complimentary, and that member will be informed of the discussion right away.

Social grove practices:

• We hold a summer reunion each year at the Lighthouse [our summer home in Idaho] and an annual Eyrealm Foundation meeting, FFFE [Fathers and Future Fathers of Eyrealm] meeting, and MFME [Mothers and Future Mothers of Eyrealm] meeting which may be part of or separate from the reunion. One automatic part of each year's reunion is to refresh and recommit to our Eyrealm "constitution" which we are now constructing. There is also usually a separate "players meeting" (no parents or "coaches") and sibling "mentor-mentee" assignments.

• In addition to the annual family reunion, we schedule one more "coming together" each year, currently a trip for married Eyrealm members and a service expedition for single members.

• We send regular e-mail updates to each other to keep everyone up to date. In these updates, we share both the events of our lives and our concerns, joys, and challenges.

• Dad does a rotating monthly Sunday interview with each child (and an augmenting monthly letter that supports Mom's weekly updates).

Financial (Physical) Empty-Nest Parenting: Finding the Balance between Assistance and Independence

An investment broker and financial counselor we know has a sign in his office that says:

If you're wealthy, don't tell your kids!

The idea, of course, is to keep kids from squabbling over your wealth, and to encourage their own initiative and independence rather than a reliance on you.

A completely opposite view of the issue was illustrated once when we were hosting a TV talk show and interviewing Dick Van Patten (from the old *Eight Is Enough* TV series) and his family. One of the sons said what he liked most about his dad was that he'd tell him anything—including exactly how much money he had and what bank it was in.

Beyond how much our children know about our finances is the bigger question of how much financial assistance we give them after they leave home, after they have a full-time job, after they are married, after they have their own children.

We have two sets of friends who approach this issue in such strikingly opposite ways that their stories really establish the two extreme ends of a spectrum.

Bill and Marge Jones each grew up with little family money, had jobs after school and all summer, and worked their way through college. They feel this made them tough and independent and they want the same "blessings" for their kids. So, even though they are quite well off, they basically give their kids nothing beyond the basics of food and shelter, expecting them to earn all their own spending money while they're young and then either get scholarships or work and take student loans to get through college. Their kids have become marvelously resourceful and independent, but it took some of them seven or eight years to get through college and there is a certain resentment about the shoestring lifestyle they've been forced into.

Pat and Liz Smith also grew up relatively poor and had to make it on their own, but their goal is to make sure their kids don't have to do the same thing. They want their children to have all the advantages they didn't have, so they basically give them everything they need (and a lot of what they don't) financially and just encourage them to take advantage of every extracurricular opportunity and to do their very best in school. Thus the Smith kids went to far better (and more expensive) colleges than the Joneses, and they finished sooner and went on to graduate school. Now that they are out of school, though, they are having some trouble living within their means and learning to live independently from their parents.

The challenge for parents who have a reasonable level of resources is to try to be honest with children about their financial position and yet not let kids rely on it so much that it diminishes their own incentive and initiative.

People try to create this differentiation in lots of different ways. Not long after one friend of ours sold his Internet company for a very large sum, his fourteen-year-old daughter asked him, "Daddy, are we rich now?" With a chuckle, he replied, "Your mother and I are rich now, but you're as poor as ever."

The ultimate goal, of course, would be to give our children the independence and self-reliance of the Jones kids and the advantages and head start of the Smith kids. That seems like an almost impossible combination, but we have tried to do it by helping our children earn and save their own money through their adolescence but supplement what they've saved through educational "loans" from our family partnership that allow them to go to the best schools they can get into and progress into their careers and families and homes as rapidly as they want to. The "loans" carry no interest and are paid back at the discretion and timing of the child. The point is that they perceive it as their borrowed money and thus value their education more.

Case Study

We concluded long ago that the goal of financial empty-nest parenting should be a balance between advantage—giving assistance, and initiative—and giving independence. Here is how we tried to convey those conclusions to our LTN children:

> To: Eyrealm
> Re: Financial Issues: Draft Agreement
> From: Mom and Dad
> There are two parts to this memo. First, an overview of the principles of financial stewardship or the "Rules for Financial Freedom" which we've tried to teach and that we've discussed together over the years, and second, a summary of our proposal for how the First Intergalactic Family Bank of Eyrealm should work in terms of your ability to borrow, invest, and repay. Please view the whole memo as a proposed financial agreement for our ongoing physical and financial family.

I. Financial Principles of Stewardship and Perspective

1. We own nothing. Everything belongs to God and we are stewards. Take care of and magnify what you are given by God.

2. Each of us comes to earth with a mission or "foreordination" of what we should accomplish here. We must strive to recognize the gifts and opportunities that enable and lead us to our mission.

3. Money is a tool, much like health or access, valuable for the freedom and opportunities it gives rather than for itself. Like money, career and occupation are not ends in themselves but the means to the ends of family, relationships, service, and personal growth.

4. In other words, broadening and contributing (learning and giving) are the goals which are facilitated and enabled by financial resources and freedom.

5. There is a financial range (which may be different for different people) in which maximum happiness lies. If our financial and material resources are too small or if they are too large, we lose freedom and thus happiness.

6. "All battles are won on reserves." The biggest opportunities and challenges of your life will depend on whether you have some reserves to draw on—financial and otherwise.

II. Financial Principles of Implementation and Application

1. Pray for enough and try to understand what that means. (Ask God to provide and guide you to enough financial resources to meet your mission and to give you the freedom to make life choices on merit rather than on cost, but not so much that your things rob you of your time and your freedom.)

2. Practice the 10-20-70 formula (donate the first 10 percent or more of everything you earn to church or charity; invest the next 20 percent; and live on the 70 percent that remains).

3. Give something back—of time and money (with the 10 percent or more you give to church)—give something of yourself. Volunteer in some capacity on a regular basis.

4. Establish a formula for your 20 percent saving (only a small part of it in high risk investments; think long-term with no "trading;" have it all in a separate account to be removed only for "absolute emergency or opportunity," not for "consumable investments"—see #6 below).

5. No credit card or consumer debt. (Have one low-limit credit card on which you pay the entire balance each month to establish credit. Other than that, use only checks or debit cards and buy no consumables—including cars—on time or on credit.)

6. Borrow only for the two "consumable investments" of house and education. (Both, as you use and enjoy them are virtually guaranteed to provide a financial return that is greater than the interest you have paid.) On everything else, practice delayed gratification and pay as you go.

III. The First Intergalactic Family Bank of Eyrealm (FIFBE)

Our "bank," so called, is legally a Family Limited Partnership which has acquired and saved assets over the years for the primary purpose of providing financial assistance to our children ("Eyrealm" members), particularly for education and first-home purchase.

For undergraduate education, we pay room and board (since we would pay for those items if you continued to live at home). Entertainment, clothing, and incidental expenses continue to be your responsibility as they have been at home. Tuition, fees, and books are your responsibility (and your chosen "consumable investment") but you may borrow FIFBE funds to cover them beyond what your part-time work and your own savings in your 20 percent investment account will cover. Your loans (on which you will sign promissory notes) will accrue no interest and will have no repayment schedule. You will repay it according to your own circumstances and judgments following graduation.

For post-graduate education, all expenses including room and board are your responsibility, but you are able to borrow from FIFBE up to half of the total you need with the same no-interest, flexible payback conditions. The other one-half you must obtain from your own resources or from regular federal or university-supplied student loans.

For first-home purchase, FIFBE will provide matching funds on a down payment, putting up an equity amount equal to what you are able to supply personally. This will not be a loan but an equity investment in proportion to the total cost of the home (i.e., if you purchased a $250,000 home and wanted to make a $50,000 down payment, you would put up $25,000. FIFBE would match it with

$25,000 and the $200,000 balance would be your regular first mort-gage on which all payments would be your responsibility, along with all upkeep, improvement, and maintenance. FIFBE would own 10 percent of the home and receive 10 percent of the selling price whenever the home was sold. Your cost of materials for home improvement (not repairs) could be added to the home's cost, thus reducing FIFBE's equity percentage.

Spouses may become full-fledged Eyrealm members with the same opportunities, options, and obligations as "natural born" members.

Repayment of loans from FIFBE is to be both flexible and optional according to circumstances. Each Eyrealm member should feel responsibility to pay back what he or she can as he or she is able (without extreme sacrifice) according to circumstance and choice of profession. (The investment bankers among you might be expected to perform a quicker payback than the teachers and social workers.)

Though we've discussed most of this agreement in some detail, please respond with your corrections, concerns, and counteroffers.

Our children had basically grown up with many of these principles in place, but the memo was the first time they'd seen the approach all written up in one place. Here are some of their responses:

Saren: I don't know if having or lacking "things" can rob you of time and/or freedom—I think it's more thinking about things that can rob us of time and free-dom. No matter how much you have, you can think too much about what you have or don't have and therefore take your thoughts away from more important areas.

I think it's important that we all understand that savings may have to fluc-tuate slightly over the years and that different things can constitute savings. For example, right now, we can't save 20 percent of our paycheck—after tithing and our mortgage we barely have enough to live on. Still, we do save—10 per-cent goes right into a stock purchase plan, 5 percent goes into a 401K, and a ton of our money goes into our mortgage payment—and since our house is a big chunk of our savings/investment, we consider that to be savings, too.

Money in a straight savings account won't grow fast. I think it'd be great if you'd encourage everyone to do their own research and ask for advice from lots of people about the best ways to make investments. You should really suggest everyone start a 401K as soon as they get a job and start a Roth IRA ASAP—I wish I'd started one right out of college—but I didn't know about it!

It might be good to have a formula for repayment of educational loans. Maybe you could propose a certain percentage of a paycheck once the education is finished—perhaps a certain percentage for while people are single or married with double income and a certain percentage for those who have kids. I'd feel better about all my loans if I'd been paying off a little every month over the past ten years since I graduated. Your proposed formula could be very flexible, but I think it would make the loans and the repayment feel more "real."

Do you want to make it clear that you guys will pay for one semester of study abroad? You paid for that for me and it was so good of you! Thanks.

I think there should be some emergency savings that we're encouraged to keep and not spend on education or down payments on houses, don't you agree?

What about paying for people to come home for special events? You should state what you're willing to pay for.

I think there should be some sort of general statement at the beginning of this saying that you guys want to use your financial assets to help us broaden and contribute.

Shawni: I am so thankful for this insight you have ingrained into our minds. I think the root of so much unhappiness lies in the inability to recognize the fact that all we have belongs to God. I've seen greed and materialism cause so many problems in the lives of so many people who are close to me. It makes me sad. But I can totally see how easy it is to get caught up in all that, and have to watch myself sometimes. We live in a world of wanting more and more. People rack up more and more credit card debt to keep up with friends and to have things they think they need. It's so refreshing when I meet someone who understands fully the principle that we are only stewards over material things. I am so thankful for the tithing we pay to the Church and the little bits we are able to give to charity. I think it's such a great tool to help us recognize over and over each month that all we have really belongs to God anyway.

I feel so sad for those who don't have the financial resources and freedom with which to facilitate broadening and contributing. I just feel extra sensitive to this since I felt so strapped financially in the early parts of my marriage. It was literally painful to feel so much freedom locked up because we were so financially unstable. Now that Dave has a better job and things are better it scares us to death to go back to living without money. Maybe that's a bad thing to be so dependent on money, but it's true that not having it takes away so much freedom to do things that broaden and contribute. Having said that, I must say that

I sure felt like we were "broadening" (or learning) when we were so financially insecure. We learned how much we want to take care of financial stewardships and how important it is to be giving and to contribute what you have when you do have financial resources because we were so thankful to people who were so generous and kind to us when we needed it.

Josh: Shouldn't the "percentage" formula really be 10-20-30-40 instead of 10-20-70? 10 percent to church, 20 percent to investment, 30 percent to the government, and 40 percent to live on? Two things you can't avoid: death and taxes. Seriously, I really believe strongly in doing this. Ever since I started earning money—way back with my paper route and picking raspberries in the summer—I have always tried to follow this advice. If it is done consistently and the 20 percent is invested wisely, it can lead to so much financial freedom down the road. Sometimes I have not been as strict with myself as I have at other times, and I later wish that I would have saved more.

I agree with most of the memo, but I don't think there is anything wrong with experimenting with stock "trading" every once in a while. It should never become a habit, but you sure do learn a lot by trying it out!

Credit cards can be so dangerous. But if they are used carefully, they can be very helpful and beneficial. I actually use credit cards quite a lot. But I am very strict on the two rules that I follow. When I use a credit card to buy something, I deduct the amount from my checking account, just as though I am using a debit card. If I don't have enough money in my checking account, I don't buy it. And the other rule is that I always, always, always pay the entire balance every month. It is never a problem, because the money is already withdrawn in my checking account records, and all I have to do is make a simple transfer on the Internet. I have never paid a penny of interest on a credit card, because I pay the full balance off every month. It is like a free thirty-day loan, but it shouldn't even be thought of as a loan, because charges should be deducted directly from your checking account. Also, you should never get a cash advance with a credit card, because interest in cash advances starts to accrue immediately. There is no thirty-day grace period as there is with purchases. My cards also have no annual fees.

There are several benefits in using credit cards like this. First, you build good credit. When the time comes to buy a house, people will be looking at your credit report, and if you have used credit cards in the manner I just explained, you will have a very high credit rating. Another good reason to use credit cards is that many of them have added benefits, such as insurance and cash-back awards. If you use them correctly, you can actually get money back depending on how much you charged to it. Products purchased with credit cards are usually insured from damage or theft, and it gives a little more peace of mind when making certain purchases. They have their own built-in return policy as well. Some have other types of included insurance. With some you can get free airline miles with every dollar spent, although these ones usually have an annual fee. And another good reason to have at least one credit card is that there are some instances, such as renting cars, where using a credit card is the only way you can get what you want.

Even with all the benefits credit cards have, they can be so dangerous. You have to be extremely disciplined and follow your own rules very strictly. If the rules are ever bent, it can lead to big, big problems.

I was always very grateful that you did this education loan thing. I think it is important to act as though you are paying for it—look for inexpensive housing, similar to what you would pay for if it were coming out of your pocket, look for good deals on food. The tuition loans from the family help us value our college experience and degrees. I have thought if this is how I will do this in my family, and I guess it really depends on my financial situation at the time.

Saydi: As a social worker I think a lot about how much good I could do and how many needy people I could help. I know there is so much that I need to do and right now it's hard to see how I won't be frustrated with all my good ideas but no means to move them to fruition! Ahhh! I need to find a rich husband (for much different reasons than most people want to marry rich!). Once I find him, he'll never be able to be one of those filthy rich people. I'll use it all before it gets to be too much! (Maybe I shouldn't tell him that until after we are married!)

I see so many people here in New York who don't understand that money is not an end in and of itself. They get so caught up in the glamour of having more than they know what to do with. Sometimes they get to a level where money is seen as a means to an end—but the end is just to get above others on the competition ladder, to play the game of who has the most! It's so sad and it doesn't bring happiness as far as I can see. The happy ones are the ones who are poor and generous! It's rare when I see a rich, generous, happy person. When I do I greatly admire them for what they have achieved.

Just a note. I don't know how this could be incorporated, but I have the coolest friend who is married and they decided that in addition to paying tithing, whatever money they use on their own personal entertainment they match it and put the funds into an account that they use for service-related activities or that they donate to humanitarian causes or give to homeless people. I thought that was a good way of balancing what you spend on yourself and what you spend on others. Good idea, huh? I think this is something that saves one's sanity when you are exposed to poverty and those who need so much. It's so hard to indulge and justify spending money on yourself after serving and seeing people with nothing. This kind of keeps that all in check somehow.

Jonah: I am so impressed by how the financial principles we have learned in our family have applied to life. I have actually been saving 40 percent for the past six months. Aja and I live on hardly anything because we were both taught to be conscious of our money and how we spend it. We have also been greatly blessed by parents who understood this principle and could help us not to go into debt and not to have big student loans to pay off for the next ten years after we graduate. What an immense blessing! I totally agree with all that is written in part 1 of this memo.

I feel bad sometimes that Eli and Charity weren't around in the days of the van and the old Mercedes. Although you can now afford to buy new cars, I remember how much you used to impress on us never to buy a new car. I have saved so much in knowing that I can get around in a less-than-perfect car.

I really think that this memo turned out the best because it can all be measured and there can be hard-and-fast rules set, where on all the other memos there are always going to be some differences between how a different child will react to different policies. Financial parameters are so much easier to set because you are dealing with numbers instead of minds. Absolutes, instead of unknowns are much easier to write about and to organize like a business.

Aja: I don't know what to say about this memo. I totally agree with saving and investments, and I like the Eyrealm bank. I still owe you a discussion of how money works in my family, but the more I think of it, the less different it seems from yours. I guess there just wasn't a very calculated contract of saving and everything when we were little—I think we just watched my parents save so much and be so frugal and still make us feel financially secure even though we lived on a dirt road in a trailer house, that we contracted the saving disease. Plus, we all had to get jobs in the summer and did babysitting during the school year, so we quickly figured out that two hours of work is not worth one stinky CD. Better to save it and get some interest. Anyway, other little differences, but not much.

The Eyrealm Financial Foundation (establishing a structure of financial independence and assistance that enables and empowers)

After wading through the emotional and social parts of our effort at an adult family constitution, the financial part seemed more straightforward. Maybe this was because, by definition, it can be reduced to numbers and formulas, and we had worked out and established many of these while the kids were still small.

Still, there were some corrections and clarifications that the kids' responses had suggested, and we now wanted to put the whole thing into the "principles, promises, and practices" format that was evolving. Also, we wanted to have an "image" or metaphor for this physical or financial part as we did for the other facets.

> Dear Eyrealm LTNs,
>
> Thanks for your memo responses which were so strong and supportive but which also pointed out the need for certain clarification. Since then, we've talked enough together that it seems we're all on the same page and that the best simplifying metaphor here is that of a foundation. You each are designing and building your own unique lives, but it may take you longer and you may not be able to build as strong or as tall if you don't have any foundation to start off with.
>
> As adult Eyrealm members, we all agree that it's best for each of us to pay our own way as much as possible, yet as your parents we don't want you to be held back or delayed by financial limitations. For example, we want you to be able to go to the best schools you can get into and graduate and move on as soon as you can rather than to compromise or delay because of financial limitations, and we want you to have a house sooner because you have a down payment rather than later because you don't.
>
> This balance between assistance and independence is the basis for the physical or financial facet of our Eyrealm constitution which, with your help, can be revised a little to fit the principles, promises, practices framework.
>
> **Financial foundation principles:**
> • We are not owners but stewards.
> • Money is a tool, a means to the ends of broadening and contributing and of finding and fulfilling foreordination.
> • There is a financial range in which maximum freedom and happiness lies.
> • All battles are won on reserves.
> **Financial foundation promises:**
> • Pray for enough (and to know what is enough).
> • Practice 10-20-70.

- Hold the 20 in an "off limits" investment account and deplete only for education or house down payment.
- No credit or consumer debt (other than one low-limit credit card).
- Go beyond the 10 by volunteering and/or having a "personal giving fund" equal in size to your entertainment budget.

Financial foundation practices:

- FIFBE covers room and board for undergraduate college and the entire cost of one semester abroad.
- All Eyrealm members can borrow interest free from FIFBE for undergraduate or graduate education as outlined in earlier memo and each establishes their own repayment schedule.
- All members can have FIFBE as a down-payment–supplying equity partner in a first home purchase as outlined in the earlier memo.
- According to your circumstances and depending on your career choice and income level, all members will attempt to repay and replenish FIFBE so it can continue to make loans to other Eyrealm members and cover travel, reunions, and other broadening and contributing Eyrealm activity.
- We hold a "finance session" at each Eyrealm conference to review FIFBE status, to share ideas and insights on individual investing, and to discuss each other's employment and career options.
- An Eyrealm trust fund is established to provide matching funds for grandkids' education.
- Each grandchild receives shares in a mutual fund at birth. At age eight, these shares are put in the child's control as the start of his or her 20 investment account and governed by the same "off limits."

Elaboration

As Jonah pointed out in his responses, this financial facet of our empty-nest family was easier to define and lay out because it deals with tangibles rather than intangibles.

For our own approach and plan, we owe a lot of acknowledgment to our attorneys and accountants who were so instrumental in setting it all up. While each family would (and should) do it differently, let us simply share our model as a "case study."

As individuals and in our own names we try to own less than what can be passed on without estate tax. The family partnership owns a summer home and other assets that we want to pass on to the kids. (Thus they already own them since they are the partners in the family partnership or LLC [limited liability corporation]). We (Linda and Richard) are the general partners so we control those assets as long as we're alive. We get assets into the partnership either by gifting them (you can give $10,000 per year to each child without tax consequences) or by creating some kind of business within the partnership that generates its own profits. The family bank is also a part of the partnership from which the kids can take educational loans or partner for the down payment on their homes. Technically these "loans" are distributions from that child's capital account within the partnership. If and when they repay it, their capital account (share of ownership) is restored.

Our retirement account's obvious purpose is to fund our retirement, should that ever actually occur. Whatever is left in it when we're gone (as well as in our own estate) goes not to the kids but first (up to a certain limit) to an educational trust fund which will provide matching funds for grandkids' college education. (The matching kicks in after their investment account funds are used. Whatever is there beyond that trust fund will go to the family charity.)

Our family charity, while it doesn't have great amounts of money (and had to be qualified as a 501 c 3 nonprofit entity) has been a real joy to us. Our adult children constitute its board of directors and meet once a year (in connection with our family reunion) to decide on what charitable gifts we should make that year. They look for small charitable causes—soup kitchens, mentoring organizations—where a few thousand dollars could make a big difference, and allocate whatever the foundation can afford for that year. Thus they are getting together with the unselfish motive of selfless giving rather than getting together as some families do to selfishly argue about who gets what from the family estate (that kind of meeting will never happen in Eyrealm since whatever estate there is will go into the family charity and be available only as gifts to charitable causes).

What the kids (and grandkids) will have financially when we're gone (other than the principles we've tried to teach them) will be some education trust funds and the summer home that has been part of our tradition and that they will hopefully keep forever as a gathering place. The grandchildren are also given a modest amount at birth, in the form of a mutual fund "birthday gift." This grows for eight years and starts off their 20-percent investment account, which they contribute to and which is off-limits except for education and first-home purchase.

Tying Service into the Formula (Giving Something Back)

I (Linda) have thought so much lately about how hard it is to really be grateful for what we have until we don't have it any more. It's hard to truly appreciate your thumb until it's broken and you can't use it. It's hard to really adore the time you have with your preschoolers until they've gone off to school. For the purposes of this chapter, we have to remind ourselves that it is hard to really appreciate money management skills until we run onto hard times or don't have it anymore—unless you are blessed with an experience that we've had in recent months that has helped us to see what might happen in a family with *no* financial skills or training.

Two months ago we decided to do a Church service mission. This involves attending church services in a new location with an inner-city ward, enjoying new associations and being assigned to care for some "special needs families" and to give them assistance in whatever way we can. What a great learning experience this has been!

At the core of the problems of many of these families is the lack of financial stability and sensibility. Even though they are on welfare, there is no way most of them can pay the rent and utilities. The Church is helping, but the families are desperately in need of a long-term solution to their long-term problems.

One of the greatest blessings for us is that these dire situations and financial disasters help us to be so very grateful for our own good, hard-working, loving, financially conservative parents who, even though they were near the poverty lines themselves, taught us principles of earning and saving that we just took for granted. When we were children, we thought everyone lived that way. Thankfully, due to this recent Church service mission, we haven't had to actually experience the loss of financial stability in order to truly appreciate it.

As your children prepare to leave your nest and you continue to work with them on financial planning, add service to the mix. Volunteer everywhere you can—from soup kitchens to ward welfare assignments. Besides the joy of service, this will give your children the opportunity to see the consequences of mishandled finances and to gain fresh appreciation for what they have. Work together with your children to teach sound financial principles to others and the teaching will reinforce the knowledge in your own children. Talk together about what you observe in the financial lives of others.

Mental Empty-Nest Parenting: Helping with Each Other's Goals—and Staying Stimulated

I (Linda) was almost in a trance as I watched one of the last high school assemblies that our youngest son Eli would be a part of. It was the last half of his senior year which had seemed to be slipping through our hands like water through a sieve. With delight, I watched the absolutely darling brigade of senior boys doing the "River Shants," a technical "dance" choreographed by the head cheerleader and performed by a bunch of senior boys, including Eli. These boys had practiced and refined to the point that even the original River Dancers would have been impressed. A smile leaked from everyone's face in the audience as we watched them all kicking and whirling in their open-necked white shirts and shants (for those who may not know, this is a cross between shorts and pants which was extremely popular at our school at that moment). Feeling like there was a knife in my heart, I realized that no matter how much I wanted to stop it or freeze it, time was marching on! Soon those great kids who had watched movies and played basketball and Nintendo at our house and had raided the food cupboard in our garage (stocked especially for them) would be gone. Even though many would keep in touch, most would be gone onto a new world of work, college, and missionary service.

My reverie was broken by one of the other mothers who slipped into the seat beside me and began to share the worries on her mind. It was the day after parent/teacher conferences. Interestingly, her concerns were not about her son who was a straight A student, but her cousin's son whose family had been transferred across the country and who she had offered to care for so that he could finish his senior year and his soccer career with a team that had a shot at the state championship. This young man was one of Eli's friends who had often been in our home.

"He's failing in every class!" she moaned. "His citizenship grades are awful too. Once the soccer season was over and he didn't have to maintain eligibility, he just dropped everything. He stays up late and goes to school only when he feels like it. I don't know if he'll even be able to graduate! Plus, I'm feeling like the Wicked Witch of the West when I try to make him do what he should. Our relationship is strained to the max. What can I do?"

I felt so sorry for this good mother who was doing her best in a difficult situation. I also felt sorry for the terrific young man who we all loved and whose soccer season had been a big disappointment. The only thing I could think to say was, "Sounds like Travis needs to set some goals."

The assembly ended and my friend and I were hurled back into our own worlds. But I couldn't help thinking about our conversation and how important setting and working toward goals is as we progress through life. This boy had probably not thought much about what he wanted in his life past the soccer championship. High school kids are especially good at living for the moment. Unfortunately there is no way we can really set goals for them. We can encourage them by providing a framework for them. We can add physical tools like paper and pencils and insist they work on their goals each week. We can ask them to consider what they want to do in the coming year: physically, socially, emotionally, mentally, and spiritually. Yet the only way they are ever going to follow through on things they think they should or would like to do is if they "own" them.

No matter how much we would like to set goals for them based on what they need to do in order to accomplish the things we want them to do, it will never work unless the goals are their ideas and the plans of how to accomplish them come from their heads. We can cajole and bribe until the cows come home, but by the time our children are ready to leave home, goals are useless unless they come out of the head of the owner!

In our house, with a father who is "a goal master" (sort of like the Yoda of Goals), our children have been setting goals since they were old enough to draw pictures. At three, every child started having what we call a "Sunday Session," which consisted of them drawing a picture on their goal chart for the week of (1) something that they could do for a family member that week: "get the diapers for the baby when Mommy needs them," (2) something they could do for a friend: "share a toy," and (3) something they can do to show that they love Heavenly Father: "say my prayers every night." The pictures that they drew were hilarious and a visual reminder of a simple goal.

As time passed, the Sunday Session became a habit (sometimes a parent-enforced one). Once a year, during the last week of August, we had the kids do a little longer session where they set their school-year goals, thought of their own personal "theme for the year" and actually made a chart that showed their goals and included a few of the plans to accomplish them.

Before you send yourself on a guilt trip, please know that we know that every parent does not have a gift or a drive for teaching their children to set goals. Those who do may have other, even better methods and those who don't are most assuredly better at some other parental responsibility. Our experience has simply taught us that kids need to set their own goals and that they benefit hugely from it. And as we've said to parents so many times, it's best to start early, but it's never too late!

If you have the luxury of a few more years with your children at home, during their junior and senior years when they are busy taking the SAT and ACT tests and thinking about college, it is important to spend some time helping them think about where they are going and what they want to do with their lives. For most, the long-term is still pretty vague, but they know what they're good at and probably need some time beyond what they might do at a college fair or a counselor's office thinking about what they dream of becoming. They can really benefit from your insights about their talents and your guiding questions about what they might want to pursue.

If your children have already left home and you haven't talked much about goals, arrange a dinner or even a phone call where the entire conversation is based on a presentation of their goals and an in-depth talk about what they think they'd like to become. It will give you a chance to hear some things that you may not have known. Though you may be dying to give advice during the conversation, remember that while advice may be important, admiration, encouragement and praise is infinitely more important. Be careful not to assume that they have already spent some time thinking about their life goals. Time to think and talk about their goals exclusively and a chance to present them to you formally will add so much to their ability to truly "own" them. If you really want them to share their goals and dreams, you may want to start by sharing your own!

The real beauty of parenting children who have set their own goals is that you become their helper and their supporter rather than their nagger or their criticizer. It's their goal which they set and you are trying to help them accomplish it. This casts you and your relationship in a completely different light than when you are just trying to get them to do what you think they should.

Herding or "Influencing"

A lot of us who like old west novels and movies aren't aware of how much the job (and the philosophy) of real cowboys has changed. "Cowboys"—those "boys" who get cows from the range to the market—used to herd them with their horses and their lariats and their dogs—keeping the herd together, moving them along, and rounding up any strays. The problem with this old-fashioned kind of cowboying was that the cattle were too stressed by the herding and harassing and lost too much weight by the time they got to market. What successful cowboys do today is called "influencing." They ride along way out on the perimeter of the herd and try, just by their presence and direction, to influence the ways in which the cattle move.

Instead of whooping and yelling and slapping and sending out the dogs, they actually sing—it seems to calm the cattle as well as letting them know where the cowboys are and influencing them to move along at their own pace in the right general direction.

Mental empty-nest parenting ought to change and evolve in similar directions. Small children, growing up in our homes, need a certain amount of correction, of management, of firm direction—of "herding." What grown children need and deserve (and the only thing they will accept over the long term) is "influencing." We should strive to be a calm and reassuring influence in their decisions, their goals, and their lives. When we push too hard, or herd, it always creates stress and often resistance or rebellion.

Of course the analogy breaks down, because in empty-nest parenting our children, not us, choose which market or destination they're going to, and there is no cowboy-cattle distinction. We are the same and they are equal with us.

When we made our first attempt at a "mental empty-nest agreement" we hadn't quite figured this out. Still, the memo was an honest attempt, and it led to some great feedback and resolutions.

It was with these thoughts in mind that we drafted our mental ENP memo:

Case Study

> To: Eyrealm
>
> From: Dad and Mom (particularly, in this case, Dad)
>
> Re: The Mental Functions of Eyrealm
>
> 1. I've always said (and felt, deeply) that the most important thing you would ever learn from your parents was a true empathy and a genuine concern for other people, which I knew you would learn 90 percent from your mother, who possesses this Christlike quality as an abiding gift. If I, on the other hand, have a corresponding gift (albeit a gift of less importance), that I've wanted to pass on to each of you, it is my ability to "bring things to pass" by setting goals and implementing plans.
>
> 2. My efforts to pass this ability on to you have ranged from helping you draw pictures of three simple weekly goals (one for school, one for self, one for family) before you were old enough to write, to the proper use of planning books, and day timers, to our personal mission statements, to hourglass-timed "Sunday Sessions,"

to the rather sophisticated yearly "theme and goal charts" that we prepare together each summer for the year ahead.

3. One of my greatest sources of pride (the good kind of pride, I hope) is to see how good each of you have become at goal setting and planning. You've each adapted and developed your own way—which matches your own personality and approach—and you're now becoming my teachers as you continue to get better and better at deciding what you want and then bringing it to pass.

4. All of which is why it's even more exciting (and mutually beneficial) to talk about and help each other with goals now that you've become an adult and moved away from home. As we consult with and advise each other on our goals and plans for our individual families, our educations, our careers, and our service, we not only synergize and refine those goals, we communicate on a whole new and fully sharing level and we stimulate and motivate each other, opening new insights and perspectives to one another.

Proposed Agreement

5. Thus, we suggest that we should all agree to continue the tradition of each creating for ourselves a large "goal and theme" chart for each new year and sharing these creations with each other for insight and enhancement. We suggest that we continue to have our "year's" start in the fall with the start of the school year. This allows us to develop our goals and themes during the summer and then to complete, refine, and share them with each other at the August Bear Lake Eyrealm reunion.

6. The individual and collective benefits of setting and sharing our yearly goals are:

A. It maximizes our chances to make each year a masterpiece of sorts by thinking it through in advance and "creating it spiritually."

B. It attracts inspiration and divine guidance; makes our prayers more specific and thus our answers.

C. It improves and deepens the communication and trust between us—because we are sharing with and helping each other on our most intimate hopes and desires.

D. It facilitates the "consulting" relationship discussed in the "social ENP memo"—and fosters the "share all, be offended by none" mentality.

E. It sets both a proactive, goal-setting example and a communication example for the next generation (your children and our grandchildren).

F. It gives us a basis and reference point for the weekly "hourglass" Sunday planning sessions to which we're all committed and makes those Sunday hours a kind of link and bond between us all as we share the practice.

7. As we take active interest in each other's goals and in the process by which those goals are set, we become more appreciative of how each other thinks and of our potential to both stimulate and be stimulated by one another's ideas and perspectives. Thus we accept the opportunity and the responsibility of sharing things we've read or heard or experienced that we think might motivate and enhance each other's minds.

Here are some of our children's responses to the "mental memo."

Saren: I don't remember us doing these "yearly theme and goal charts" at our reunions. I've only seen Eli and Charity's goal and theme charts—does anyone else do them? I think it's an idea that came along after I had left. It sounds like a good idea and it probably works well for some people. Doing school-year-based goals is also a good idea for some people. For Jared and me, the school year has no real meaning right now so we're doing Jan-Dec goals. I don't think it's a good idea to state here that you think this is the best way for us all to be setting goals, especially after you just said that we all do things in our own ways and you think it's great.

I propose that this summer, we all share our methods of goal setting—both long- and short-term. I'd be very interested to hear what everyone else is doing these days, especially the other married couples. Maybe we need to just ask open-ended questions about how people do goals and glean ideas from each other rather than saying that we should all do goals for a certain time frame in a shared manner. It would be great to share our goals when we get together this summer as well as talk about processes we use.

I also propose that we take some time this summer to talk about how we can help each other reach our goals. One idea might be to find "goal buddies" who have a similar goal to us so that we can check up on each other. Shawni and I have shared goals lots of times about eating right or doing other things and it's great to check up on each other.

With this memo, I think it would be good to do a list of principles of goal setting that we can all agree on (sort of like you did in the financial memo) and then propose a list of practices that could support these principles. Something like:

Lifetime, era, yearly, monthly, and weekly goals help us to consciously and consistently move forward in our lives, fully embracing the concept of eternal progression.

Setting goals in specific priority areas helps us maintain balance in our lives (i.e., family, career/school/projects, personal, others).

Setting aside time each week and extra time once a month to review and set goals is vital to the goal-setting and reaching process.

Sharing our goals with spouses and with family members helps us to reach them.

To support these principles, we propose:

All members of Eyrealm have weekly Sunday Sessions.

Once a year, Eyrealm members share their yearly goals, talk about their goal-setting processes and strategize together about how they can help each other reach certain goals.

Once a year, Eyrealm members make a few specific goals for what they'd like to collectively accomplish during the year (a service project, a family newsletter, help for some extended family members—a couple of cousins need help right now).

I also think that this memo needs to address some of the other aspects of "mental ENP" which might include:

How can we stimulate each other's minds (book reviews, quote exchanges, and so on)?

How can we learn from each other (maybe report at conferences on the most important things we've learned that year [about the world, people, ourselves, the gospel] or a new subject or book that we think everyone would be interested in?)

What can we do to make sure everyone's getting enough mental stimulation (especially those at home with young children who may feel at times that their intellectual minds are underutilized)?

Shawni: Neither Dave nor I has ever done this type of "goal and theme" chart before. This is something that you started after I left home and I've seen them before but have never been involved in the steps to doing them.

When we get married off into our own families it just has to change a little somehow. It's not the same as when we were just one individual family unit and we shared everything in life. Maybe it's not all healthy to always "share all" because sometimes new family units need their own unique bond and things they only share with each other.

It's weird but as you get married and spin off into your own little planet family, things aren't as "public" as they are when you're still in your little home orbit around the sun with no one else to pull you in another direction. This is not to say that Dave pulls me in a bad way away from you, but he has his own way of doing things and sometimes I think he needs to figure out his own way for his own sanity. Our family has so many systems and traditions and unique ideas that I think others who join in want to find another way to do things—not because they don't agree with what's being done, but because they would feel helpless and insignificant if they just followed along with the status quo, never questioning, never reevaluating.

So I guess what I'm trying to say is that I really agree with and love the idea in this memo, but I have to take my own new family into account too and we need to figure out a system that works well for us. I think it's great to help each other out and be aware of what everyone else in the family is striving for—and it definitely makes us feel closer and more bonded so I will commit to try my best to do this. But I don't think we can just expect everyone who joins in the family to jump right in and follow the current.

I totally agree with Saren's comment about stimulating each other's minds. We all have such different and diverse interests and curiosities thus we can gain so much by sharing with each other. We can (and do, I think) help each other become the best we can be by observing each other and learning from each other.

Josh: I have a problem with this proposal. In item 3, you say "You've each adapted and developed your own way—which matches your own personality and approach, and you're now becoming my teachers as you continue to get better and better at deciding what you want and then bringing it to pass." But then you suggest that we all should do our goals your way—with the charts. How are we going to learn from what we've adapted and developed if we revert back to a system that many of us were never even a part of? I think that if we are going to do any sharing (which in itself I am a little uneasy about), it should be the sharing of our own systems, and how we each individually bring things to pass.

The "goal and theme" chart sounds like a good thing for visual people. Dad is very visual and he likes to make charts and things that he can look at. I would have a hard time coming up with a large chart, and it wouldn't be something that I would hang on my wall and look at. I am more of a mental person. I agree that it is important to write goals down, but I like to structure them in my mind rather than on a poster. And I always set my yearly goals at the beginning of the year now that I am not in school. Perhaps when my own kids start school I will go back to beginning in the fall.

I don't want this to sound negative, but I really feel that there are many goals that are personal, only between me and Heavenly Father, that I don't want to share with everyone. It is good to share some goals, but I would feel uncomfortable sharing all of my goals with the family. I don't mind sharing goals after I have achieved them, but there are some that I just feel should not be shared.

There are some things I want to do in life because I personally made that decision and did it all myself, not because people are expecting it of me because they heard I was going to do it or because they are watching me and following up on me. If people always knew what I wanted to do, it would take much of the spontaneity and surprise out of life. "Congratulations, you did it, but I already knew you were going to do it." It's a hard thought to explain, but one that I feel strongly about.

Jonah: This one is a hard one for me. I know that I am good at goal setting and I have really adapted a lot of what I have been taught by you, but I just feel like I am not doing it quite right all the time because you made it such a system. I feel like you addressed this well in 3. Right now in my life I really don't feel like I have a lot of goals—but I really do. Actually I guess that they are all plans and I know what I am working toward. Aja makes goals in a completely different way than I and she seems to be effective in reaching each one of her goals. She just makes lists and crosses things off each day as she finishes them. Her goals are what we would call plans. Our goals together are strong and solid but we are just trying to integrate the different ways that we get things done.

I think that we should totally be able to share our goals because in many cases I think that we can help each other to reach the goals that are set. Because we are all going to have very different professions I think we will be able to have our own "networking" only it will be much more effective than business networking because we have better communication and experience together than any business could ever develop.

I know that Aja and I will eventually develop some kind of perfect goal-making and striving process but I really think that we are going to have to create the method ourselves. We should share it all but need to realize that the methods for setting and reaching goals are and will be different for each of us. There will be some common threads because of our upbringing, but we will bring strength and variation because of our ability to adapt to the way that our spouses were taught.

Talmadge: The bottom line on this whole part is that we've (the children) got to step it up and really broaden and contribute. I imagine the amazing synergy if we could all step it up and be a little more aggressive in our own individual goal setting.

Aja: I like this memo, even though I'm not totally used to this whole formulated goal-setting program yet, because it's so different than what I'm used to. I obviously could comment on some of the "fully sharing level" and "consulting" comments because I think they are a little too formulated, but all-and-all, I say Gung-Ho! Oh, one question: What should happen when someone doesn't like or has misgivings about someone's goals or lack of a specific goal? Are we just going to tell each other straight out?

The Mental "Watchtower" of Eyrealm (synergizing with and stimulating each other in the arts of mental creation and perspective expansion)

Well, our "mental" memo stimulated lots of important feedback and brought out some important issues. After trying to digest it all, we made our attempt to reduce the "mental facet" of our adult family agreement to a memorable metaphor and to the principles, promises, and practices format.

Dear Children:

Once again, your response, this time to the "mental memo" was illuminating. It's interesting that we all appreciate each other's interest in and support of our individual dreams and goals, but none of us want to be stereotyped or confined in how we do our goal setting and planning and we each want to make the choice as to which goals we share and how we share them. And we all see the "mental" facet of Eyrealm as broader than just the sharing of goals; it includes stimulating and educating each other and sharing everything from ideas and perspectives to favorite books.

What it really seems that we want to do for each other is to elevate and expand our perspectives—to lengthen and broaden our views. By ourselves, each of us has a limited, ground-level view of the terrain around us and even of where we want to go in that terrain. But together, and with the individual and collective mental resources of Eyrealm, we can boost each other up onto a "watchtower" and see further and with more perspective, thus understanding the world around us better and also having a sharper vision of what we each might be able to accomplish and where we might be able to go in the world.

With that image in mind, and drawing from the ideas each of us gave, perhaps we can all arrive at the following strategy or agreements for the mental Eyrealm.

Mental watchtower principles:

• Desires and dreams must become goals and plans in the mind before they can become realities in the world.

• Sharing your goals with those who love you unconditionally refines the goals, commits you to their pursuit, and increases their chance of being accomplished.

• Lifebalance results from goalbalance. The three prime stewardships are family, work, and self ("self" includes the service you choose to give others). Both our goals and our life should balance them.

• From foreordination insights and from eternal and lifetime goals, we can "draw down" goals for the seasons and eras of our lives. From these we can draw down yearly, monthly, and weekly goals.

Mental watchtower practices:

• We will each seek divine guidance in laying out our lives according to God's will.

• We will each share selected yearly goals and their derivation (and our own unique goal-setting methods) at the annual Eyrealm conference—establishing commitment and seeking suggestions.

• We will each hold a weekly "hourglass Sunday Session" that reflects yearly and monthly goals for family, work, and self.

• We will be aware of, and offer help and support for, the goals of each other Eyrealm member.

• We will each share in the responsibility for the ongoing mental stimulation and education of each Eyrealm member, and support and celebrate each other's pursuit of knowledge and know-how.

Mental watchtower practices:

• We each create (and selectively share) our own unique approaches to and methods for goal setting, planning, and time management, and share the goals themselves as we see fit, looking to each other for support and for ideas on implementation.

• We share (formally once a year at Eyrealm conference and informally via e-mail) what we are each learning (about our own profession or discipline, about the world, and so on).

• We share brief summaries of favorite books and articles via e-mail. Each of us is assigned one month of the year during which we share, via a more detailed summary, our favorite book of the year.

Any parent who feels that he or she is good at something wants his or her children to emulate the skill. The only thing better than emulating is when children develop their own unique approach, borrowing what they like from "your way" but adding and modifying according to their own gifts and perspectives. That is exactly what happened in our family regarding goal setting.

And what a blessing it is to have unique, individualist children who pursue their own interests, read their own books, see the world from their own vantage points, and then share their particular perspectives with each other and with you!

Spiritual Empty-Nest Parenting: Understanding That All of the Real Answers Are Spiritual

It was our annual family reunion—the time we are supposed to come together, to share, to have fun in the joy of being together. And we were having fun on the afternoon I'm going to refer to. Several of us were water-skiing on the mirror surface of our beloved Bear Lake, and were in the process of teaching a little cousin to water-ski. I thought I was doing the teaching. Sixteen-year-old Eli thought, since he's a better skier than I, that he was doing the teaching. I reminded him who it was that had taught him to ski. He reminded me that that was a very long time ago. I chose to ignore everything Eli said and proceeded to teach the kid my way. Eli responded with some angry, rude comments, one of which got to me enough that I pulled the boat into the shallows near shore, turned the driving and teaching over to Talmadge and Saydi, and told Eli to get out and walk to the beach with me. The two of us walked in through the shallow water, continuing our argument. Jonah, twenty-one at the time and feeling that Eli needed some support (or possibly some protection), got out before the boat pulled away and followed us. The two boys basically ganged up on me, and said, in essence: "You've always taught us to have our own opinions and do things our way—but you don't listen to our opinions—you just plow ahead with your way."

"This isn't about opinions," I said. "It's about respect. You just don't talk to a parent the way Eli was talking in the boat."

"Well, you'd better decide what you want—kids with their own opinions or kids who just shut up and let you do everything your way."

"I just said it's not about opinions, it's about respect."

I also told Jonah that Eli didn't need his help with the argument and that it was between the two of us. Jonah's response was, "Well, yeah, but you're so overbearing, and it gave me a chance to make a point."

"What point?"

"Just that, you say you want us to think for ourselves, but you smother us with your view of things and it's so strong and so persuasive that we feel like we don't have a choice or an opinion!"

"Like when?"

"Okay, like when I wanted to go for a semester in Boston and you thought I should wait and stay near home until graduate school. Part of the reason I went was to defy you—because it wasn't your idea."

Suddenly the waterskiing issue had escalated to defiance, independence, and the whole sweep of who we each were to each other.

With hindsight, I'm so glad we were on vacation so that we had time for the talk that followed. (Isn't that the real reason for vacations and reunions?) We spent the rest of the day talking heart to heart, first the three of us, then me alone with Eli, sitting on the sand. Then me alone with Jonah, walking along the beach. Then with the whole family sitting around our big table and offering a family prayer for better understanding of each other's feelings.

What we all ended up doing (along with venting and explaining and apologizing and resolving) was to recommit ourselves to more open and more spiritual communication. We realized anew that we are a family of strong individual wills and opinions, and that only the Spirit can truly unite us and calm us to where we learn from each other rather than arguing and competing.

"Spiritual empty-nest parenting" is last in this book's format because it is the ultimate answer and the facet that can help with and pull together the other four.

Three- and Four-Generation Families

As mentioned earlier, nowhere in the scriptures, when the word "family" is used, does it refer to a two-generation family—to children and parents alone. The word always refers to three generations or more. The modern American idea of a two-generation nuclear family—parents and kids living in one house—is a new and limiting definition of the word.

Family should mean more than that—especially spiritually. Family should, on a practical and daily basis, mean at least three and maybe four generations. As an empty-nest parent, your spiritual concept of family should include your adult children and their children as well as your own parents if they are still alive. "Cousins" and "uncles" and "aunts" and "nieces" and "nephews" and "grandchildren" and "grandparents" and even "great grand-parents" and "great grandkids" should be important and functional words in the concept and operation of family.

Is this possible, people ask, in our modern, mobile, transient world? Answer: Yes—and it is more important and more needed than ever before. The harder the wind blows, the more we need our "roots" and our "grove"— not only for protection, but for peace and for security. The deepest and most spiritual view of a family is that it is made up of relationships and bonds that can outlast this world.

Everyone defines "spiritual" differently, yet Gallup tells us that 80 percent of Americans describe themselves as "spiritual people" and 95 percent believe in some kind of higher being. Certainly for those of us in the Church who do believe in a personal and interested God, the spiritual aspects of empty-nest parenting are the most important of all. Many parents find that they pray more about a child after he or she has left home than they did before. Perhaps because the danger and challenges the child faces are bigger, or perhaps because when he or she is gone—out of our sight—and further from our influence—we feel more need for God's involvement.

Maybe right there is the real key to understanding spiritual empty-nest parenting. Just as we tend to depend more on God to watch over our children when they leave our home, perhaps God depends more on us to watch over His children when they leave Him and come to this earth. God is our Heavenly Father, the true Father of our spirits; thus we are mere "babysitters" for the children he sends to us. In that context, we should be constantly asking the true parent for help and guidance in raising and caring for His children. And we should expect God to answer that kind of direct-stewardship prayer.

In the turmoil and materialistic complexity of today's world, most believing parents acknowledge the need they have for God's help. And we do often feel that need most keenly when a child has moved on and no longer lives under our direct care. In that mind frame, we drafted our first attempt at a "spiritual agreement" with our adult children.

Case Study

> To: Eyrealm
> From: Mom and Dad
> Re: The Spiritual Center of Eyrealm
>
> 1. As our family grows—as each of you spin off into your own orbits with your own unique interests, individual careers, and families of your own—it could be thought of as "the great diversification or decentralization," "the pulling apart," "the breaking up" or even "the redundancy" of Eyrealm.
>
> 2. We all choose not to think of it this way, however; quite the contrary. We think of it as expansion, as growth, as the maturing and seasoning and ripening of our family kingdom, as the harvesting of our joy and as the increasing opportunity for family synergy

and for mutual help and chosen interdependence that magnifies both our individual and our collective broadening and contributing.

3. The reason we can live far apart and progress with our own individual lives without jeopardizing the unity and sanctity of our family is that we have a dense spiritual core whose powerful gravity holds each of us in dependable, coordinated orbit. (We must like that metaphor, having used it twice, perhaps because there are nine planets in our solar system.)

4. That dense, spiritual core, of course, is Christ. What could be more uniting than our shared (yet individual) belief that He is our Creator, our Savior, our Advocate and our Judge?

5. His spiritual gravity "holds" us in a number of beautiful ways. (An alternative metaphor from one of our two favorite hymns, "Come Thou Fount of Every Blessing," [the other one—"If You Could Hie to Kolob"—stays with the first metaphor] is that of a long and benevolent leash that keeps us from straying into darkness and danger. For though we are "prone to wander, Lord I feel it" we can ask Him to "let thy goodness, as a fetter, bind my wandering heart to thee.")

6. What are the ways we have personally found in which His gravity and his fetter holds us close (both to Him and to each other)?

A. Because of Him we try to see everyone and everything spiritually. Each person is a brother or a sister, and each thing (or challenge or opportunity) is a gift from Him.

B. Because of Him, there is a focal point for our worship, and we unite ourselves by thinking about the same aspect of His character each Sunday, each of us, wherever we are as we partake of the sacrament (by focusing on the same chapter in *What Manner of Man*).

C. Because of Him we value each other eternally. We believe we were close brothers and sisters in our spiritual existence before this life and that we are here together to help each other return to Him. Thus we prioritize each other and take responsibility for each other. (An unending extension of when you, as eight year olds, were "tutors" for a younger "tutee.")

D. Because of Him we concentrate on learning and teaching and living the values He taught and exemplified and the joys He gave and made possible. We've structured and organized these joys and values and taught them to you as you will teach them to the next generation of Eyrealm.

E. Because of Him and His example, we are oriented to service, both collectively and individually. Our idea of a great family vacation is a humanitarian expedition to some place with great needs, and each of us looks for service opportunities and factors "contributing" heavily into the choices of career and profession.

F. Because of Him we pray and study and testify together and separately. Our monthly family testimony meetings which we do in our own orbits and together whenever we can allow formal expressions of love and belief. We try to coordinate scriptural study to motivate and share with each other and we pray together when we can, even by phone.

7. Isn't it great (and important to remember) that all the preceding points begin with "Because of Him"? Think how weak and powerless we would be as a family if we were left to our own devices or plans or schemes for staying united and committed to each other. It is our allegiance, commitment, and loyalty to Christ that makes possible our deepest unity with each other.

8. *Proposed agreement draft:* Our goal is nothing less than spiritual unity and character unity. This is our center and our priority. It has always been so. When we used to make up our "school year goals" together at Bear Lake each summer (and as we still do when we gather there for summer reunions), we structured and clustered our goals by category. For students, "category 2" was always academics and grades and "category 3" was extracurricular things from student government to sports to music. "Category 1" was always character—giving service to others and developing your testimony and spirituality. May it always be so!

Some of the kids' responses to this draft memo:

Saren: This memo, like the mental one, really needs some more concrete principles and suggestions for practices stated. It's nice, but it's vague. How do you, as our parents, want to continue to guide us spiritually? How will you continue to contribute to our ongoing spiritual development? What is our role, as we become more "interdependent," in helping you guys increase your spirituality? How can we all help each other draw closer to Christ and thus closer to each other? Do we want to talk about and maybe all commit to some basic principles about living the gospel to a high standard (such as how we observe the Sabbath Day, how we share the gospel, how we read the scriptures, how we help others around us)?

I think we need to come up with some more concrete methods. Reading What Manner of Man together and having testimony meetings together when we get a chance are two great methods that we should never abandon. But I think we need to address all the questions I've just asked in this memo. I'm very interested in what you think about our roles in each other's spirituality and salvation.

Shawni: I totally agree with this memo, so I'm having a hard time figuring out what to write that isn't just a reiteration of what you have said. So I thought I'd just mention something this memo made me think about. Reading this made me wonder how our family would be without Christ. Are our personalities the way they are because we do have that inner-core belief in the gospel? Would we be different people if we didn't believe in Christ? Would we not care about each other as much? Thinking about that makes me realize how true it is what you say about Christ being the one who unites us. He does create that dense spiritual core whose gravity pulls us even closer together.

I thought about the fact that Christ unites us and brings us closer a lot when I was going to Boston University. I made a lot of really nice friends—some of whom I still keep in touch with. I loved the fact that they were different from me and we had some great discussions. But the whole feeling was different when I was surrounded by people with my same belief in Christ. Somehow that just made me so much closer to them. Some people I would meet I would click with from the first moment because we had so much in common—and we shared the same deep-down beliefs. So do you think we would lose a lot of our strong relationship as family members if we didn't believe in Christ? There are some families I have met who are very close who don't believe in God, but I really don't think it's the same kind of closeness.

So I think that having Christlike love is the key for any family to stay together—as you say—Christ is the key, the gravitational core. Trying to gain that Christlike love takes a lot of effort—a lot of reaching out to hold that hand that is "continually stretched out" to us as Isaiah says so many times. It takes a lot of effort to always be aware of the needs and concerns of each family member. And of course some family members are a lot easier to give that Christlike love to than others. But if we can continually strive to have it for each and every family member then we will really always have all that this memo promises. Christ is the core, the center, our Savior—and He has made our family possible.

We need to always strive to stay so close to Him and if we do we will always be close as a family.

Jonah: Christ truly is the center and core of who we are and who we can become and that is such a central part of our family. This is the most important part of Eyrealm because it is really what binds us all together—it is our testimonies that have led to missions and to callings but mostly just to a deep and abiding belief. I really like the concept of spiritual gravity and the imagery that it brings up with our all holding together and being close to the center.

Aja: Through all this empty-nest stuff I always wonder about the fate of the in-laws. Not just Jared and Dave and me but all the six others that will shortly come. I feel like my entry into the family has been nothing but smooth and warm and fun and joyful, but I'm still not too used to everything, and I still appreciate my past with my family and feel infinitely emotionally, spiritually, and physically attached to them in a way that I'm sure could never be duplicated. So, how am I supposed to really get totally into the Eyrealm conversation? I'm still trying to figure it out—I'm new at this whole thing. But, I'll let you know.

The Spiritual Omniscient Partner of Eyrealm (forging a common character and developing personal faith, hope, and charity)

While there was little disagreement or controversy in the kids' response to this memo, there was the sense and suggestion that it would be more meaningful and have more actual affect on each of us if it were more pointed and prescriptive. So we attempted to work it into the now standard "metaphor and the three Ps" format.

Dear children:

What a profound blessing it is to feel as much spiritual unity as we do. It is so remarkable that a group of people as individually strong-willed and opinionated as we are can agree in a humble and united way on the preeminent importance of Christ.

Deep down we know that the best advice, the best answers, and the best approaches are always spiritual. All of the other facets of our adult Eyrealm agreements (the emotional, the social, the financial, and the mental) work best and accomplish their intention if they are spiritually guided. And our vision statement we'll work on next should really be about building an extended family structure that helps each of us return to God.

Therefore, the image we should all carry is that of a partnership that includes and values each of us but that is managed by an omniscient managing partner who we submit to humbly and petition constantly for direction and guidance.

Omniscience is such an awesome word—all seeing, all knowing. Our own perspective is so limited, and God's is so total. It has been said that the essential difference between God and man is awareness. He is all-aware and thus omniscient and omnipotent. If we can, in every aspect of our personal and family lives, seek His inspiration and His will, we may still have setbacks but we cannot ultimately fail.

The marriages, the families within Eyrealm, and Eyrealm itself are all partnerships. If we can include in each of them the managing omniscient partner, they will each become more than we could have imagined. With that in mind, we set forth our "spiritual agreements."

Spiritual omniscient partner principles:

• Christ is the focus of all we do, the light that leads us, the ultimate example we follow.

• Spiritual serendipity: Guidance is a more worthy goal than control and spiritual awareness can get us to where God wants us to be.

• Spiritual stewardship: Since all things belong to God, we should seek His will in all things.

• Spiritual synergy: It is not independence we seek, but dependence on God and interdependence with those we love.

Spiritual omniscient partner promises:

• We will put Christ and Heavenly Father first in all things and seek their will above our own.

• We will serve God by individually and collectively serving each other and our fellowman.

• We will take upon us Christ's name, remember Him, and keep His commandments.

• We will be our "brother's keepers," safeguarding and strengthening each other's testimonies in every possible way.

Spiritual omniscient partner practices:

• We each read the same chapter (about the same aspect of Christ) of *What Manner of Man* in church each Sunday.

- We fast and hold family testimony meetings on the first Sunday of each month.
- We donate, volunteer, and give service together and individually. Both Eyrealm charity gifts and some kind of service expedition are agreed on and participated in yearly.
- We teach each other spiritual principles at the annual Eyrealm reunion.
- We each receive a priesthood or father's blessing on our birthday.
- We pray constantly for each other and ask each other to pray for specific needs we may have.

It was this fifth facet—the spiritual aspect of empty-nest parenting—that really pulled us together and reassured us that we were on the right track. We felt that we now had a five-part family constitution that included and combined the emotional safe harbor, the spiritual grove, the physical or financial foundation, the mental watchtower, and the spiritual omniscient partner. The process we'd gone through to arrive at each one had pulled us together and taught us a lot about each other. It was far from perfect (the process or the product), but it was ours, and we all shared in it.

With a family constitution in hand, we felt like we were ready to go for "the simplicity that lies beyond complexity" by attempting to formulate a family vision or mission statement.

An Adult Family Mission Statement: Putting It All Together into a Form That Becomes Part of Us

Walk into most any corporate office—companies large and small—and you are likely to see a nicely framed "mission statement" or "vision statement" hanging on the wall. Business executives have found that a clearly stated, attractively worded summary of the firm's principal purposes and attitudes can have a powerful unifying and motivating effect on employees.

It is the same in families. Stephen Covey says that bringing one's family together to write a family mission statement is "the single most important and effective exercise of leadership that parents can undertake." He also explains that in the absence of parental leadership a mission or purpose will be established in kids' minds by the media, the peer group, and the broader society—one that certainly will not reflect the values and principles parents want for their children.

But the goals and the vision statement of a young family with small children in the home are fundamentally different from those for an empty-nest family. It is a little like comparing a small, centralized, on-location company with a larger more decentralized company where most of the authority and decision making has shifted out to the branch offices. When our own family was young and all the kids were at home, our mission statement had more to do with the things we wanted to do together and with how we wanted to treat each other within the walls of our own home. As kids grew up and left, we began to feel the need to establish communication patterns and common interest projects that would preserve our love and bonds and help each other and our diverse individual pursuits. The process of establishing our Eyrealm constitution put us in a position to get at the heart of what we wanted our ongoing family to be. Like a distilling process, we felt that out of our efforts on a constitution, a "mission statement" could drip down.

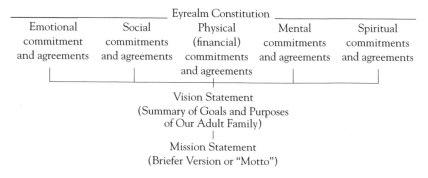

Eyrealm Constitution				
Emotional commitment and agreements	Social commitments and agreements	Physical (financial) commitments and agreements	Mental commitments and agreements	Spiritual commitments and agreements

Vision Statement
(Summary of Goals and Purposes
of Our Adult Family)

Mission Statement
(Briefer Version or "Motto")

Case Study

With the background of all the earlier memos and responses and after talking about it on the phone, through e-mail and personally whenever any of us were together, we (Linda and Richard) took a crack at drafting an adult family mission statement—something we hoped reflected what we'd discussed with the kids and that would give us a goal or target to aim at as we further worked out our approach to empty-nest parenting. We would have preferred to hammer all this out in person at some great all-inclusive meeting, but with kids living all over the world, we decided to let the process unfold through writing and through e-mail.

> To: Our Children
> From: Mom and Dad
> Re: Eyrealm Adult Family Vision Statement (draft)
> 1. We choose to continue to strengthen our family relationships. Whatever distances or differences may separate us, we choose to continue to love and prioritize each other, together with our spouses and children, forever.
> 2. We see our ongoing family as a chance to further develop Godlike attributes. We believe that it is possible to return to God as a family, for we see the family as the organization and government of God in the hereafter and we appreciate that our roles within our family bring us as close as we can get to the Godlike attributes of self-sacrifice and unconditional love. We call our expanding and ongoing family "Eyrealm" because we view it as a sub-realm of God's kingdom and because we seek to live by standards and with a unity that elevates each of us to a higher realm.
> 3. We vow to support each other in our individual efforts to broaden ourselves and contribute to the world around us. Our vision of the mission of the family in general and Eyrealm in particular encompasses two broad and eternally important roles. Its "internal" role is to provide the support and the strength that allow each individual member to reach his/her potential and to discover and fulfill his/her foreordination. Its "external" role is to use its collective commitment and synergy to work as a family for good causes in the outside world. These two roles are natural extensions of the "broaden and contribute" motto we've always had in our family. The adult Eyrealm should be designed, structured, and maintained as a vehicle that helps each of us within it to broaden into the best

people we can be, and it should be organized into an entity that contributes effectively to individuals in need and to the broader society.

4. We will work to make Eyrealm a protecting and nourishing membrane within which we each flourish and grow. Actually, any good organization has some form of dual internal and external purposes. Strong companies, for example, must be concerned about the "inner" individual growth and well-being of each of their employees as well as about the "outer" sales or distribution of their product. What elevates Eyrealm above this norm is the permanence of its commitments and the freeness of its contributions. In a sense, Eyrealm is a magical encircling membrane, flexible enough to allow each of us, though still inside, to go as far as we wish in our own way while still surrounded by its protection and its support. The membrane also serves to concentrate and mix our collective abilities in synergistic ways so that Eyrealm may contribute more to the outside than could the sum of its parts.

5. We understand that, in order to be an effective facilitator of both inner growth and outer contribution, Eyrealm must work or function efficiently in five planes:

• It must work physically or financially in terms of providing a foundation of resources for education and other "broadening," as well as the resources for humanitarian work and other "contributing," all without undermining the independence of its members.

• It must work emotionally by giving confidence and by encouraging uniqueness and individuality, even as it provides support and a safe harbor of acceptance when things don't go well. Our unconditional acceptance within the family also makes us emotionally equipped to notice and listen to the concerns of people outside the family.

• It must work socially to keep members both in close touch and in constant trust, and to maintain a communication that is open and positive. It thus allows roles and relationships to evolve and mature so that we respect each other's differences, stay always open to each other's advice, and relish each other's achievements as if they were our own. This inner "social security" emboldens us to reach out to others who need a friend.

• It must work mentally to where we freely and fearlessly share our goals and dreams with each other and take responsibility for keeping each other mentally stimulated, broadly interested, and fully aware of new ways to give and to serve.

• Finally, it must work spiritually, with Eyrealm undergirding our individual faith and holding us to an inner unity of belief and of purpose which can spill out to meet the spiritual needs of others.

6. We see Eyrealm as both our cradle and our catalyst, both our center and our circumference. We want to continue to live as part of it even as we build our own families apart from it. We will draw strength and support from it and we will combine our talents within it. We will formulate physical, emotional, social, mental, and spiritual agreements that serve our individual needs and preserve our union. Eyrealm will endure eternally because it is made of the unbreakable bonds of unconditional love.

Reactions and feedback:

Saren: I like the concept of "Eyrealm" as a subset kingdom within God's kingdom. But what about our in-laws? If we're part of the "Eyrealm," then can we also be a part of the Loosli-realm and the Pothier-realm (Dave) and the Fegert-realm (Aja)? I think we need to be careful that the concept of Eyrealm does not override our focus on our own mini-realms that we're building and the realms of our in-laws and their great families. I'm curious to see how everything will work beyond this life—what eternal families will really mean, and how they'll all fit together.

Maybe what you're saying, in simpler terms, is that our family mission as we go forward is to support each other's individual broadening and contributing (through encouragement, advice, and sharing insights, knowledge, and ideas) while capitalizing on opportunities to broaden and contribute collectively as we combine our talents, resources, and ideas to learn together and make the world a better place together.

I like the "membrane" imagery a lot. However, it brings to mind again the question of how in-law families fit in. If we're all inside this wonderful Eyrealm membrane, can we also be inside a membrane of another family? I think we can—but I think that the importance of our "other families" (in-laws) needs to be brought up in this memo.

I think it might be nice to finish this off with a one-sentence mission statement that encapsulates the great ideas included here. We all love "broaden and contribute." Maybe we could simply expand on that a little and add in the concept of loving more. Here's one quick idea:

"Build a realm of unconditional love where everyone works to broaden each other's minds, talents and possibilities so that we can collectively and individually contribute all that we have and are to the world and to each other."

It might be nice to ask everyone to write up a one-sentence mission statement for what they see as the mission of Eyrealm and then combine concepts and phrases to make one statement we can all share.

Shawni: I feel that we have such a huge responsibility to search diligently to figure out our stewardships and eternal individual potentials as well as make a very significant contribution to the world.

I suggest that we come up with something short and sweet to sum everything up—maybe just a short statement that we can all post in a place we can always remember all this important stuff and be reminded of it daily. A sign we put on our fridge or maybe even something we want to frame in our homes to remind us always of the importance of Eyrealm and our stewardship to our family and to the world.

Josh: I just wonder how our relationships will be in the future compared to other relationships in our current extended family. Obviously each of us will come up with our own mission/vision statement for our own families.

I think that the "emotional" paragraph should be listed first, even if they are not in order of importance. Although the financial one is important, this one is a million times more important. Money can come from anywhere, but the emotional support of a family can only come from one place. Some of the others below should also be put before the financial one.

Talmadge: I really like this way of explaining the Eyrealm and its possibilities, but we have to consider marriage as a top priority that doesn't have to be five or ten years after we leave home.

If we put more emphasis on this, I think it will help the unmarried of the family to have a different perspective.

Reading the kids' responses, we realized that our first draft was both too long and too limited. They wanted a clearer, more concise statement—one they could memorize or put on a plaque—one that really represented "the simplicity that lies beyond complexity." But they also wanted it to be about more than what Eyrealm would do for them. It needed to be about what each of us would do within Eyrealm for each other and for others.

We realized that we really hadn't defined what our adult family was. We had named it Eyrealm, but was Eyrealm us (Linda and Richard)? Or was it all of us? Or was it the relationships and agreements between us—our family structure? In a way it was all three, but we had to clarify that before we could be clear on the purpose of Eyrealm or on our vision of what it should become.

Vision Statement

After some thought and some further discussion with the kids, we asked each of them to try to come up with a draft of a very condensed adult family mission statement and to e-mail it to us. We, in the meantime (and without seeing theirs), sent the following e-mail to each of them.

Dear Children:

Thanks for your responses on that draft "vision statement." We agree with your consensus that it needs to be refined and "boiled down" to something shorter and more pithy. Here are some thoughts and then an attempt to boil.

We didn't create you (you came from God and were already you) but we did (with God's will and help) create this family—this Eyrealm which has raised you and which can now evolve and become what we and you want it to be. The vision statement we are now trying to condense should state the ongoing purpose for the family structure we call the adult Eyrealm.

Each of you are in the process of creating your own family, and Eyrealm, for one thing, should be a helpful resource to you in that process. It should enhance our individual happiness, freedom, and potential and be a safe harbor of acceptance. It should help us each to become all that we can be and to give all that we can give. And it should retain and expand the "broaden and contribute" mentality of our original family mission statement.

But again, Eyrealm itself is not just a structure, it is the individuals within the structure and the commitments of each of us to each other. Therefore, the vision statement should give us some motivation, some guidance, some vision in terms of (1) What each of us within Eyrealm try to do for each other (emotionally or otherwise); (2) What Eyrealm, as a structure, does for each of us (financially or otherwise); and (3) What Eyrealm made up of all of us, does for others, for society, for the world (charity, service expeditions, our work to strengthen families).

We want a brief statement that speaks volumes to us because we know what's behind each of the words. Here is an attempt:

Eyrealm Vision Statement

"As we each create our own families, we will build an extended family realm of unconditional love wherein, regardless of distance or difference, we all strive to enhance and broaden our own and each other's minds, possibilities, and faith, so that we can deepen our joy, discover our individual destinies, contribute individually and collectively (particularly to the strength and well-being of other families), and return, together, to God."

This is probably still a little too long for a mission statement, but we'll "refine and combine" as your drafts come in and maybe we can have a briefer "mission statement" to just trigger all these concepts in our heads.

We were glad you all seemed to like the image of the magical, encircling membrane of love which is so totally flexible that it doesn't restrict or restrain any of us in any way, allowing everyone to do their own thing in their own way and their own place and yet still holding all of us in its embrace. The membrane, as you pointed out, is not only flexible but "intersectable" so each of us can also be inside the membrane of other families—like the one we join when we marry. In any case, this encircling concept helps us think of Eyrealm in the three ways mentioned earlier: (1) Each of us helping and serving and being there for each of the others within; (2) The membrane itself having certain financial and other resources to nourish (womb-like) those within it; and (3) Combining our strengths and gifts within so that, as the combined Eyrealm, we can contribute more outside than we could individually.

Before our children received our draft, several of them sent us their drafts.

Talmadge: Dear Dad: Here's a shot at a concise adult family mission statement:

"To have each member of Eyrealm work together in the cause of Eternal Families. To help other families as we go along and be a fortress of strength always."

Jonah: In trying to get something really brief, I've been thinking about getting down to action!

I think that the catch word phrase should be "talk but do." We really need to be aware of the things that we need to do. I love how much we get together and talk, but I am wanting to be sure it happens!

334

Aja: I don't know if you're looking for a catch phrase, or what, but I'm all about the short two- or three-word mission statements.

I really like the simple two-word phrase you attribute to your father: "Love more." It relates to all realms of Eyrealm—physical, emotional, spiritual, social, mental—and it also encompasses inner/innie (i.e. broaden) and outer/outie (contribute) focuses. It's simple, yet so awesome that it is a very noble and difficult goal. Plus, we can work on it as individuals and as a family!

I also still like broaden and contribute, especially now that I understand that broaden means broadening the mind, not broadening the family through getting married and having children. Perhaps both meanings of broaden should be included: broaden and contribute.

Others received our draft and responded:

Shawni: Mom and Dad, I really like the vision statement you wrote—I really think it sums things up perfectly and wouldn't have anything to add or take away. I think the essence of it all of course is simply what we have talked about—"Love More." But I really like what you wrote—a little more descriptive and explanatory to help us remember the real reason for families here on earth.

At this stage, we felt it was time to get on the phone and on the computer and push our collective thinking until we had collectively condensed all the hopes and thoughts we had down into the essential code words we were trying to incorporate. After one last flurry of communication, we came up with:

> Broaden and Contribute,
> Love More,
> and
> Return Together

To each of us, these few words summarized and captured what we wanted to do for each other within our family, what we wanted to do together as a family for others, and what we wanted our family organization to facilitate and do for each of us and for all of us. It embodied our desires to grow together, to serve together, to increase in real love together, and to spiritually return to God together.

Our family's process had taken several months, but it had been well worth it. It had caused us to think and to communicate on a whole new level, and we came out of it feeling like we knew each other better.

We all realized that our family will never be static. Each of us will always be changing and growing, as will our relationships with each other. Thus, we know that our family vision statement and constitution will need adjustments and additions. We hope the ongoing process will continue to be enjoyable and productive and continue to cause us to think about who we are to each other.

But for now, we were where we wanted to be, and we tried to pull it all together in a summarizing e-mail to our children:

Case Study (Conclusion)

Dear LTN Children:

Thanks! Despite your busy and demanding lives, you have rolled up your sleeves and together we have hammered out an adult family vision statement, mission statement, and an Eyrealm "constitution." We think these will serve us (and help us to serve others) forever!

Through the process of our back-and-forth interchanges we have gradually distilled the simplicity that lies beyond complexity. We've all read each other's ideas and mentally merged them with our own. Because of this process, we all know the pages of meaning that are condensed into "Broaden and Contribute, Love More, and Return Together"; and we know exactly what the Eyrealm membrane does to protect, nourish, and support us within even as we combine our gifts to contribute without. Because of the process, we know the symbolism as well as the principles, the promises, and the practices of our emotional safe harbor, our social grove, our financial foundation, our mental watchtower, and our spiritual omniscient partner. And because we recorded the process (wrote it, e-mailed it, etc.) we can go back and remind ourselves of the meanings, the symbols and the commitments whenever we want to.

Several of you, throughout the process, reminded us all that what we wanted to end up with was something simple and symbolic enough to frame on our walls or post on our refrigerators or our screen savers. We now have, because of all of your efforts, that beyond-complexity simplicity:

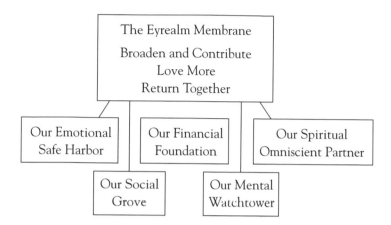

Appendix Conclusion:
"It's All About the Process of Agreement"

There are two key words here: "Process" and "Agreement."

The best ideas in the world for empty-nest parenting will fail unless there is a process of development and discussion with your adult children— a process wherein their needs and ideas are talked about and dealt with as much as yours, and where you all truly empathize with each other's perspectives and feelings. This process may take months or even years, and so long as it is active, there is no urgency or pressure to complete or conclude it, because the process is actually the ongoing answer.

The goal of the process, the thing you are working toward together, is an agreement or a series of agreements that will be a guide and a channel for your adult relationships with your children. By definition, an agreement reflects the needs and wishes of each party. It ought to be written (for clarity and consistency) and it may need to go through several drafts before it "works" for everyone. You may call it an adult family mission statement, a family credo or pact, a basic series of family agreements, or, as we have, a vision statement or a "constitution."

None of the time you spent in this process of agreement is wasted. It is time spent thinking and talking about life—about the needs and hopes and dreams of life and about how family members can help each other with them. How could time be better spent?

Your process may involve letters or phone calls or family meetings or long one-on-one drives or e-mail or family reunions or chat rooms or family vacations. It may start after you read this book and after all of your children are gone; or it may start a few months (or even a couple of years) before your first child leaves—preparing him or her and preparing yourself.

The adult mission statements and agreements you come to don't have to be final or static. Let them evolve and be adjusted, altered, or added to as time passes and needs and situations change. Keep the process alive, because the process and the agreements are your passport to a beautiful and fulfilling autumn and winter of your own life.

Saren's Suggestion:

Okay, I loved the process our family went through, but, with hindsight, it could have been much simpler and more streamlined (and I think I'd change the order a bit, too). Here are a few suggestions ("If we were doing it again . . . ")

1. Vision statement and mission statement: In a family meeting or via e-mail, have all the adult members of your family draft a basic statement of what

they see as the purpose of your adult family. What is your basic role in each other's lives as you move forward? What do you want to "be" to each other? Work together to "boil down" these ideas into one all-encompassing vision statement and a short, catchy mission statement that captures the essence of your adult family's functions in a few words. Make sure that everyone has a chance to review and edit these statements.

2. Questions: Talk about the fifty questions in section e with your kids. Maybe you could set aside time at a reunion, plan a special family meeting or conference call, or use e-mail. You might want to just work on five questions at a time, so no one gets overwhelmed or burned out on the process. Take careful notes on these conversations!

3. "Facets" or main topics: Using the answers you get on these questions, decide on several areas or "facets" of your adult family that you'll focus on. You can choose the facets we chose (emotional, spiritual, mental, social, financial . . .) or you may come up with other main topics that work better for your family (communicating with each other, advising each other, helping each other financially, seeing each other, and so on).

4. Agreements: Under each "facet," come up with "agreements" on each one—a list of principles, promises and practices that take everyone's ideas and answers from your discussions into account. You, as the parents, could come up with these agreements yourselves or you could ask each of your adult children to take one of the facets and write up the agreement for it. Either way, everyone needs to see the drafted agreements and edit them and agree to them before they can be finalized.

5. Adult family constitution: Combine the vision statement, mission statements, and all the agreements into one document and make sure everyone has a copy.

6. Review and revise: On at least a yearly basis, go over your family constitution and make additions and changes.

In our family, we ended up with a great family constitution that everyone's pretty excited about. In the process, we learned a lot about each other and discovered a lot of feelings and issues that had been smoldering or simply ignored. We all felt that the process was pretty tedious, though. If we had it to do over, I think we'd have gone for the more simplified process suggested above. If this process still seems a bit overwhelming to you, don't worry. There are so many ways you can create your own unique and happy empty-nest family. The most important thing is that you're reading this, thinking about these issues, learning from reading over our family's case study, and coming up with your own ways to address the important questions of empty-nest parenting with your children. If nothing else, we hope you will use this appendix as a catalyst for figuring out what you need from your children and what they need from you—and that you'll ask them some questions and use their answers to clarify what everyone hopes and intends to do in each others' lives.

Good luck! If you learn even a fraction of what we learned in our family through your own family's process, it'll be well worth your effort!

Postscript (and Best Wishes): An Invitation for Further Interaction at emptynestparenting.com

As we watched our grown children interact with each other and with us during the process of trying to better establish our adult relationships, we thought a little about how our Heavenly Father must feel as He watches us relate one with another.

We don't want out children to compete and compare themselves with each other—rather, we want them to support and magnify each other. God must feel the same way, and it must please Him when we learn and interact in ways that help each other to grow and progress.

With that in mind, we would love for this book to be the beginning of an ongoing interaction between *you* and *us*. No one is an expert in this challenge of empty-nest parenting—it's new to all of us and we're all "fellow strugglers" trying to understand and deal with new situations. We wish we could have sat with you as you read this book, and heard your reactions and your ideas.

The two of us love to write about what we're currently thinking about, experiencing, struggling with, and gradually resolving. We all feel most passionately about what we're involved in at the moment. We seem to think better and write better (or at least *easier*) when the subject is something that is personally relevant and timely in our lives.

Nothing fits that criteria better than the topic of *Empty-Nest Parenting*. As this book goes to press, ten of our eleven children have left the nest, and we are vitally interested in improving every aspect of our own empty-nest parenting. *We need help!* All empty-nest parents do—help in the form of good ideas and motivation from and synergy with other ENPs.

Wouldn't it be great if we could form a big Empty-Nest Parenting group or club, where we could meet together and share our worries and dilemmas and get suggestions, sympathy, and ideas from other ENPs?

Well, guess what? We have, and we can! And it's a club with which you can meet any day at any time. It's a growing group of very diverse parents who are united by their love and continuing interest in their "grown and departed" children. It's a process that is only possible on the Internet. We've worked with some other ENPs that we respect and established *emptynestparenting.com*. You're invited to log on anytime, to become a member, and to ask questions and get answers—to give and to receive.

Here's what we believe: How well parents and their grown children handle their evolving roles, responsibilities, and relationships will have more to do with their collective happiness than any other factor. Empty-nest parenting is simply too big an issue to leave to chance. The most typical approach is just "trying to deal with things as they come up," and that approach just isn't good enough anymore. As parents today, we need a philosophy—*a clear* understanding *of what we want to do for our grown kids and a thoughtful* strategy *of how we will go about it. It is the pursuit of that philosophy, understanding, and strategy that motivated this book and that we now hope will draw us together on emptynestparenting.com.*

Best wishes now, in this new ENP phase of life. May it be a joyful adventure for us all!